AMERICAN RELIGIOUS
RESPONSES TO KRISTALLNACHT

AMERICAN RELIGIOUS RESPONSES TO KRISTALLNACHT

Edited by

Maria Mazzenga

AMERICAN RELIGIOUS RESPONSES TO KRISTALLNACHT
Copyright © Maria Mazzenga, 2009.

First published in 2009 by PALGRAVE MACMILLAN® in the United States - a division of St. Martin's Press LLC, 175 Fifth Avenue, New York, NY 10010.

Where this book is distributed in the UK, Europe and the rest of the world, this is by Palgrave Macmillan, a division of Macmillan Publishers Limited, registered in England, company number 785998, of Houndmills, Basingstoke, Hampshire RG21 6XS.

Palgrave Macmillan is the global academic imprint of the above companies and has companies and representatives throughout the world.

Palgrave® and Macmillan® are registered trademarks in the United States, the United Kingdom, Europe and other countries.

ISBN: 978-0-230-61806-0

Library of Congress Cataloging-in-Publication Data

American religious responses to Kristallnacht/edited by Maria Mazzenga.
    p. cm.
  Includes bibliographical references and index.
  ISBN 0-230-61806-5
  1. Kristallnacht, 1938—Public opinion. 2. Jews—Persecutions—
Germany—Public opinion. 3. Germany—Foreign public opinion,
American. 4. Public opinion—United States—History—20th century.
5. United States—Religion—20th century. 6. Religions—Relations—
History—20th century. 7. Antisemitism—History—20th century.
8. Antisemitism—United States—History—20th century. 9. Theology—
United States—History—20th century. 10. Judaism—United States—
Doctrines—History—20th century. I. Mazzenga, Maria.

    DS134.255.A64 2009
    940.53'1842—dc22   2008055758

A catalogue record of the book is available from the British Library.

Design by Macmillan Publishing Solutions

First edition: August 2009

10 9 8 7 6 5 4 3 2 1

Printed in the United States of America.

CONTENTS

INTRODUCTION: AMERICAN RELIGIOUS GROUPS AND KRISTALLNACHT

MARIA MAZZENGA

News of Kristallnacht, the anti-Jewish pogrom that transpired in Germany on November 9–10, 1938, shocked the people of the United States. The pogrom followed the shooting on November 7 of the third secretary at the German Embassy in Paris, Ernst vom Rath, by Herschel Grynszpan, a young man devastated by news of the deportation of his family from Germany to Poland by the Nazis weeks before. In the Nazi-sanctioned violence following vom Rath's death on November 9, 91 Jews were killed, and hundreds more beaten. Thousands of Jewish shops and homes were smashed. More than 1,000 synagogues were destroyed. Thirty thousand Jewish men were arrested and sent to concentration camps—where more than 1,000 died. Due to the systematic, thorough, and widespread nature of the violence against Jews during the Kristallnacht pogrom, most scholars now view it as the beginning of the Holocaust.[1]

The U.S. press promptly and accurately reported the pogrom to the American people. "The greatest wave of anti-Jewish violence since Adolf Hitler came to power in 1933 swept Nazi Germany today," reported the *Washington Post* on November 11, 1938. The *New York Times* gave a city-by-city account of the attacks on Jews, their businesses, and their synagogues.[2] Nearly every American newspaper condemned Germany for its actions. President Franklin Roosevelt declared that he "could scarcely believe that such things could occur in a twentieth century civilization" and announced the recall of the U.S. ambassador to Germany. As Deborah Lipstadt shows, the immediate response in the United States as reflected in the press was nearly universally one of alarm and anger.[3] The Gallup organization polled a cross section of voters in every state just after the pogrom. When asked "Do you approve or disapprove of the Nazis' treatment of Jews in Germany?" 94 percent expressed disapproval. Indeed, George Gallup believed the "vote of condemnation so nearly unanimous as to constitute one of the most decisive expressions of opinion in any of the more than 800 surveys conducted by the [Gallup] organization in the last three years."[4]

Religious organizations were at the forefront of this protest. Indeed, the events of November 1938 precipitated the first joint statement ever issued by all Christian denominations—Protestant and Catholic—in the United States. In "a profound spirit of Christian justice we protest the flagrant denials of rights which the National Socialist party specifically guaranteed when seeking the support of the churches in Germany," the statement read. Protestants, Jews, and Catholics also spoke out individually. Dr. Henry Ward of Union Theological Seminary told a New York crowd of more than 20,000 that Germany's Jews should be evacuated and a trade embargo instituted against the Reich. Reuben Grainer, a former head of the World Zionist Organization, told the same crowd that it was naïve to leave the protest against Germany to non-Jews because we think "that will impress the Nazis—we, Jews, repeat our defiance of the Nazis." One *Washington Post* report relayed the local response that came from the pulpits across the District of Columbia on the Sunday following the pogrom. Michael Curley, the archbishop of Baltimore, told an assemblage of priests and lay Catholics at Holy Comforter Church that Hitler was a "madman" with "delusions of divinity." Hitler had been baptized a Catholic, said Curley, but good Catholics "do not forget that Jesus was Jew. Catholics remember that Jesus founded their church." Dr. Ulysses G. B. Pierce at All Souls Unitarian Church called for "aggressive and persistent goodwill" and asserted that "we must stand fast against all bigotry, all intolerance, all fanaticism, ever keeping in mind that no matter what our difference, we are all bound together in one worldwide brotherhood." Reverend R.P. Robertson of the First Baptist Church of Hyattsville, Maryland, said that Nazism could never "hope to bring peace to the world," because it is "founded on the principles of racial hatred."[5] New amalgams of religious and national ideals emerged spontaneously in the days following the Kristallnacht pogrom.

As we know today, such outrage did not result in measures that might have stopped Hitler's murder of 6 million Jews. A combination of factors, among them economic insecurity, diplomatic isolationism, and antisemitism, kept the United States from assisting Germany's Jews in ways that might have saved substantial numbers of them. Six months after the November pogrom, a poll published in *Fortune* magazine revealed that 83 percent of Americans were against changing immigration quotas to allow more Europeans into the nation. Legislation proposed by the senators Robert Wagner and Edith Rogers just after Kristallnacht to bring 20,000 German refugee children under the age of 14 to the United States never made it out of committee. Moreover, thousands of endangered Jews who might have secured refuge under existing quotas were denied entry into the country due to the barriers raised by bureaucratic officials, many of whom were antisemitic. When reports of mass killings of German Jews began trickling through government institutions and the media, they were often greeted with disbelief. American religious organizations, for their part, failed to assist not only Jews, but Christians persecuted by the Nazis in any significant numbers.[6]

While America's failure to rescue sizable numbers of Jews suffering under Nazism is irrefutable, scholars have more recently emphasized that the expectation of a successful large-scale U.S. rescue operation for Europe's Jews is not rooted in historical reality. Henry Feingold suggests that those who indict the Roosevelt administration for not doing more to assist the Jews read history more idealistically than realistically. To "observe that not enough was done is simply to recite a self-evident truth. Enough can never be done where such catastrophes are concerned."[7] For Feingold, however, the idea that an effective rescue of the Jews never materialized wholly due, as David Wyman's work in particular has suggested, to deceit and indifference on the U.S. front isn't historically accurate. In the case of Breckinridge Long, a State Department employee and antisemite who was intent on blocking the entrance of Jewish refugees, deliberate deceit was involved. However, Feingold and others suggest that the failure to assist the Jews was less deliberate and more related to mitigating circumstances. For example, no cogent policy of rescue for Germany's Jews resulted from the 1938 Evian Conference more due to general anti-immigration sentiments in the Depression-ravaged countries than any specific malice toward Jews on the part of conference attendees. Roosevelt, the consummate politician, was well aware that he would be unable to convince Congress to relax such restrictions (the failure of the Wagner-Rogers Bill in the year following the Evian Conference would prove him correct). Additionally, while it was clear that the Nazis had singled out the Jews for particularly deplorable treatment, the policy of extermination that would be implemented during the war was still unknown during the period between 1933 and 1941when rescue was most feasible. When the truth about the camps did become known during the war, many simply refused to believe human beings were capable of such actions. Even after the news of the camps began to trickle in, the U.S. public could not believe that the Germans (often distinguished as a people from the Nazi leadership that had supposedly hijacked the country) could allow the Jews to be treated so horrifically. A poll of December 1944 showed that a majority of Americans thought Hitler had killed some Jews, "but could not accept the idea that a mass-murder operation in which millions had died, had occurred."[8]

Hence, while we know that the United States failed to respond to the catastrophe unfolding in Europe in ways that would have saved European Jews from extermination, this was, to borrow a phrase from volume contributor Victoria Barnett, a "complex failure" with unique aspects and implications for American religious groups. The essays in this volume strive to gain a fuller picture of the religious response to Kristallnacht by examining the immediate responses of three American religious groups—Protestants, Catholics, and Jews. Originating with a two-week summer workshop on organized American religious responses to Kristallnacht, sponsored by the Center for Advanced Holocaust Studies at the United States Holocaust Memorial Museum, the essays bring a wide range of previously unexamined evidence to bear on the subject.

Kristallnacht generated a flurry of uniquely American activity among the Protestants, Catholics, and Jews of the United States. Taken together, these essays suggest four themes evident in the American religious reaction to Kristallnacht, with broader implications for viewing the responses of those groups to the Holocaust itself. First, responses to the pogrom were negotiated within an American political and cultural framework. Second, each tradition grappled with the sometimes thorny issue of interfaith relations in its response to the pogrom. Third, religious groups felt compelled to reevaluate where they placed Judaism in relation to their own traditions and teachings—with American Jews undergoing self-evaluation—in the wake of the tragedy. Finally, Kristallnacht generated distinct theological developments among certain groups, especially fundamentalist Protestants and Orthodox Jews, but to a certain extent among Catholics and mainstream Protestants as well. At the heart of each of these themes is a deep ambivalence. How inclusive can one be toward those of other faiths without losing a sense of one's own community? Adding national identity to the equation complicates the picture further: for many Christian and Jewish Americans, denouncing the persecution of Jews presented a reinforcement of their American and religious ideals, while at the same time allowing non-American Jews into their nation may have presented not only a religious threat, but a social and economic one as well. When did interfaith cooperation jeopardize one's own religious values? When did the disproportionate suffering of Jews call for words and actions outside the boundaries of typical religious activities? Did the Nazi targeting of Jews for particularly vicious persecution as Jews alter notions of religious hierarchy and scriptural interpretation among Christians? While the essays here do not definitively answer these questions, they do address them in a number of ways.

One of the most prominent themes here is that the American context shaped reactions to the Nazi treatment of the Jews. As Matthew Bowman notes, Americanism interacted with religious theology and organization to prompt particular reactions to Kristallnacht. Bowman draws from the work of Michael Kazin and Joseph McCartin in defining Americanism as "'a cultural style imbued with political meaning;' that is, an understanding of how society should work and a way of both talking about and living it that Americans have sought to enshrine in law." Here, "Americanism revolves around an adherence to personal liberty and suspicion of authority in rhetoric and cultural practice." American religious leaders and their followers, in particular, believed that they should be able to choose and practice faith freely and have historically been suspicious of any power that sought to deny them that choice. At the same time, as Bowman points out, "Americanism is more than this negative definition; it is also a celebration of itself, a confidence in the possibilities and progress offered by American cultural norms, and a conviction that they endow American citizens with unique virtue and promise."[9]

The three religious traditions examined here reveal an absorption of this politically imbued cultural style in range of ways. In an illuminating comparison between the ecumenical efforts of Christians and Jews in Europe and of those in North America, Victoria Barnett finds that American-style ecumenism was rooted in a pragmatic desire to transcend denominational boundaries toward building consensus on social and political issues. In Europe, ecumenism was characterized less by pragmatism and interfaith cooperation than by theological debate toward finding places where Protestants could legitimately take a stand in terms of doctrine and tradition. By the late 1930s, as the Nazi program was implemented in Germany and many European nations fell under the grip of fascism, ecumenism became associated with political democracy and religious freedom. In his examination of the Protestant response to the Kristallnacht pogrom, as expressed through the mainstream secular media, Kyle Jantzen finds that mainstream Protestantism had "recast itself as an ethical way of life, intimately connected with the freedom of democracies and the culture of western civilization." Both Barnett and Jantzen, moreover, touch on where the Canadian and U.S. Christian churches found points of unity in opposing Nazism. These points of unity were based on shared Christian *and* democratic ideals. Their essays open the volume, as they express a North Americanist response to Nazism broadly conceived, examining how democratic idealism shaped the mainstream ecumenism underpinning many of the early denunciations of the Nazis by religious groups.

That the essays here attempt to reveal the ways in which American democratic idealism shaped religious responses to Kristallnacht is not to posit a wholly celebratory American exceptionalism in contradistinction to Nazi fascism. The United States has its own varieties of ethnic discrimination and antisemitism that served again and again to build national community. As Jantzen notes, a key inhibiting factor to more substantive Protestant responses to Nazi persecutions was native racism and antisemitism. John Higham and David Gerber have described how the mass migration of Eastern European Jews to the United States in the late nineteenth and early twentieth centuries resulted in an intensification of antisemitism, complicated by the fact that it usually took less apparent forms and was practiced more informally in America than in fascist Europe, so as not to overtly contradict the pluralist and democratic ideals enshrined in the nation's founding documents. Publicly expressed democratic ideals of equality and religious pluralism, then, accompanied informally expressed antisemitism. The Jewish population in the United States jumped 16-fold over four decades, reaching 3.9 million by 1917, the eve of the passage of the immigration laws that would restrict their numbers well into the Nazi era. As these Jews became upwardly mobile, the Patrician antisemitism (an upper-class version mobilized to protect white Anglo-Saxon privilege) of individuals like the State Department's Breckinridge Long intensified. Long's obstructionism, along with that of his subordinates, enabled him to block the entry of thousands of Jewish refugees to a devastating effect: 90 percent of the quotas open to Italian and German immigrants went unfilled during the war.[10]

American antisemitism was not, of course, just a Patrician phenomenon. As Maria Mazzenga's essay on Catholic institutional responses to the pogrom shows, there was also a more populist American variety that blended with Catholic theological antisemitism in the writings and radio broadcasts of Father Charles Coughlin. Coughlin shockingly responded to Kristallnacht with increased support for the Nazis and their antisemitic program. Nonetheless, Coughlin's position in the church became increasingly marginal as another group of Catholic leaders began asserting a Catholic Americanism that saw the Jewish and Catholic traditions as part of a single continuum and the acceptance of religious pluralism as a positive development for the future of the Church in the United States. Drawing from evidence in previously untapped archives, Mazzenga describes two competing strains of Catholic Americanism at work in the

1930s that characterized a response to the pogrom differing from the European Catholic. The competing strains produced an ambivalence within the Catholic community, splitting those who hoped to maintain a closed border from those who felt an obligation to help their coreligionists escape Nazi tyranny, as Patrick Hayes's essay on Catholic refugee efforts in the 1930s shows. First, American Catholics charged with coordinating German refugee policy in the late 1930s were unable to create an adequate institutional structure that would facilitate the intake of refugees by the United States. The Jewish community was not a priority for Catholic assistance, based in part on the Jewish claims and abilities to aid their own people. Instead, these Catholics worked with German bishops who asked for assistance in rescuing "non-Aryan Catholic" refugees. "Non-Aryan Catholics" were those individuals who, while Catholic by faith, were nonetheless legally designated as racially Jewish by the Nazis, because they were converted from Judaism or descended from Jews. Hayes's essay is a fascinating account of how American Catholic leaders of immigration policy sought to negotiate the fate of German Catholics that fell into a Nazi-created category. The Catholic Church may be a global church, but the national political structures in which the American hierarchy operated clearly conditioned the way they responded to the plight of the Jews.

Matthew Bowman's work reveals that an overt linking of religious concepts and Americanism is not necessary to prove the Protestant fundamentalists' debt to national ideals—precisely because Americanness offers a fairly substantial space in which religious identity can be constructed. Early on, American fundamentalists were wary of Hitler's antisemitism, as the Jews were the chosen people according to scripture, but they were appreciative of his repression of communism and ability to bring stability to Germany. On balance, their opinions of the dictator were ambivalent at worst. This uneasy acceptance was shattered by the church crisis that began in late 1933, when the Nazi German Christian movement attempted to take over the German Protestant churches. For the fundamentalists, Bowman shows, the "heart religion" of personal relationship to the Deity could not exist in tandem with Nazi-controlled religious institutions. True religion, in short, was religion untrammeled by the state, based on freedom of conscience and the right to practice as the individual saw fit.

Michael Berkowitz's civic-minded American Jewish War Veterans clearly drew from American ideals in their reaction to Nazism in general. They were a larger and more active group than their British brothers, the British-Jewish Ex-Servicemen. While Jewish veterans in both the United States and Britain had been engaging in anti-Nazi activity since Hitler came to power in the early 1930s, the pogrom generated intensified calls for the enforcement of a boycott of German goods and for the admission of Jewish refugees in both the United States and Britain, and caused Jewish veterans to offer practical support for the emigration of Jewish war veterans from Europe. The Jewish war veterans' story illuminates yet another facet of anti-Nazi activism in the United States and Britain, ultimately revealing how Jews in both countries had come to absorb respective national ideals, and how they put those ideals to work for their German coreligionists.

By contrast, the Orthodox Jews at the center of Gershon Greenberg's essay were wary of America, though they highly respected President Franklin Roosevelt, and this affinity grew as the Nazi program for the Jews became clearer. While the Jewish War Veterans of the United States proudly embraced American customs, their Orthodox brothers and sisters frowned upon such accommodation. Indeed, as Greenberg shows, some Orthodox Jews saw the rise of Hitler and the Kristallnacht pogrom as a punishment for Jewish assimilation into America. In this sense, Greenberg's Orthodox Jews are comparable to Bowman's fundamentalist Protestants, appreciative of the freedom of religious expression that allowed them to practice their faith unfettered, though wary of what they saw as the secularism that corroded religious practices. Catholics' and mainstream Protestants' absorption of national democratic values, on the other hand, had enabled them to more readily express sympathy for Jews. A comparison between these groups' understanding of what the persecution of Jews meant is especially interesting, because it reveals that interpretations of events in largely religious terms do not necessarily function to exclude faiths other than one's own. Conversely, strong identification with national values does not necessarily dilute religious expression. Certain Catholics and mainstream Protestants were able to strengthen and clarify their own religious views *because* they expressed support for Jews, not in spite of such support. Similarly, the freedom of Orthodox Jews and fundamentalist Protestants to engage in nonmainstream religious practices that rejected American secular values was affirmed rather than denied by Nazi discrimination against Germany's Jews.

Accordingly, expressions of interfaith solidarity were extremely complex. Orthodox Jews and fundamentalist Protestants were far less likely than their more mainstream counterparts to engage in interfaith activity. Members of both groups were deeply disturbed by the Nazi persecution of the Jews, but because they tended to interpret the world and its phenomena in more strictly religious terms than their mainstream Protestant fellow citizens, they were less likely to engage in the kind of interfaith activity described by Barnett. Their support was expressed through prayer and theological reevaluation. For Barnett's and Jantzen's mainstream American Protestants, however, the fact of the crossing of denominational boundaries was itself a rebuke to the Nazis, because they identified faith with religious pluralism—something the Nazis obviously rejected. Denunciations of the pogrom, for the groups involved, generated a transcendence of religious boundaries, a move away from American prejudice, an acknowledgment that Nazism was as pernicious as communism. Non-Orthodox Jews and Protestants often engaged in anti-Nazi protest jointly. The Jewish War Veterans in the United States, as Berkowitz's research shows, were very successful at coalition-building among those of other faiths and appear to have been the organizational force behind a widely publicized late-1938 interdenominational radio broadcast denouncing the Nazi treatment of Jews.

That prominent Catholic clerics participated in this broadcast underscores the fact that Kristallnacht is a landmark moment in American Catholic interfaith history. As both Hayes and Mazzenga detail, by tradition, church law, and papal pronouncement, Catholics were prohibited from participation in interfaith activity, as such activity threatened to undermine Catholicism as "the one true faith." The Vatican had made clear in a formal pronouncement directed at the American hierarchy, decades before Kristallnacht, that neither religious liberty nor the separation of church and state was reconcilable with Catholic teaching. Ideally, the state would be Catholic, as would all of its citizens. However, as Mazzenga shows, many Catholic clerical leaders had come to absorb the American democratic ideals of their nation in spite of Catholic teaching, and these individuals found ways of denouncing the Nazi persecution of the Jews without overtly violating Church teaching and law. One way around the restrictions was to make pronouncements of support for Jews separately from Protestant and Jewish groups. This happened in dioceses all over the country after Kristallnacht. In some cases, Catholic clerics felt so strongly on the matter that they signed statements and did indeed appear with members of other faiths in spite of the rules. Such interfaith activity by Catholics is commonly seen as originating with the onset of the Second World War, but the evidence presented here suggests that this activity occurred before the war, and the Nazi persecution of Jews (as opposed to American wartime nationalism) had a role in precipitating it.[11]

For those Jews and Protestants who viewed events entirely in religious terms, Kristallnacht was world-altering. Interpretations of the Nazi persecution of Jews came as a result of their religious views, not out of respect for freedom of religion or brotherhood of man. The Jews were the chosen people. Orthodox Jews, therefore, comprehended Nazi actions as an expression of God's wrath, and their response was prayer. Where many Americans saw Kristallnacht as a crisis of Western civilization or a humanitarian tragedy, these individuals saw it through the prism of their relationship with God.

The fundamentalists, for their part, as Bowman shows, had a particularly religious stake in the persecution of the Jews. Unlike most American Christians, fundamentalists were not supersessionists; that is, they did not believe that the Atonement of Christ supplanted or replaced God's covenant with Abraham. This meant that the Jews were still the chosen people; they had a relationship with God that was unique, and that would ultimately exalt them above any Gentile in heaven. The fundamentalists' worldview also meant that they wrestled with antisemitism, however. "Corrupted Jews," those who had abandoned their faith, were viewed as responsible for the rise of atheistic communism, as the forged *Protocols of the Elders of Zion* taught. This meant that, initially, many were ready to believe that Hitler was merely assaulting communist conspirators, and here the fundamentalists were in agreement with the Catholic Fr. Coughlin and his followers. However, while Coughlin's belief that the Nazis served to rid the world of communists was reinforced by the pogrom, the fundamentalists' was not. Instead, most of them renounced the *Protocols* and viewed the pogrom as evidence of the Nazi regime's corruption by Satan. Nazism, for them, had become as evil as any threat presented by communism.

Mainstream Protestants also saw their worldview altered by the Kristallnacht pogrom. Because they were so identified with secular values, however, their religious sentiment was strongly associated with democratic freedom and Western civilization. As Europe succumbed to totalitarianism, mainstream American Protestants saw themselves as preserving western humanistic values—their response to the treatment of the Jews in German-occupied territories affirmed this position. Their interfaith activity was an expression of the sense that they were preserving values under siege in Nazi Germany.

Greenberg discerns four levels of response among Orthodox Jews indicating an alteration in religious consciousness precipitated by the pogrom. The first transpired in the arena of public ritual. At the November 20, 1938, gatherings of American Orthodox Jews for fasting and prayer, the pogrom was viewed as a religious disaster, and emphasis was placed on mourning it as an event during which the shedding of blood, the burning of Torah scrolls, and the destruction of holy structures signified God's anger. Jews viewed what had happened in Germany as punishment for their sins, and believed that fasting and begging God's forgiveness would restore their relationship with God. There was also a sermonic response.

Individuals such as Rabbi Tobias Geffen of Atlanta spoke of the need to hope for eventual redemption. He assured his audience that Hitler would be isolated for his venality, using references to the Torah to reinforce his point. He called for the unity of all Jews, for example, as Esther did in response to Haman. In the "apocalyptic" reaction, Orthodox Jews viewed Hitler as an instrument of God, punishing them for their assimilation into America and movement away from the faith. Suffering would return them to God and the observance of the Torah. Finally, an "apocalyptic-Kabbalistic" response also viewed the pogrom as unprecedented, adding Kabbalistic numerology to interpretations of its meaning. In contrast with the wholly apocalyptic view, Hitler was not seen as an instrument of God here, rather, his actions exceeded any kind of measure-for-measure punishment. In this view the pogrom was ushering in redemption and eternity, and Jews were advised to pray and fast in the interim between world history and messianic reality. Greenberg's essay reveals the ways in which a significant portion of the Jewish population viewed Kristallnacht through an almost exclusively religious lens.

Ultimately, these essays show that for most Catholics, mainstream Protestants, and non-Orthodox Jews, an embrace of American democratic values and renewal of religious belief occurred simultaneously in the wake of the Kristallnacht pogrom. For the more Orthodox Jews and fundamentalist Protestants, religious views were altered but affirmed, with a confirmation of American values occurring negatively, meaning that many of them gained a new appreciation for the American ideal of freedom of religious expression, because it enabled them to practice their religion freely, unlike in Nazi Germany. The essays here present us with a snapshot of American religious traditions grappling with an unfolding and expanding tragedy, its future path still unfathomable.

NOTES

1. Kristallnacht statistics are from Martin Gilbert, *Kristallnacht: Prelude to Destruction* (New York: HarperCollins, 2006), 14–16; see also Mitchell G. Bard, *48 Hours of Kristallnacht: Night of Destruction, Dawn of the Holocaust* (Guilford, CT: Lyons, 2008); Saul Friedlander, *Nazi Germany and the Jews,* vol. 1, *The Years of Persecution, 1933–1939* (New York: Harper Perennial, 1998).

2. "Nazis Burn, Pillage," *Washington Post*, November 11, 1938, X1; "Jews Are Ordered to Leave Munich," *New York Times*, November 11, 1938, 3; "American Press Comment on Nazi Riots" *New York Times*, November 12, 1938.

3. Deborah Lipstadt, *Beyond Belief: The American Press and the Coming of the Holocaust, 1933–1945* (New York: Free Press, 1986), 98, 105.

4. Dr. George Gallup, "The Gallup Poll: Nazi Treatment of Jews and Catholics Overwhelmingly Deplored by U.S. Public," *Washington Post*, December 9, 1938.

5. "The Churches' United Front," *New York Times*, December 27, 1938; "20,000 Jam Garden in Reich Protest" *New York Times*, November 22, 1938; "Divinity Delusions' Lauds 2 Cardinals Hoover 'Indignant' Others Join Protest," *Washington Post*, November 14, 1938.

6. See Arthur D. Morse, *While Six Million Died: A Chronicle of American Apathy* (New York: Random House, 1967), 260–261; David Wyman, *The Abandonment of the Jews: America and the Holocaust, 1941–1945* (New York: Pantheon Books, 1984), 105–106, and David Wyman, *Paper Walls: America and the Refugee Crisis, 1938–1941* (New York: Pantheon, 1985); David Gerber, ed., *Antisemitism in American History* (Urbana: University of Illinois Press, 1986), 29–31; Lipstadt, *Beyond Belief*, chapter 4; Haskell Lookstein, *Were We Our Brothers' Keepers? The Public Response of American Jews to the Holocaust, 1938–1944* (New York: e-reads, 2002); Haim Genizi, *American Apathy: The Plight of Christian Refugees from Nazism* (Ramat-Gan, Israel: Bar-Ilan University, 1983).

7. Henry Feingold, *Bearing Witness: How America and Its Jews Responded to the Holocaust* (Syracuse: Syracuse University Press), 74.

8. Quote from Feingold, *Bearing Witness*, 92, on the question of Americans' refusal to believe that the German people, as opposed to their government leaders, were capable of the atrocities committed during the war, Steven Casey's work is particularly good, see Steven Casey, *Cautious Crusade: Franklin D. Roosevelt, American Public Opinion, and the War against Nazi Germany* (Oxford: Oxford University Press, 2001), 211–213 and passim; William D. Rubinstein, *The Myth of Rescue: Why the Democracies Could Not Have Saved More Jews from the Nazis* (New York: Routledge, 2000); for a different perspective on the rescue question see John Dippel, *Bound Upon a Wheel of Fire: Why So Many German Jews Made the Tragic Decision to Remain in Nazi Germany* (New York: BasicBooks, 1996).

9. Matthew Bowman, public comments following summer workshop, "American Religious Organizations and Responses to the Holocaust in the United States: Kristallnacht as a Case Study," August 24, 2007, United States Holocaust Memorial Museum, Washington, D.C. See also, Michael Kazin and Joseph A. McCartin, eds., *Americanism: New Perspectives on the History of an Ideal* (Chapel Hill: University of North Carolina Press, 2006).

10. Gerber, *Antisemitism in American History*, 30; John Higham, *Send These To Me: Jews and Other Immigrants in Urban America* (Baltimore: Johns Hopkins University Press, 1984); Wyman, *The Abandonment of the Jews*, 106–109, chapter 7.

11. Partially in response to the Holocaust, Catholic restrictions on interfaith activity were eventually lifted (this would officially take place with the issuance of *Nostra Aetate* by the Second Vatican Council in 1965).

CHAPTER 1

CHRISTIAN AND JEWISH INTERFAITH EFFORTS DURING THE HOLOCAUST: THE ECUMENICAL CONTEXT[*]

VICTORIA BARNETT

One of the many tragic aspects of the period between 1933 and 1945 is the failure of the Christian churches, in the United States and in Europe, to rescue more Jews from Nazism. This failure is especially striking since a few religious leaders in both North America and Europe tried to create genuine interfaith cooperation to help those fleeing Nazism. In addition, some of the earliest and most forthright condemnations of the persecution and genocide of the European Jews came from religious leaders, including Christian leaders, in both continents.

Despite this, religious aid to refugees (and the churches' advocacy on behalf of the European Jews) proved to be piecemeal and ineffective. It remained the initiative of a progressive minority that was unable to generate commitment and support for this work among the church members. Ultimately, Christian refugee organizations in the United States and Europe—most of whom focused their relief efforts on "non-Aryan" Christians—received far more financial support from Jewish organizations than from their own member congregations.

---

[*] This chapter is based upon a paper originally delivered at the twenty-eighth Annual Scholars Conference on the Churches and the Holocaust at the University of Seattle, Washington, in 1998.

There are several excellent studies that deal with this history, and I will not repeat them here.[1] Here I will review an important element of this history that is often overlooked: the ecumenical context of religious efforts to help refugees. I want to look especially at the relationship between ecumenical efforts in the United States and in Europe, and at some of the differences in theological and political perspectives that shaped the churches' actions on both continents. A comparative look at the key ecumenical developments on the two continents might give us some deeper insights into what happened—in particular, into why the early ecumenical efforts on behalf of European Jews failed to find wider resonance and be more effective. While most of the churches' efforts on behalf of refugees were on behalf of Christian refugees—who comprised some 30 percent of those who fled Nazism—I want today to look at the churches' activity with respect to Jewish refugees and Jewish organizations.

I

Both in their refugee efforts and their response to the German church struggle, the U.S. churches were influenced by their ecumenical relationships with churches in Europe. These relationships were complex; they had been shaped by the very different experiences of the respective churches, as well as by their theological and institutional differences.

Despite these differences, ecumenical leaders on both continents shared the same goals. One was the creation of a Christian unity that would transcend denominational and national boundaries. The other was the creation of a viable church witness on social and political issues.

These issues took different forms in the United States and Europe. In the United States, the Federal Council of Churches (FCC) was founded in 1908. It initially consisted of 33 denominations, and in its early years, it worked to establish a network of state and local councils of churches throughout the country. It also reached out to establish relations with the Catholic, Canadian, and European churches.[2]

Much of its early focus was on the so-called social gospel questions: labor issues, race relations, and cooperation with international pacifist groups. In all these endeavors, the emphasis was on religious unity: not just among different denominations, but among different religions. Indeed, one factor that characterized ecumenical work in the United States was its emphasis on using consensus on social and political issues to build ecumenical relationships. Doctrinal or theological differences were secondary—as the German theologian (and subsequent resistance figure) Dietrich Bonhoeffer observed when he came to United States as a student in 1930:

> I wanted to tell you before about the Federal Council. I got to know personally all the leading figures here. People talked about everything, except about theology. . . . They talk as if all the basic questions have already been answered. But that's not even remotely the case.[3]

Thus, when U.S. churches worked on issues like racism and unemployment during the 1920s—especially on the local level—they were often joined by Catholic and Jewish organizations. As Lerond Curry puts it in his study of Catholic and Protestant relations, Americans "tended not so much to have religion in the sense of strong convictions as to use religion to further their own social and political desires."[4] In the United States, the enemy of ecumenism was denominationalism and provincialism.

The early ecumenical tone in Europe was quite different. Although there were international Christian organizations in the nineteenth century, the world ecumenical movement really began with the World Mission Conference in Edinburgh in 1910. Like their counterparts in the United States, the Europeans also wrestled with the social issues of the day. Their approach to these issues, however, was not characterized by the pragmatism and interfaith cooperation of the groups in the United States, but by lengthy theological debates to discern where they could legitimately take a stand in terms of doctrine and tradition. In Europe, the ecumenical task was not to unite different denominations in common cause, but to foster understanding among the church representatives of different traditions and nations. In the wake of the First World War, this was not an easy task. An early meeting in 1923 in Zurich, for example, almost ended in a fight between French and German delegates about the occupation of the Ruhr region.[5]

Thus, the enemy faced by the early ecumenical leaders in Europe was not denominationalism, but nationalism. As Andrew Chandler writes, "Humane, liberal minds saw that nationalism led to suspicion, hostility, and conflict."[6] The early ecumenists joined the internationalists of the era and the founders of the League of Nations in the belief that nationalism had caused the First World War and continued to jeopardize relations among their countries during the 1920s. The experience of the First World War made a number of them confirmed pacifists. Many of them hoped that the ecumenical movement would create ties that would transcend national boundaries and foster permanent reconciliation, not just among the churches, but also among the nations.

The issue was not just political nationalism, but also its variations that arose during the 1920s. The European ecumenical leader Adolf Keller described these variations as "a kind of a religion—the religion of blood."[7] The ecumenical enterprise, he wrote, was opposed by a "rival, hostile, secular ecumenism" that sought not common religious ground, but rather the establishment of churches along the divisive boundaries of race and nationalism.[8] The European debate over this kind of nationalism predated the German church struggle—but it involved the same cast of characters.[9] Some of the strongest theological opposition to the ecumenical movement, in fact, emerged from within Germany, and many of the names involved are familiar. They include Emanuel Hirsch and Paul Althaus, who subsequently became theological apologists for some aspects of Nazism. The German theologian Emanuel Hirsch opposed the ecumenical movement in 1925, "charging that the call for church unity across national boundaries was politically motivated, and suggesting that the boundaries of the Volk and the church should ideally coincide."[10] In 1931, Hirsch and Althaus "published a joint protest against German participation" in any ecumenical movement.[11]

The opposing viewpoint was represented by Germans like Dietrich Bonhoeffer, who had already written in *Sanctorum Communio* in 1927 that "there is a moment when the church dare not continue to be a national church."[12] Other supporters of the ecumenical spirit in Germany included Paul Tillich, Hans Ehrenberg, and Friedrich Siegmund-Schultze, all of whom were forced to leave Nazi Germany (in Siegmund-Schultze's case, in the summer of 1933, after the Gestapo arrested him and charged him on 93 counts of helping Jews).

This background shaped the ways in which the churches abroad responded to some of the issues that arose in the German church struggle. It also shaped the attitudes of Jews, Protestants, and Catholics toward one another. There was virtually no history of interfaith work in Europe, nor had such cooperation or dialogue emerged during the 1920s.

In the United States, however, there was some precedent for interfaith cooperation among Jews, Protestants, and Catholics. This work arose out of the common ground of social issues; in 1919, for example, the Roman Catholic Church, FCC, and Central Conference of American Rabbis released a joint statement about labor issues such as the 12-hour day and working conditions in the steel industry.[13] The National Conference of Christians and Jews (NCCJ), founded in 1928, grew out of the early attempts at Christian and Jewish cooperation during the 1920s. These attempts ranged from pulpit exchanges to discussion groups where Catholics, Protestants, and Jews explained points of doctrine to one another.[14] In 1923, the FCC had established a subcommittee, the

Commission on International Justice and Goodwill, to reduce anti-Jewish, anti-Catholic, and racial prejudice. This commission worked throughout the 1920s to promote increased local contacts among the three major faiths.

The National Conference of Christians and Jews emerged from this work; early participants included the FCC leader Samuel Cavert, Rabbi Stephen Wise, Jonah Wise, and Felix Warburg. During the 1930s, it was led by Rev. Everett Clinchy. In 1934, it sponsored a national Brotherhood Day, and its "Ten Commandments of Good Will" was read in about 2,000 U.S. communities. It also sponsored local discussion groups with representatives of different races and religions; by 1938, there were 1,150 of them.[15]

From the beginning the NCCJ was committed not just to cooperation around social issues, but also to changing Christian theological attitudes toward Judaism. In its founding statement, it recognized that "Perhaps no page of history, called Christian, bears more blots and stains on it than that which records the relations of Christians and Jews during almost two thousand years."[16] At a board meeting of the group in February 1930, Dr. Ernest Halliday of the Congregation Board of Home Missions spoke on proselytizing. Was it possible, he asked, to "work with (my rabbi colleagues) as I would with the minister of another Protestant communion and with a Roman priest, or shall I work against him? It scarcely seems possible that I can do both."[17] If Christians were to join Jews in working for tolerance and social justice, he concluded, they had to abandon attempts to convert them. Christians could only proselytize among those Jews, he said, who "after fair trial . . . cannot be won back to the faith of their fathers."[18]

This theological rethinking was not simply based on the shared battle against racism and prejudice. The essence of the "Ten Commandments of Good Will" was its deep commitment to democratic principles. Its underlying assumption was that since racism, religious prejudice, and injustice undermined the democratic system, religious leaders were called to oppose these things, whatever their theological differences.

After 1933, U.S. Christian leaders did not consciously follow the blueprint set by the National Conference of Christians and Jews. But the statements about the persecution of Jews in Germany that emerged from the FCC and from leading Christians like Reinhold Niebuhr were striking for their emphasis on civil liberties and the role of Christians in a democracy.

This was in marked contrast to the situation in Germany, of course, and in Europe as a whole. In the German churches, on all points of the ideological spectrum, the perception existed that there was indeed a

"Jewish question." Those who joined the Confessing Church (and many of their allies in the European churches) argued that this was a theological, not a racial, issue. But it was still an issue. The question was when the Jews would finally achieve salvation through Christ. The larger question, which we find in the church statements of the period, concerned issues of assimilation, national identity, and Christian culture.

This perspective was articulated even by some in the ecumenical movement. In 1933, Hans Schönfeld, who worked for the Council for Life and Work in Geneva, sent a confidential report to Samuel Cavert at the FCC, in which he wrote:

> Regarding the Jewish question. One must realize that it had become a real problem in Germany, due to two factors. The first is that the Jews in the post-war period had gained an influence which was in fact out of proportion, not only to their numbers in the total population, but also to their significance as a cultural factor. . . . The second factor, and this is the more important one, is the considerable number of Jews who immigrated from Eastern Europe. They were in many cases of an undesirable type, as alien to German Jews as to the country as a whole. It cannot, I believe, be denied that their influence in numerous instances has been unfortunate and harmful. This is for an explanation—not as a justification—of the persecution of Jews in Germany.[19]

Outside Germany, such statements drew criticism from some ecumenical leaders but found a sympathetic hearing among others. The strong desire for unity and reconciliation among the churches meant a strong commitment, both in North America and Europe, to preserving relations with the German churches.[20] Thus, particularly in the early stages, there was considerable caution toward the Confessing Church, especially its more radical members. In England, because of Bishop George Bell's respect for Siegmund-Schultze and Dietrich Bonhoeffer, Bell became a strong proponent of the Confessing Church in Britain. But even in his church, there was by no means agreement on whom to support, especially during the turbulent early period of the church struggle.

This was also true of the FCC. Its leaders, such as William Adams Brown, Henry Leiper, Samuel Cavert, and S. Parkes Cadman issued strong statements against Nazi anti-Jewish measures and demanded a response from the German Evangelical Church. At the same time, they continued to work for cooperation with the official leaders of the German church, including Reich Bishop Ludwig Müller, and tried to keep their options open. In the late summer of 1933, Henry Smith Leiper visited Germany and reported back to Cavert, after meeting with Müller and a number of German Christian leaders, that they were "all most anxious for the closest relations with us and with the Ecumenical Movement." Having heard the German Christian side of the story, Leiper wrote that he realized that he had been given "some very basic misrepresentations of the German situation":

> Gleichschaltung apparently does not mean in the minds of such men a weak conformity. . . . It does mean trying to tune together, in the radio or musical sense, the various organs of social expression in the land . . . means the search for like disposition, similar will, cooperative relations, and coordination of effort. In that sense it is not so evil a thing as it has been made to appear. . . . I learn, apparently on unimpeachable authority, that contrary to our impression the victory of the 'German Christians' in the recent (July) elections was not simply the result of pressure or intimidation or manipulation of the voting. . . . Mueller and his most vociferous supporters are not impressive as close followers of Jesus; they tend, while rejecting the Old Testament emphasis on the Hebrew contribution to religious history, to be very much like the Old Testament in spirit. What the Jews of the Old Testament did to non-Jews with religious zeal and inhuman ferocity many of the 'German Christians' are quite prepared to do to the Jews, as we know to our sorrow. . . . The general feeling is that Germany hangs still in the balance. . . . The stability of the mark depends on American support financially and they fear what Jewish influence in banking may do in these circumstances. The eventual success of Hitler is not assured and German leaders know it. But they see only chaos if he fails.[21]

Thus, although they continued to feel strongly that Nazi measures against the Jews and the churches were antidemocratic, church leaders remained cautious about statements that could endanger their relations with the German churches. This attitude, while not directly tied to subsequent refugee efforts, did have an effect on what the churches were willing to do publicly to support the refugees. In March 1933, for example, the FCC board member Walter Van Kirk wrote to Leiper:

> I have been talking with [Everett] Clinchy and James G. MacDonald regarding the possibility of having the Federal Council take action on the Hitler persecution of the Jews. . . . European churchmen have been in a measure critical of the so-called intrusion of American churchmen into strictly European matters. . . . The Protestant forces of Germany, in the main, seem to be in substantial agreement with the Hitler movement. Is it not likely, therefore, that any action on our part would be deeply resented by the German Protestant Church?[22]

During this period, the German church struggle was so delicate that even Siegmund-Schultze warned Cavert, in 1933, that the FCC should be cautious. In a confidential letter to the U.S. church leaders Cavert, Rushbrooke, and Macfarland, Siegmund-Schultze argued against statements by foreign churches about what was happening in Germany, saying that he feared it would drive the German churches to leave the ecumenical movement, just as the Nazi state had left the international organizations.[23] In 1938, British Bishop Headlam wrote Archbishop Cosmo Lang that the British "attitude toward the German Church has been very largely a mistaken one. The important thing is that Hitler should learn to respect Christianity. He will not do that if Christianity is used to oppose National Socialism, and if scatterbrained English divines flirt with Bolshevism."[24] As late as 1939, Bishop Berggrav of Norway warned against isolating the German church and creating "a Maginot line of churches."[25]

II

The ecumenical context of religious efforts on behalf of refugees, therefore, was complex. But the early signals that came from churches in Europe and the United States suggested a basic opposition to the Nazi measures against the Jews and a readiness to do something on behalf of the refugees from Germany. Throughout 1933, European and U.S. ecumenical leaders pleaded with German church leaders for a clear condemnation of the Nazi measures against the Jews.[26] In March, the FCC sent a protest letter to German Church Council member August Schreiber demanding a condemnation of the attacks on the Jews. In a letter the same month to Professor Julius Richter in Berlin, the FCC associate general secretary Henry Smith Leiper stated the American case succinctly: "The Jew does not always have an easy time in the United States to be sure, but as you know there is a very deep rooted conviction in the American mind that religious freedom is an inalienable right of man."[27]

By the beginning of April 1933, when 3,000 Jewish refugees had arrived in Switzerland, the Swiss church president Henriod sent a message to the German churches asking for a clear position.[28] In April, the French Protestant leader Wilfred Monod published an open letter welcoming the Jews coming from Germany to France.[29] In May, British Bishop George Bell wrote German Church President Kapler of his concern about actions against the Jews.[30] At the ecumenical World Alliance conference in Sofia, Bulgaria, in September 1933, the delegates passed a resolution condemning the Nazi actions against the Jews:

> We especially deplore the fact that the state measures against the Jews in Germany have had such an effect on public opinion that in some circles the Jewish race is considered a race of inferior status.[31]

In both the United States and Europe, of course, these concerns for the Jews of Germany were triggered not just by reports of what was happening in Germany but also by the numbers of refugees that began to flee. In Europe, Friedrich Siegmund-Schultze made an early attempt to create a coalition of Jews, Protestants, and Catholics in Berlin in 1933. This failed not only because of his early exile, but also because, even outside Germany, "Protestant, Catholic, and Jewish authorities showed a reluctance to collaborate with one another on such a broad venture."[32]

In the United States, the response to the refugee crisis was initially, albeit briefly, marked by interfaith interest. Eventually, as Genizi's book shows, the religious organizations aiding refugees essentially split along religious lines, with Christian organizations aiding Christians and Jewish organizations helping Jews. Nonetheless, the early meetings of some of these organizations, notably the American Committee for Christian German Refugees, deliberately included representatives of Jewish, Catholic, and Protestant groups.

There was one organization that continued to try to build both an interfaith and an international consensus—the National Conference of Christians and Jews, mentioned earlier. While it was never officially active in refugee work, it became very active unofficially in trying to create an ecumenical network that could help refugees. This network extended into Europe. These efforts coincided both with the brief tenure of James McDonald as High Commissioner for Refugees and with the early efforts of some European Jews to create a network of aid for those trying to escape Nazism.

The intensity of James McDonald's disappointment and bitterness against religious apathy, addressed when he resigned as High Commissioner of Refugees in 1936, may have been due in part to his expectations when he began his work in 1933. His early correspondence illustrates that he viewed the churches as important potential allies and hoped to create a network in United States and abroad that could confront the refugee problem. Thus, shortly after he began his work, he sought out representatives of religious groups in the United States and Europe, including the National Conference of Christians and Jews.[33]

McDonald soon discovered the limits of the churches' readiness to really work with other faiths. The U.S. Catholics were represented briefly on the American Committee for Christian German Refugees; by 1934, however, they had withdrawn to form their own committees. The attempts of Robert Ashworth at the National Conference of Christians and Jews and Christians to win Catholic involvement were thwarted. In March 1934, McDonald wrote to Ashworth:

> This is to acknowledge your telegram in which you suggested I get in touch with the Apostolic Delegate in Washington, with a view to securing his possible endorsement of the effort to raise funds through the American Christian Committee for German refugees. After conferring with a number of important Catholics in Washington, I decided not to attempt to take this matter up with the Apostolic Delegate. It seemed to my Catholic friends that there was no chance at all that your suggestion would be accepted, and more of a fear was expressed that it would seem inappropriate that the issue be raised in precisely that form.[34]

McDonald's efforts to set up an interfaith network were not confined to the United States. In addition to contacting Canadian religious and political leaders, he made an early journey to Europe, where he hoped to establish an interfaith European committee that could distribute funds for the American Christian Committee for German refugees (ACGR). Among the members that McDonald suggested for this committee were Bishop George Bell and representatives of the Quakers and Catholics.[35]

One of McDonald's Jewish contacts in Europe was a doctor named Bernhard Kahn. Kahn was born in Sweden in 1876 but studied and settled in Germany, where he founded the German Aid Association of German Jews (Hilfsverein der deutschen Juden) in 1901, in response to the pogroms in Eastern Europe. In the years before the First World War, he became a leader in refugee and immigration affairs. He traveled throughout Eastern Europe in areas where Jews had fallen victim to pogroms, and also intervened on behalf of Russian prisoners during the First World War in Germany and set up an interconfessional committee to help them. He met with governmental representatives to arrange exchanges of prisoners and became well known in Poland, Russia, and France for his efforts.[36] In 1920, he was asked to lead European refugee work for the United States Jewish Distribution Committee; and he later represented that organization at the conference in Evian.

Kahn left Nazi Germany in 1933 for France. Early in 1934, John McDonald, on his first trip to Europe as High Commissioner for Refugees, met with Kahn in London and gave him a check for 500,000

French francs from the American Jewish Joint Distribution Committee for refugee work.[37]

McDonald was not the only American to meet with Kahn. In May 1935, Rabbi Morris Lazaron of Baltimore traveled to Europe for the National Conference of Christians and Jews and stayed with Kahn in Paris. Lazaron also traveled to Germany and sent a detailed report of his impressions to Everett Clinchy, who passed the letter on to Henry Smith Leiper at the FCC: "Many Protestant pastors are still in prison. . . . I had a message from Cardinal Faulhaber that he is virtually in prison. . . . For the first time Catholic official cooperation is authorized. Dr. Baeck meets this week with a Catholic who will contact Protestants."[38]

The prospects of such interfaith efforts, however, were undercut by the same factors that plagued religious refugee efforts as a whole, including a lack of widespread support among church members and the tendency of different churches to establish their own organizations. The very existence of the National Conference of Christians and Jews as an interfaith organization depended on its maintaining a certain distance from the FCC. As Henry Smith Leiper explained in 1939:

> In the case of the National Conference of Christians and Jews the case is different because of course to do its work this organization has to be independent. As you know, it was founded by the Federal Council and made independent when it became clear that only so could it get real solid cooperation from bodies not in the Federal Council—both Jewish and Catholic.[39]

While Lazaron reported on his meetings with European leaders of all faiths, most of his report emphasized this interfaith work in terms of its relevance to democratic values. His main concern was that Protestant, Catholic, and Jewish leaders unite to combat Nazi propaganda. Only such unity had a chance of saving the victims of Nazism. "We are fighting with our backs to the wall," he wrote, "and daily the situation grows worse. As I told you in Rome: it is no longer a question of Jews; it's the larger issue of the destruction of an entire generation so far as our traditional ideals are concerned."[40]

III

To some extent, the alliance of Christian faith with the political ideals of democracy had influenced the ecumenical movement from the beginning. Underneath the concept of unity among churches was the firm belief that Western civilization embodied certain ideals that were consistent with Christian faith, and that the time had come for the Church to witness these ideals in its life in the world.

In the United States, this conviction was at the heart of religious efforts during the 1920s to create an interfaith network. Among Europeans, it manifested itself during the 1920s in some of the debates about pacifism and nationalism. Between 1939 and 1945, the identification of the ecumenical spirit with the spirit of democracy was a theme that permeated the ecumenical documents of the period. It comes up especially in the documents written during the war that sought to define prerequisites for a just postwar peace, including documents that emerged from the World Council of Churches (WCC) in Geneva, as well as John Foster Dulles's "Six Pillars of Peace" paper.

In 1939, President Roosevelt had stressed the need for cooperation between the "seekers of light" (religious groups) and "seekers of peace" (governmental leaders). In the bitter years that followed, many religious leaders put great hope in this cooperative effort.

The result was that, once the war began, religious refugee work became a "political orphan."[41] The priority of the Allied governments was to win the war, and "religious groups were expected to conform to Allied military policy."[42] It was not that religious refugee work stopped. On the contrary, the events in Eastern Europe and the deportations of the German Jews beginning in 1941 alarmed religious leaders throughout the world. Especially in the United States and Great Britain, they lobbied their governments to allow more refugees in and to prevent restrictive immigration laws.[43] By the end of 1941, they certainly realized that their efforts literally meant life and death for the European Jews. Even as the deportations to the east began, some leaders still hoped to save parts of the Jewish population. In February 1940, 1,200 German Jews were deported without warning from the town of Stettin. In the foreign protests that followed, Adolf Freudenberg, director of the refugee office at the WCC in Geneva, wired the FCC for money. He estimated that he needed $4,400 a month to enable more refugees to enter Switzerland. The reply from New York, a telegram from Henry Smith Leiper, is one of the bleakest documents of the period: "Deeply regret funds dependent on receipts impossible estimate large amounts improbable stop can you use two steamship tickets Geneva-New York."[44]

When, in March 1943, the Protestant ecumenical leader William Visser 't Hooft telegraphed Archbishop of Canterbury William Temple that 15,000 Jews had been deported from Berlin, Temple gave an impassioned speech in the House of Lords asking the British government to let more refugees in.[45]

With the war going on and the onset of genocide on an unprecedented scale, however, the positions taken by the churches increasingly became shaped by the political realities and by their own attempts to shape those realities. As the persecution of the Jews intensified, the differences between Jewish and Christian leaders became painfully clear. The letters and telegrams of Jewish leaders like Stephen Wise in New York and Gerhart Riegner in Geneva urged church leaders to do more; they responded that they were doing all they could.[46] To be sure, there were statements that represent ecumenical milestones. One was the December 1938 condemnation of the so-called Kristallnacht pogrom issued jointly by the FCC and the Catholic Church.[47] The declaration condemning the genocide of the Jews, issued on March 19, 1943, by the WCC and the World Jewish Congress in Geneva, was another milestone. Not only was this sent to Christian and Jewish bodies, but copies were also sent to the British and U.S. governments, the Papal Nuncio in Bern, and Allen Dulles at the Office of Strategic Intelligence.[48]

Its reception among church leaders was mixed. In England, for example, William Paton, the general secretary of the International Mission Council, remarked that the WCC leader Visser 't Hooft had come under the sway of the Zionists.[49] Yet the statement had some effect on member churches: the amount of money sent by the FCC to the refugee offices in Switzerland increased.[50]

In general, however, none of it was enough. The history of the world's religious communities and the refugees from Nazism is a very complex one, and here I have only been able to outline one part of it. There are many parts of this history that I have not touched on, and that are crucial in any understanding of what the churches were doing: the apathy and antisemitism of many church members; the theological anti-Judaism that emerges even in some of the ecumenical writings of people who were helping refugees; the role of the Catholic and Protestant churches in Europe in receiving and conveying messages from the German resistance, and the effect this had on what the churches were willing to say publicly; and the various visions for the postwar period that emerge from Christian and Jewish documents during the final years of the war.

Yet I hope that I have given a glimpse of what Visser 't Hooft called the "war behind the war"—"a war of spirits, a war in which great spiritual powers struggle for the possession of the human soul."[51] Henry Feingold has observed that during the Holocaust, many people believed "that there exists such a spirit of civilization, a sense of humanitarian concern in the world, which could have been mobilized to save Jewish lives during the Holocaust." But such a spirit, says Feingold, "did not in fact exist."[52] The irony is that the ecumenical movement, at its best, hoped and attempted to embody such a spirit. If we are to understand its failures, we must reflect on the complexity of that failure.

NOTES

1. Several studies on this topic already exist, and there is a considerable amount of literature on the specific issues that faced the churches on both continents. The works of Haim Genizi (*American Apathy*) and William Nawyn (*American Protestantism's Response to Germany's Jews and Refugees, 1933–1941*) offer detailed studies of Christian refugee attempts in the United States. J. N. Nichols's study of religious refugee work (*The Uneasy Alliance*) has an analysis of work in this field before 1933, as well as an excellent chapter on the Nazi era. Robert Ross's study of the U.S. religious press (*So It Was True*) during the period, while not about refugee efforts per se, offers much insight into the mentality and apathy of church members.

   In Europe, the role played by the churches in refugee work and rescue is usually discussed in the broader context of their ties to the Confessing Church and the church struggle and, during the war, to the German resistance. In addition to the numerous memoirs and accounts of individual Christian rescue activities, Adolf Freudenberg's *Rettet sie doch* and Armin Boyens's two-volume work *Kirchenkampf und Ökumene* look at the ecumenical efforts to help refugees. Winfried Meyer's *Unternehmen Sieben* and Klemens von Klemperer's *German Resistance against Hitler: The Search for Allies Abroad* shed additional light on the German resistance's attempts to use church connections to gain support abroad and to assist the small networks in Europe that were rescuing Jews from Nazism. More recently, two excellent studies of ecumenical networks in Europe have appeared: Uta Gerdes, *Ökumenische Solidarität mit christlichen und jüdischen Verfolgten: Die Cimade in Vichy-Frankreich 1940–1944* (Göttingen: Vandenhoeck & Ruprecht, 2005) and Jörg Ernesti, *Ökumene im Dritten Reich* (Paderborn: Bornifatius, 2007), which looks particularly at the Catholics' connections to other networks.

2. The minutes of U.S. Executive Committee of the World Alliance. Federal Council of Churches (FCC) papers, Presbyterian Historical Archive (PHA), RG 18 Box 44 F 10: "World Alliance for International Friendship, Correspondence, Jan 1917–Dec 1945." For a study of earlier interfaith efforts in this country, see Lawrence G. Charap, "'Accept the Truth from Whomsoever [*sic*] Gives It': Jewish-Protestant Dialogue, Interfaith Alliances, and Pluralism, 1880–1910," *American Jewish History* 89, no.3 (Sept. 2001): 261–77.

3. Letter of 12.26.1930, published in *Barcelona, Berlin, New York: 1928–1931,* in Dietrich Bonhoeffer Works, vol. 10 (Minneapolis: Fortress Press, 2008), 267.

4. Lerond Curry, *Protestant-Catholic Relations in America: World War II through Vatican II* (Lexington: University Press of Kentucky, 1972), 23.

5. Report by William Adams Brown, May 16, 1923. FCC papers, PHA, RG 18 Box 44 F 10: "World Alliance for International Friendship, Correspondence, Jan 1917–Dec 1945."

6. Andrew Chandler, ed., *Brethren in Adversity: Bishop George Bell, the Church of England, and the Crisis of German Protestantism, 1933–1939* (Suffolk: Church of England Record Society, 1997), 3.

7. Report from Adolf Keller, Geneva, January 19, 1933. FCC papers, PHA, RG 18 Box 9 F 15: "General Secretary Foreign Correspondence, Jan–May 1933."

8. Adolf Keller, *Church and State on the European Continent* (London: Epworth, 1936), 361.

9. See A. James Reimer, *The Emanuel Hirsch and Paul Tillich Debate: A Study in the Political Ramifications of Theology,* Toronto Studies in Theology, vol. 42. (Lewiston: Edwin Mellen, 1989).

10. Ibid., 61.

11. Ibid.

12. Dietrich Bonhoeffer, *The Communion of the Saints* (New York: Harper and Row, 1963), 189.

13. William J. Schmidt, *Architect of Unity: A Biography of Samuel McCrea Cavert* (New York: Friendship Press, 1978), 120.

14. FCC information service, May 8, 1926, press release on "The Literature of Understanding." FCC papers, PHA, RG 18 Box 10 F 18: "Goodwill between Jews and Christians."

15. Curry, *Protestant-Catholic Relations*, 30.

16. Document, October 26, 1928. FCC papers, PHA, RG 18 Box 10 F 18: "Goodwill between Jews and Christians."

17. Ibid., minutes of the National Conference of Christians and Jews meeting, February 21, 1930.

18. Ibid.

19. "The Situation in Germany," by H. Schoenfeld, dated April 25, 1933. FCC papers, PHA, RG 18 Box 9 F 15: "General Secretary Foreign Correspondence, Jan–May 1933."

20. See especially the reports by A. J. Macdonald and Bishop Batty in Chandler, *Brethren in Adversity*.

21. Henry Smith Leiper papers, Burke Library, Union Theological Seminary, New York: Folder, Correspondence—Federal Council of Churches 1934–39, Letter, Leiper to Cavert, en route to Copenhagen, September 2, 1933.

22. Ibid., Letter Walter Van Kirk to Leiper, March 20, 1933.

23. Letter, Siegmund-Schultze to Cavert, October 17, 1933. FCC papers, PHA, RG 18 Box 9 F 15: "General Secretary Foreign Correspondence."

24. In Chandler, *Brethren in Adversity*, 152.

25. Klemens von Klemperer, *German Resistance against Hitler: The Search for Allies Abroad 1938–1945* (Oxford: Clarendon, 1992), 45.

26. See Boyens, *Kirchenkampf und Oikumene 1933–1939* (Munich: Chr. Kaiser, 1969), 43–44, 290.

27. Burke Library, UTS Archive, Henry Smith Leiper papers, Letter March 15, 1933.

28. Ibid., 43.

29. "European Survey," Keller, Geneva, April 6, 1933, FCC papers, PHA, RG 18 Box 9 F 15: "General Secretary Foreign Correspondence, Jan–May 1933."

30. Ibid., 309.

31. Eberhard Bethge, *Dietrich Bonhoeffer: Theologian, Christian, Man for His Times,* New revised English edition, ed. Victoria J. Barnett (Minneapolis: Fortress Press, 2000), 315.

32. See John S. Conway, "Pacifism and Patriotism: Friedrich Siegmund-Schultze," in Nicosia and Stokes, eds., *Germans against Nazism: Nonconformity, Opposition, and Resistance in the Third Reich* (Oxford: Berg, 1990), 91–92 and 110 nn. 8–9.

33. Archive, Leo Baeck Institute (LBI), New York, "High Commission for Refugees: Correspondence, Dec 7, 1933–Feb 1934." (AR 7162).

34. Ibid., March 18, 1934.

35. Ibid., letter to Robert Ashworth, American Christian Committee for German Refugees, April 3, 1934; letter, December 13, 1933, to George Bell, Bishop of Chichester.

36. Archive, LBI, New York, Bernhard Kahn collection, Folder I, "Biographische Notizen 1936." (Ar-CA 187–416)

37. Archive, LBI, New York, High Commission for Refugees, letter to Bernard Kahn in London, February 9, 1934; Text of telegram, January 22, 1934, to Bernhard Kahn in Paris, setting up the London meeting with him.

38. Burke Library, UTS, Henry Smith Leiper papers. Letter, Lazaron to Clinchy, from Amsterdam, May 13, 1935. Leiper's reply to Lazaron (c/o Kahn in Paris), June 7, 1935.

39. Letter, Leiper to Roy McCorkel, May 23, 1939. FCC papers, PHA, RG9 B 64 F 2: "Interseminary Movement, Henry Smith Leiper."

40. Burke Library, UTS, Henry Smith Leiper papers. Letter, Lazaron to Clinchy, May 13, 1935.

41. J. Bruce Nichols, *The Uneasy Alliance: Religion, Refugee work, and U.S. Foreign Policy* (New York: Oxford University Press, 1988), 53.

42. Ibid., 55.

43. See the correspondence between Samuel Cavert and William Paton (May–August 1941) about lobbying in both countries and Canada against the Allen bill, which attempted to bar refugees who had been in Nazi prisons or camps. FCC papers, PHA, RG 18 Box 9 F 18: "General Secretary Foreign Correspondence Nov 29, 1939–1941." There is additional material in the FCC papers in RG 18 Box 33 F 18: "Immigration June 1919–1947."

44. Armin Boyens, *Kirchenkampf und Ökumene 1939–1945* (Munich: Chr. Kaiser Verlag, 1973), 45–46.

45. Boyens, *Kirchenkampf und Oikumene 1939–1945*, 130–131.

46. An example is the exchange of letters between Stephen Wise and Henry Smith Leiper in October 1937. Burke Library, UTS, Henry Smith Leiper papers: Folder, Correspondence—Federal Council of Churches 1934–39.

47. "Joint Resolution which was adopted relative to the totalitarian attacks on religious minorities," "signed by both Roman Catholic and Protestant Christians," December 23, 1938. It was signed by all member churches of FCC, as well as by the Orthodox, Southern Baptists, United Church of Canada (affiliated), Catholics, and Episcopalians. It was the first time that Roman Catholic, Anglican, and Protestant Christians had issued a formal declaration on a contemporary issue.

48. Boyens, *Kirchenkampf und Oikumene 1939–1945*, 127ff.

49. Ibid., 127 n. 153.

50. See Boyens, *Kirchenkampf und Oikumene 1939–1945,* 129ff.

51. Library of Congress, Reinhold Niebuhr papers, File: World Council of Churches, 1940–48. Visser 't Hooft, "The Ecumenical Church and the International Situation," April 1940.

52. Henry Feingold, "Who Shall Bear Guilt for the Holocaust: The Human Dilemma," in Michael Marrus, ed., *The Nazi Holocaust*, vol. 8, *Bystanders to the Holocaust* (Westport: Meckler, 1989) 141–142.

CHAPTER 2

"THE FATHERHOOD OF GOD AND BROTHERHOOD OF MAN": MAINLINE AMERICAN PROTESTANTS AND THE KRISTALLNACHT POGROM

KYLE JANTZEN

Within the literature that concerns itself with North American responses to the Holocaust, there exists a wide range of opinion. On one end of the spectrum is David Wyman's verdict that the American reaction to Jewish plight amounted to abandonment, and on the other end is William Rubinstein's insistence that it was a myth that anything significant could have been done to rescue Jews. Amid the lamentations over the weakness of North American responses to the Holocaust, it has been asserted that the Christian churches were especially culpable for their ambivalence toward and neglect of the Jews suffering persecution in Nazi Germany. To use a Canadian example, Irving Abella and Harold Troper argued that "most Canadians seemed indifferent to the suffering of German Jews and hostile to their admission to Canada," then went on to assert that "the churches remained silent."[1]

In the case of Protestantism, the Canadian historians Alan Davies and Marilyn F. Nefsky have surveyed a variety of denominations in response to the charges of Abella and Troper, while American scholars like William Nawyn and Robert Ross have explored aspects of the American response to the Holocaust.[2] Their gloomy conclusions suggest that the Protestant churches fared little better than other institutions or social groups in responding to the tremendous moral and political challenges of the Holocaust.

It is my intention to follow of these initial forays into the responses of North American Christians to the Holocaust, and to begin from a very specific point of departure, namely, the protests and petitions of liberal or mainline Protestants in the United States and Canada concerning the atrocities committed during Kristallnacht, the Nazi antisemitic pogrom of November 9–10, 1938.

First, let me provide some explanation for the parameters of my investigation.

Why study Kristallnacht? Quite simply, the November pogrom was and is widely regarded as a watershed—an event after which no reasonable person (either within Germany or internationally) could downplay the ideological importance or political radicalism of the National Socialist Jewish policy. It marks a point of transition between the escalating antisemitic measures of the 1930s and the increasing violence we associate with the wartime Holocaust. It is, therefore, a key moment at which to measure North American attitudes and actions.

Why study mainline (or liberal) Protestantism? Simply put, it was at the time the most prominent branch of Protestant Christianity in North America. It included Episcopalians (Anglicans in Canada), Presbyterians, Congregationalists, and some Methodists, along with members of the United Church of Canada—in short, the Protestant traditions most deeply rooted in North American society.

Why study initial reactions to Kristallnacht? While I am interested in the wider activities of the churches between the German annexation of Austria in March 1938 and the outbreak of the Second World War in September 1939, I have chosen to emphasize the immediate aftermath of Kristallnacht in the belief that the first few weeks after the November pogrom reveal most clearly the moral and theological strengths and weaknesses of these Protestant communities.

And finally, why study the public reporting of church reactions? Given that the churches had no direct control over the levers of political power—they could not recall ambassadors, seize German assets, increase refugee quotas, or declare war—the best measure of the churches' response would seem to be the extent to which they participated in and helped to shape the public debate around Nazi German brutality and the growing refugee crisis in Europe. For this reason, I have chosen to rely chiefly on public statements reported in leading daily newspapers in the United States and Canada, including the *New York Times*, *Washington Post*, and *Chicago Daily Tribune*, along with the *Toronto Star* and the *Globe and Mail*. This is based on the assumption that public addresses, press releases, and the news coverage of church-sponsored events were the chief means by which liberal Protestant church leaders achieved the widest audience for their message. I have supplemented this with some examples from the church press and the results of various public opinion polls of the day.

What I have found is that, in contrast to the "silence" so often attributed to the Christian churches of North America, liberal Protestant reactions to Kristallnacht were swift, energetic, and widely publicized. They were, to be sure, largely rhetorical in nature, and intentionally embedded within the broader public outcry against the brutal events in Germany. While more than a few liberal Protestant leaders called for aid to Jewish and other "non-Aryan" refugees from Germany, their most common responses revolved around condemning the Nazi attacks on Jews and pleading with the governments of the United States and Canada to make emphatic protests to Hitler and the German government.

In this chapter, I will examine three aspects of this liberal Christian response to Kristallnacht. First, I want to discuss the sociopolitical context in which mainline Protestants initially received news of the violence and mayhem of Kristallnacht. Second, I will outline four key moments between November 10 and 20, during which mainline American Protestants first voiced their disbelief and outrage, and then roundly condemned the National Socialist regime for its treatment of German Jews. While I will deal primarily with churches in the United States, I will also make some observations about the Canadian scene. Third, I will address, if only briefly, the question of practical aid for Jewish refugees.

CONTEXT

The sociopolitical and cultural context into which news of the Kristallnacht pogrom broke was filled with ambivalent and contradictory attitudes to both Germany and Jews. To be sure, even before Kristallnacht, Germany was very much on the minds of the American public. Widespread concern over Hitler's aggressive foreign and repressive domestic policies meant that Americans were already wary of the Führer and his regime. In a March 1938 poll, 65 percent of Americans regarded Germany as the nation that could least be trusted to keep the treaties it made.[3]

By the autumn of 1938, dozens of articles each week in leading American dailies were adding to Americans' unease about Germany. Only six weeks before Kristallnacht, the war scare in Europe was temporarily forestalled by the Munich Agreement, in which the English prime minister Chamberlain, French premier Daladier, Italian prime minister Mussolini, and German chancellor Hitler partitioned Czechoslovakia. Ostensibly, this sacrifice of the only functioning democracy in the heart of Europe had satiated Hitler's expansionist appetite, though neither Europeans nor Americans could be sure. Indeed, when the pollster George Gallup asked Britons and Americans whether they believed that Hitler had no more territorial ambitions in Europe, as the German dictator had promised, 93 and 92 percent, respectively, answered no.[4]

More ominous still were arresting articles like "Nazi Propaganda" in the *Chicago Daily Tribune*, which carried a reproduction of maps taken from Nazi leaflets distributed in the Sudeten region just prior to its occupation by German forces. The maps showed a year-by-year progression in which Germany conquered Poland and Hungary in 1939; Rumania, Bulgaria, and Yugoslavia in 1940; and Ukraine, Switzerland, and the northern half of France in 1941. As the article explained, the propaganda maps continued right through 1948, by which time Germany and Italy were to have divided up all of Europe (Great Britain included) into their two spheres of influence.[5]

Editorials in various papers early in November 1938 argued that Germany had essentially won control of Central Europe—all without firing a shot. Barnet Nover of the *Washington Post* exclaimed, "The balance of power that obtained in Europe before the Munich settlement has been upset beyond any possibility of restoration. Germany bestrides the Old World like a colossus; there is none to oppose her."[6] The same day, in the *New York Times*, Anne O'Hare McCormack's column on "Europe" contained the subheadline "Decisions at Vienna Mark New Axis of Power."[7] Over at the *Christian Science Monitor*, Demaree Bess described the Munich Agreement as a "comparatively bloodless and cheap" victory for Hitler: "Germany now dominates eastern and central Europe. To all the smaller countries east of the Rhine it appears to be clear that Germany has fought and won a 'war.'"[8]

Other articles in the days leading up to Kristallnacht discussed Nazi press attacks on America, French proposals for additional fortifications on the Maginot Line, President Roosevelt's plan for an emergency budget to pay for 7,000 to 10,000 planes and 400,000 troops, new British designs for bombproof shelters, German demands for the return of African colonies seized by Britain and France in the Treaty of Versailles, and the tragic

Polish refugee crisis precipitated by the Nazi expulsion of thousands of Polish Jews across the eastern German border with Poland.

At the *New York Times*, writers looked ahead to the upcoming celebration of the twentieth anniversary of the Armistice of 1918 with dismay. Under the headline "Armistice Day: The Drama Unfolds" Samuel T. Williamson wrote a four-page recollection of the closing months of the World War, after which he reflected on the recent resurrection of German power in Europe. Under the subheadline "Twenty Years After the Humbling of Imperial Germany A Powerful Reich Flings Out a Challenge to the World," Williamson lamented that the Treaty of Versailles had been "chewed to pieces," that the recent redrawing of the map of Europe had given Germany more territory in 1938 that it had possessed in 1914, and that Germany was once again the "best-armed nation in the world." He went on to describe the new German soldiers as the "undernourished German children of the World War," who were hardened by hardship and sacrifice and "electrified" by a new voice: "A voice of anger, resentment, grievance, hatred—yet to them a voice of promise, a voice of power, a voice of pride—a voice of command. They may die for that voice. Yes, the armistice is over!"[9]

This gloomy survey was accompanied by another article under the headlines "Germany Wipes Out World War Defeat," followed by "On the Twentieth Anniversary of the Armistice She Is Victor in Europe," and "Won All Without Test." As the article concluded, "there is no possible doubt that twenty years after the armistice which sealed her military defeat Germany won the World War after all."[10]

Despite this growing concern with Germany, however, public opinion was not universally set against the Hitler state. Indeed, Russian communism was deemed by Americans to be a far greater threat that German National Socialism. A July 1937 poll asked Americans—if they were forced to choose—whether they would prefer to live under the kind of government in Germany or in Russia. Over 60 percent of the respondents favored Germany over Russia, a sentiment echoed in a June 1938 poll asking Americans which was worse: communism or fascism. Even in February 1939, after the Munich Agreement and Kristallnacht, more Americans believed communists in America to be a greater threat than Nazis. Given these views, Hitler's hard-line campaign against communists in Germany and Spain (and eventually, it was assumed, in Russia) made it difficult for Americans to criticize the National Socialist regime too harshly. This was all the more the case for Protestants (and Catholics too, of course), for whom the atheistic materialism of the Soviet Union meant that any nation or movement that attacked communism was automatically at least a nominal ally.

If American attitudes toward Germany were mixed, ambivalence and confusion also marked perceptions of Jews in the United States. Even when public opinion turned strongly against Hitler and his regime—and it clearly did during the period just before and after Kristallnacht—it did not imply that there was widespread sympathy for Jews. On the one hand, over half of the Americans polled by Elmo Roper in January 1936 believed that Germany would be worse off if it drove out its Jewish population. Two-and-one-half years later, in November 1938, another Roper poll revealed that over half of the population believed that there was very little hostility to Jewish people in the United States. In the wake of Kristallnacht, fully 94 percent of Americans polled disapproved of the Nazis' treatment of German Jews, and 72 percent approved of the temporary withdrawal of the American ambassador from Berlin.[11]

On the other hand, the same November poll in which over half of the Americans surveyed believed that there was little hostility toward Jews in the United States also found that almost one-third of respondents felt that this hostility was growing. By March 1939, this number had risen to 45 percent. In answer to follow-up questions, Jews surveyed blamed the increasing hostility they faced on external factors such as jealousy over Jewish accomplishments; propaganda directed against Jews; or meanness, narrow-mindedness, and ignorance. In contrast to this, the survey sample as a whole focused far more on Jewish financial power, business practices, and avarice.[12]

Moreover, in an April 1938 poll, fully 48 percent of the Americans surveyed believed that the persecution of Jews in Europe was at least partly their fault, and 10 percent felt that it was entirely their fault. Three polls conducted throughout 1938 and 1939 discovered consistently that 12 percent of the Americans surveyed favored a campaign against Jews in America, while another poll taken in July 1939 found that 42 percent of Americans who were asked wanted either to take measures to prevent Jews from gaining too much economic power in America, or (less often) to deport them as fast as humanely possible.[13]

With such high levels of prejudice toward Jews, it is unsurprising that the general public in the United States was in no mood to hear talk of increases in immigration for Jews, or even for other European refugees created by the Nazi annexation of Austrian and Czech territory. Two famous Roper polls taken immediately after Kristallnacht determined that 77 percent of respondents rejected the idea of allowing "a larger number of Jewish exiles from Germany to come to the United States to live," while 43 percent opposed even the idea of the U.S. government contributing "money to help Jewish and Catholic exiles from Germany settle in lands like Africa and South America." Most surprisingly, fully two-thirds of the Americans surveyed opposed a proposal to permit 10,000 refugee children from Germany to be brought into the United States to be taken care of in American homes. The simple truth was that in the populace at large, the refugee crisis was a concern only to Jews. While roughly 85 percent of Protestants and Catholics polled in April 1939 stated they would vote against a bill to increase immigration quotas for European refugees, 70 percent of Jews surveyed declared that they would vote for such a measure. Such a gap between sentiments is telling.[14]

In stark contrast to this background of ambivalence about Germany and prejudice toward Jews in American society at large, the mainline Protestant church press proved to be consistently anti-German and pro-Jewish. Articles in church periodicals regularly condemned Nazi barbarism, denounced American antisemitism, and lamented the plight of Jewish and other so-called non-Aryan refugees caught in Hitler's grasp. While this was true of publications like *Advance* (Congregationalist), *Zion's Herald* (Methodist), and *The Presbyterian*, the most striking example of all came from the *Churchman*, a leading Episcopalian magazine edited by Rev. Guy Emery Shipler and issued, generally, twice each month. Lead editorials, editorial cartoons, reprinted speeches and resolutions, and multicolumn or multipage articles addressed the subjects of antisemitism, German brutality, and the refugee crisis in no less than 20 of 22 issues of the *Churchman* published in 1938. This was not including the many letters to the editor and smaller notes that were also regularly printed. Indeed, with various discussions carried forward from issue to issue, it is no exaggeration to assert that this cluster of topics comprised the single most important agenda of the *Churchman* over the course of the year. Prominent in this coverage were reports about the work of organizations like the National Conference of Jews and Christians and the American Committee for Christian German Refugees, as well as the editorial cartoons of Charles A. Wells, who regularly and creatively produced images asserting the importance of liberal religion as the guardian of tolerance, freedom, democracy, and civilization.

Another element of the mainline Protestant press that deserves mention was its emphasis on pacifism as a principle on which liberal Christians ought to face the growing international crisis. Deeply divided concerning the participation of the United States in the World War of 1914–1918 and embarrassed by the triumphalist and militaristic rhetoric of clergy during that conflict, American Protestant clergy turned decisively toward pacifism during the 1920s and early 1930s. In 1934, a survey of over 20,000 Protestant clergy sponsored by several leading denominations (Congregationalists, Baptists, Methodists, and Episcopalians) revealed that two-thirds of clergy "expressed the opinion that the Churches should not sanction or support any future war," and declared that as individuals they would not sanction it either. Over 80 percent opposed military training in high schools, and 77 percent supported a reduction in American armaments, irrespective of any action taken by other countries. Not surprisingly, seminary students were even more radically opposed to war than clergy in general. By 1937, however, the impulse for pacifism had begun to wane. As a survey sponsored by the Oxford Conference on Church and State discovered, American religious leaders who responded were almost evenly split between pacifist and nonpacifist points of view.[15] This was due in no small part to rising concerns about the political state of Europe, especially the rise of totalitarianism in Germany. That said, mainline Protestant publications like the *Churchman* retained their commitment to pacifism throughout the political crises of 1938. For instance, in "The Pacifist's Dilemma," an editorial from October 1, Rev. Guy Emery Shipler admitted that many had begun to question whether pacifism would still work in a time in which the power of Hitler and the Japanese was growing, and in which other world leaders kept giving them what they wanted. Was pacifism, he wondered, really just cowardice. In response to his own line of inquiry, Shipler noted that diplomatic strategies such as a boycott of German commerce and international isolation of Germany had never been sufficiently attempted against Hitler, and until they had been tested and found wanting, it was perfectly justified for pacifists to continue to oppose any decision for war in Europe.[16]

It was this mixture of factors—public mistrust and criticism of Hitler and the German government, an even greater fear of communism, and antipathy and hostility toward Jews, contrasted (at least in part) by mainline Protestant press coverage that was almost unequivocally anti-Nazi, concerned for Jewish and "Non-Aryan" refugees, critical of American antisemitism, and pacifist by conviction—that formed the context in which American mainline Protestants encountered news of the Kristallnacht pogrom.

RESPONSE

Under bold headlines like "Nazi Mobs Riot In Wild Orgy" and "Hitler Seizes 20,000 Jews," news of the Kristallnacht pogrom spread across North America within hours of the violence, and received full coverage in the newspapers of November 11.[17] In the English-speaking world, reactions in the general media were of shock and outrage.[18] Beginning immediately, political, economic, and cultural leaders began denouncing Hitler and his regime for their inhumanity and barbarism.

Mainline Protestant leaders also reacted very quickly and continued to speak out over the ensuing days and weeks. In the United States, over the course of the ten days immediately following Kristallnacht, liberal Christian protests erupted in four key moments: first, the Armistice Day remembrances of November 11; second, the Sunday services and Federal Council of Churches' (FCC) statements of November 13; third, the FCC-sponsored national radio broadcast of November 14; and fourth, the ecumenical and interfaith day of prayer held on Sunday, November 20. In most cases, responses focused on outrage at German brutality, the threat to Western civilization, and the call for humane treatment of Jews and other victims of Nazism.

Both ideologically and practically, these Protestant responses were enmeshed in broader public reactions to the German persecution of Jews. This is not surprising given the extent to which mainline Protestants came to understand the world in largely secular terms, based on their confidence in reason and their adoption of bourgeois, reformist values. In short, over the course of the nineteenth century, liberal Protestantism recast itself as an ethical way of life, intimately connected with the freedom of democracies and the culture of Western civilization. The rise of the Social Gospel movement led liberal Protestants to believe that Christianity could, and should, provide answers for the many systemic social ills of modern society, whether the economic antagonisms of the class struggle or the political and military conflicts between nations. This worldview was captured in the oft-repeated slogan "Fatherhood of God and Brotherhood of Man."

FRIDAY, NOVEMBER 11, 1938—ARMISTICE DAY

Hours before any North American Armistice celebrations would begin, British church leaders used the commemorative occasion to decry the brutality of the Kristallnacht pogrom. The archbishop of Canterbury, speaking on behalf of the Christian people of Britain, gave "immediate expression to the feelings of indignation with which we read of the deeds of cruelty and destruction which were perpetrated Thursday in Germany and Austria." He added, "Whatever provocation may have been given by the deplorable act of a single irresponsible Jewish youth, reprisals on such a scale so fierce, cruel, and vindictive cannot possibly be justified." Setting the tone for the Church of England, the archbishop instructed, "I trust that in our churches Sunday and thereafter remembrance may be made in our prayers of those who have suffered this fresh onset of persecution and whose future seems to be so dark and hopeless."[19] In London, "prayers for the Jewish people 'in their trouble' were said by Bishop Paul de Labilliere, dean of Westminster, in a last-minute change in the Abbey's Armistice Day remembrance services."[20]

In the United States, many Armistice Day celebrations referenced the tragic events in Germany. In Washington, as speakers honored the service and sacrifice of participants in the World War of 1914–1918, they also called for vigorous action in the face of the political situation in Europe. "It is of little worth that we kneel reverently in our cathedrals and churches to do homage to Him who died for human redemption unless we are prepared at any cost to press His claims upon a reluctant, disobedient, and war-crazed world," declared Bishop James E. Freeman, as he spoke from near the former president Woodrow Wilson's tomb in the Washington Cathedral. A number of churches, including President Roosevelt's church (St. Thomas'), announced they were planning special services for Sunday.[21]

In New York, the Very Reverend Milo H. Gates, Dean of the Episcopal Cathedral of St. John the Divine, hastily altered his Armistice Day service to include a vigorous condemnation of the Kristallnacht pogrom. Declaring that the European persecution of the Jews and the German revival of the ghetto augured ill for the future peace of the world, Gates depicted German antisemitism as a tragic return to the Middle Ages. Noting pointedly that there was less peace 20 years after the end of the (First) World War than in 1918, Gates added that the "tyranny of the so-called tyrants is worse than the tyranny of the so-called proletariat," a clear assertion to his audience that they ought to regard Nazism as a greater threat to America than Russian communism.[22]

Responding to the urgency of the situation, the Anti-Nazi League to Champion Human Rights hastily organized a broadcast on the radio station WMCA and the Intercity Broadcasting network for the evening of Armistice Day. District Attorney Thomas E. Dewey and the former New York governor Alfred E. Smith were the main speakers, tasked with responding to the question, "Has Germany gone mad?" The *New York Times* gave the broadcast front-page coverage and included lengthy descriptions of the speeches.

Mainline Protestant leaders also figured prominently in this broadcast, most notably the Reverend Elmore M. McKee, rector of St. George's Protestant Episcopal Church and former chaplain of Yale University. As the *New York Times* reported, McKee "declared that the church generally has a common responsibility in the plight of Jewish people and declared that, much as the Jews are suffering in Germany, it is the doers of iniquity who suffer most." Later in the article, the description of the rector's speech continued:

> Dr. McKee asserted that the Christian community throughout the world was deeply saddened by this latest phase of "madness run riot." He said his first reaction was a feeling of definite personal responsibility for the plight of the Jew in the modern world, who has to face such things as not even being considered in this city for membership in certain clubs or who finds it harder to get a job than those who are Christians.
>
> Dr. McKee declared that there was no basis in science "for the myth of Nordic supremacy." He contended that there could be no sanity, no order and no peace unless there was "universalism under one God."
>
> He said that the tragedy that is taking place in Germany did not represent the feeling of all the German people and pointed out that Germany had a great many Christians and religious leaders. Praying God to lead Germany 'to her true spiritual destiny,' Dr. McKee asked that, out of the broken homes and cruelty of Germany, a new day would come when the Christian church shall seek by study and prayer and humility to atone for its sins and set about healing the breaches between peoples.[23]

Because the broadcast had been organized only a couple of hours before it was aired, the network agreed to rebroadcast it on the evening of Monday, November 14.

Other church leaders also reacted quickly to amend their Armistice Day services, or to issue statements that gave voice to their outrage over the events of Kristallnacht. As the Rt. Reverend. Robert L. Padock, episcopal bishop of Oregon; William B. Spafford, executive secretary of the Church League for Industrial Democracy; and Rev. Guy Emery Shipler, editor of the *Churchman*; expressed the matter in a joint statement they issued, "the bestial brutality of the Nazi persecution of the Jews is so great that no decent person can avoid giving an expression of hatred for Fascism."[24]

One vital component of the November 11 response to Kristallnacht was a call for further protest. Dr. Everett R. Clinchy, director of the National Conference of Jews and Christians, announced that Catholic, Protestant, and Jewish organizations had already issued calls for special prayer and intercession the following weekend for the victims of "racial and religious oppression" throughout the world. Initiated by the FCC two months earlier,[25] this prayer movement, which had taken on new urgency since Kristallnacht, was endorsed by the heads of 17 major American churches. As Clinchy explained:

> We unite in inviting all Christian people to join in prayer and intercession on Sunday, Nov. 20, for the victims of racial and religious oppression,

who, because of loyalty to conscience or the accident of birth, are forced
to endure persecution or exile.

This inhumane treatment falls heavily on many groups in many lands
and occasions acute distress of spirit in all who believe in justice and
brotherhood. We would direct special attention, however, to the plight of
those of Jewish blood in Europe, whether Jewish or Christian in faith.

The inclusion of Austria and parts of Czechoslovakia in the German
Reich has added greatly to the number of 'non-Aryans' who suffer grievous civic and vocational abilities and have to endure all kinds of public
ignominy.

We plead also for a united effort on the part of all the people of God to
combat the hateful anti-Semitism which prevails in many lands and even
in our own country. We must recognize anti-Semitism, at home as well as
abroad, as a plain denial of the spirit of our Lord who was himself a Hebrew
according to the flesh and who taught us that all men are brothers.[26]

On a separate note, bishops from the Methodist Episcopal Church,
who happened to have been meeting to choose delegates for a national
Methodist conference, also paused to issue a public condemnation of
the Nazi pogrom. Declaring that their clergy in Europe would not be
silenced, they castigated the Nazi idolatry of race: "When paganism
lifts its voice, be it in the concept of the totalitarian State, in economic
theories or in racial theories that deny brotherhood, Methodism is
determined to preach a gospel that insists that all men are brothers and
children of one Father to whom final loyalty is due."[27] The next day,
in a rare move, the Methodist bishops focused their efforts on moving
the American political authorities to act. On behalf of their 4,669,000
church members, they called on the U.S. government to lodge an official
protest over the anti-Jewish riots:

We protest such incredible, inhuman and unjustifiable deeds. . . . We
urge the German Government to compel them to cease, both in justice
to the Jews and as evidence to the world that such actions do not reflect
the opinion of the German people and are not supported by them.

We urge our own government to protest to the German Government
and to make such representation in behalf of the sufferers from these riots
as may be possible. We believe that governments and peoples must seek
to make a public opinion in the world that will help prevent such outrageous excesses.

They are a sharp warning of the growth of racial and religious prejudice and intolerance. We pledge ourselves to make every possible effort
to develop a spirit of humane and understanding brotherhood in which
anti-Semitic feeling can have no place. We further declare our intention,
so long as anti-Semitic attacks continue, to join in seeking effective ways
of protest and action.[28]

SUNDAY, NOVEMBER 13, 1938—SERVICES AND FCC STATEMENTS

Having noted the tragedy of Kristallnacht already on Friday's Armistice anniversary, the Protestant clergy also used their Sunday services to condemn German barbarism. In an event that was widely reported, the Reverend. John Haynes Holmes of New York's Community Church led his independent Protestant congregation of 1,100 in a collective protest directed to the German Ambassador Dieckhoff in Washington. Standing up together to show their solidarity, they affirmed the following statement:

> We, the members and friends of the Community Church of New York, have assembled this day for the worship of God, Whom we have been taught to reverence as the Father of all mankind, without distinction of race, nationality or creed. . . .
>
> We have prayed to God for mercy and rescue of our brethren, the Jews of Germany, stricken by such horrors of persecution as outrage all sense of human decency, profane the divine ordinances of love and justice and carry the world back to that jungle savagery from which we had believed that men had escaped forever.
>
> So, to our prayers to God, we would add our protests to you, the official representative in this country of the government responsible for this monstrous crime against our brethren, the Jews. We ask you to instruct your government of the abhorrence felt by Americans, as we believe also by Germans, for its bloody deeds. We bid you to remind your government of the outlawry it decrees upon itself by these offenses.
>
> We beg you to teach your government what it should know, that those who would heal the hostilities and still the hatreds of our time by restoring a peace of justice for all nations are rendered helpless either to speak or act in the face of these abominations against the Jews.
>
> Sir, you will be faithless to your office if you fail to inform your Fuehrer and his associates in authority that they stand condemned by the conscience of mankind, and can themselves neither ask nor receive cooperation to any end until they have purged their country and their own hearts of these assaults upon the innocent and helpless multitudes of Israel.[29]

As clear as the Community Church's protest was, it was dwarfed by the effort of the FCC to solicit public statements of protest by civic and ecclesiastical leaders, which were then released on Sunday, November 13. As the *Los Angeles Times* reported, "Clergy and lay leaders in the United States and abroad, using language of unspared strength, yesterday denounced the German government's subjugation of its Jewish citizens. 'Mad' . . . 'Inhuman' . . . 'Bestial' . . . 'Barbaric'. . . . Those are words from sermons and other public utterances on the first Sunday since the newest Nazi oppressive movement, aftermath of a Jew's slaying of

a Nazi diplomatic official."[30] The list of public figures participating in
the FCC endeavor included the former president Herbert Hoover; the
Right Reverend. William T. Manning, bishop of the Protestant Episcopal
New York Diocese; the Reverend. Dr. Harry Emerson Fosdick, pastor
of the Riverside Church; William Green, president of the American
Federation of Labor; Dr. Edgar De Witt Jones, president of the FCC;
Dr. Henry Sloan Coffin, president of the Union Theological Seminary;
Mrs. Eugene F. Itemann, chairman of the New York State Branch,
Women's International League for Peace and Freedom; Dr. Samuel
McCrea Cavert, general secretary of the FCC, and the Reverend. Ralph
W. Sockman, pastor of Christ Church.

Hoover's statement, which quite naturally received the most attention,
is instructive for the way in which it illustrates how mainline Protestant
responses to Kristallnacht centered on Nazi barbarism as a threat to
Western civilization, and for how Protestant and civic responses tended
to blend together:

> I am glad to again evidence my own indignation and to join in an expres-
> sion of public protest at the treatment of the Jews in Germany.
>
> It is not the German people at large who are to be blamed for this
> action. The blame is squarely up to the political agencies in power. These
> individuals are taking Germany back 450 years in civilization to [Spanish
> Inquisitor General] Torquemada's expulsion of the Jews from Spain.
>
> They are bringing to Germany not alone the condemnation of the
> public opinion of the world. These men are building their own condem-
> nation by mankind for centuries to come. . . .
>
> It is still my belief that the German people if they could express
> themselves would not approve these acts against Jews. But as they can-
> not so express themselves it is the duty of men everywhere to express
> our indignation not alone at the suffering these men are imposing on
> an innocent people but at the blow they are striking at civilization
> itself.[31]

Fosdick, the famous New York preacher, said much the same thing
in his response: "The appalling persecution of the Jews in Germany
is an outrage to the conscience of the civilized world. It is a tragedy
if nothing can be done to prevent this cold-blooded, brutal pogrom.
Decent people of all faiths and races join in protesting the cruel
barbarities."[32] Nor were the words of Manning, episcopal bishop of
New York, any different:

> Such action as that which is now taking place in Germany is an open
> defiance of God and a shame to humanity. It is an amazing and shocking

thing that in this day in which we are living such crimes can be permitted. They violate every principle not only of religion but of common humanity and decency and will stand condemned by every reputable government and by the whole civilized world. Such barbarous and inhuman acts cannot long continue. Any government guilty of such acts will fall through its own wickedness.[33]

Even the FCC president Jones echoed the humanistic tone of the other statements when he declared, "I protest against this inhuman spirit and practice first because the Jew is a human being. I protest in the name of Christianity, freedom and common decency."[34]

MONDAY, NOVEMBER 14, 1938—FCC BROADCAST

As the FCC mobilized important Protestants to condemn Hitler and the National Socialist regime in Germany, it also worked very broadly, drawing in public personalities and even a Roman Catholic voice in a national broadcast held on the evening of Monday, November 14. Once again, the former President Herbert Hoover was the main speaker on a panel that also included Alfred M. Landon, the last Republican candidate for the presidency; Edwin H. Hughes, a bishop of the Methodist Episcopal Church; the Reverend. Robert I. Gannon, the Jesuit president of Fordham University; Harold Ickes, secretary of the Interior; and William H. King, United States senator. Bishop Edwin H. Hughes's speech is typical of the Christian but humanitarian response to the events in Germany:

Ladies and gentlemen, I speak as a representative of the Federal Council of the Churches of Christ and of my own church. . . .

In the German Reich the outrages appear to have two forms.

The first is represented by a deliberate legal process intended to hinder the Jews in a commercial way and doubtless so to harry them as to drive them from the land. If today's papers report truly some of these poor people are at this moment trembling at the borders of other countries praying for the refuge of exile.

Who of us can believe that the God and Father of our Lord Jesus Christ, who was, speaking earthwise, a Jew, can look with approval upon the heartless proposals in law that would work such hardships?

The second form is mob-like rather than law-like. A poor, misguided boy, tormented and probably demented, fires a hasty shot and drops the spark into the magazine of terror. At once the revenge speeds away to visit itself upon the innocent who had no more to do with the youth's mad deed than did any one of my radio listeners.

Reversion to Savagery

Soon we have, according to all the dispatches, a mob of stonethrowing men and women who revert to savagery and with a pitiable lack of self-control fall back on tigerish behavior toward persons and on sacrilegious treatment to sanctuaries where fellow-human beings have been reverently worshiping the One God. Cannot the autocracy that represents a totalitarian State quickly stop conduct that being brutal is far more than childish?

Many of us who have traveled in Germany cannot believe that these dreadful happenings are sanctioned by the people who have laid emphasis upon the glory of their culture. We have every right to expect that a speedy popular demand will arise in the German Reich not only for the cessation of these brutalities but for the punishment of those who have wildly made themselves legislatures, laws, courts and judges, and have thus given out terrible sentences of unmerited punishment.

A plea for our Jewish people now is in reality a moral plea for ourselves. Humanity simply cannot afford to be silent. We must all think of a story in the Hebrew scriptures. Mordecai in the book of Esther is marked for death because his religious conscience refuses to be assimilated. Haman hated the Jews and prepared a gallows for his hanging, and in the end the gibbet was not for Mordecai. The final result was recorded in the words: "So they hanged Haman on the gallows that he had prepared for Mordecai."

This story remains a spiritual parable applicable to the present débâcle. We all wish to believe that the German people prefer to accept the role of Esther rather than the role of Haman, and in so doing to save themselves and the world from the dreadful reaction that always follows after injustice and cruelty. All good people may pray that this may be the religious outcome.[35]

Hughes's speech is instructive. While he included the biblical story of Esther, Mordecai, and Haman, he interpreted it largely as a matter of Mordecai's freedom of religious belief and practice, and not as a matter of Jewish worship of the God of Abraham, Isaac, and Jacob. Similarly, Germany's participation in persecution was less a case of collective sin against the Jews as God's people and more the abandonment of the German customary high level of culture and civilization—a descent into savagery. Interpretations such as these illustrate that the mainline Protestant leaders who responded to Kristallnacht did so from an ideological position very similar to that of liberal Catholics or the public at large, concerned as they were with the rights and freedoms of liberal democracy as the pinnacle of both Western civilization and the religion of Christ.

SUNDAY, NOVEMBER 20, 1938—DAY OF PRAYER

In the days leading up to the November 20 day of prayer, American Protestant leaders continued to speak out against Nazism and on behalf of the Jews. Various Methodists and Baptists released statements, and the Washington Federation of Churches called on clergy in the D.C. area to participate in the upcoming day of prayer.

The leadership of the FCC in the November 20 day of prayer meant that the event tended to be ecumenical in nature. In Detroit, for example, 5,000 people "representing various faiths and races" met at the naval armory, where clergy and labor leaders addressed the crowd and called for a ban on German trade.[36] In Boston, Christians joined Jews at a local synagogue for a service to mark the beginning of a three-day period of mourning for the suffering of German Jews. "Prayers were said for peace, tolerance and brotherhood and for the enlightenment and salvation of the Jews' persecutors."[37]

In Washington, spiritual leaders called for a "united Jewish-Gentile front in facing the Nazi persecution crisis and in fighting the possible spread of anti-Semitism in this nation as thousands here joined the Nation in a day of prayer for victims of persecution and oppression." Speaker Dr. Howard Stone Anderson spoke at the First Congregational Church, calling Hitler a "madman" and the Jews of Germany "scapegoats." Dr. Albert J. McCartney spoke at the Covenant-First Presbyterian Church, where he declared, "The maltreatment of the Jews is not a Jewish question, but a humanitarian problem that transcends borders, creeds and nationalities." Meanwhile, at Calvary Baptist Church, Dr. W. S. Abernathy warned against indifference "when wrongs and injustices are being perpetrated." And at the Brightwood Methodist Episcopal Church, the Reverend. Carroll S. Coale urged the children of his congregation "to pray for the unfortunate boys and girls in Germany, and give thanks that you live in a land where you have freedom to pray."[38] Other papers reported similar meetings in New York and other leading American cities.

CANADIAN PROTESTANT RESPONSES

Much about the Canadian liberal Christian response to Kristallnacht mirrored what was happening across the United States. Public sentiments were similar, and mainline Protestant spokespersons echoed their American counterparts. One important contrast was the importance of the Canadian Jewish Congress in sponsoring the November 20 "Day of Public Sorrow" events held in at least 60 towns and cities from coast to coast. As the advertisement for the Toronto gathering explained, "citizens of Toronto, of all religious denominations, will meet . . . to express their grief at the misfortunes which are befalling the victims of Nazi brutalities." The announcement went on to state that the event would feature "prayers and liturgical renderings, messages and addresses by Church, Rabbinical, and lay leaders."[39] Perhaps because of this, the public protest gatherings in Canada not only condemned Nazi brutality but also, more strongly than in the United States, it appears, called on the Canadian government to open the doors of Canada to Jewish refugees.[40]

In the *Globe and Mail*, the leading Canadian daily newspaper, front-page headlines read "20,000 Told All Religion Threatened" and "Toronto Rally Expresses Sympathy With German Jews, and Hears Nazis Are Danger to Church." Readers were informed how "Jew and Gentile, rabbi and Christian minister, made common cause yesterday with nearly 20,000 Toronto citizens of both faiths in expressing sympathy with the victims of Nazi persecution in Germany." With 17,000 people gathered in Maple Leaf Gardens and 3,000 more assembled at nearby overflow meetings, the report went on to describe how Torontonians from all parts of the city—both men and women, rich and poor—were drawn to the rally, filling the arena an hour ahead of time: "It was not so much a protest meeting," the *Globe and Mail* suggested, "as a gathering of citizens of divergent religious beliefs, but possessed of a joint conviction—which the speakers stressed—that the right of all religious belief was being threatened. Speaker after speaker stepped to the front of the platform and emphasized that the Nazi regime constituted a real danger to the Church as well as the Synagogue." In short, the paper reported, this was a call for all races and creeds to come together to preserve the freedom of religious thought and expression. The loudest applause came when Rev. Crossley Hunter of First United Church and other speakers urged "that Canada adopt an 'open door' policy in dealing with the Jewish refugee problem."[41]

The *Toronto Star* also carried news of the rally on its front page, noting how "the main gathering was one of the most cosmopolitan Toronto has ever witnessed. Seated side by side on the platform, financier and workingman, rabbi, Protestant clergyman and Roman Catholic layman voiced heartfelt sympathy for the hundreds of thousands crushed beneath the swastika." Under the headline, "Jews Sob In Sorrow 20,000 Torontonians Protest Persecution," the story captured the spontaneous power of the demonstration, and the prominent role of Protestant leaders as speakers.[42] While the Toronto gathering was by far the largest of the 60 or more such events held across the country, many ranged between 800 and 2,500 people in size.[43]

PRACTICAL AID

As laudable as these ecumenical and interfaith gatherings were, and as active as groups like the U.S. Federal Council of Churches had been in the first two weeks following Kristallnacht, their protests were almost entirely rhetorical in nature. A few urged the American and Canadians governments to pressure the Germans, or appealed directly to Hitler through the German ambassador Dieckhoff. Only rarely, however, did the practical matter of aid to the victims of Nazi persecution emerge as a theme.

The fact that many of the Jews suffering under Hitler were not even Jews by faith seems to have almost entirely escaped the American Protestant community, though it was a regular point made by Frank Ritchie and his colleagues in the American Committee for Christian German Refugees, and taken up regularly in the *Churchman* and other liberal Protestant publications.

For instance, the *Christian Science Monitor* publicized a Foreign Policy Association report, which released in Washington just before Kristallnacht. Denying that the refugee problem was solely a Jewish one, the author of the report, David Popper, stated, "The number of Christian 'non-Aryans' is believed to equal or surpass the total of actual or potential Jewish refugees." His estimate was that the total number of refugees amounted to 660,816, which included 198,000 Jews in "Old Germany," and 102,300 in former Austria. Another 285,516 refugees were 'non-Aryans' (ethnic Jews converted to Protestant Christianity), while 75,000 were classified as Roman Catholics.[44]

In fact, the *Christian Science Monitor* was likely simply echoing the message of Frank Ritchie, the executive director of the American Committee for Christian German Refugees, who regularly corresponded with leading newspapers and church publications about the refugee crisis. In a forceful letter to the editor of the *Washington Post*, published even as the Kristallnacht pogrom was taking place in Germany, Ritchie blamed German propaganda for creating a false impression. Ritchie argued that Americans needed to know that "the problem of persecution in Germany is not confined to those of the Jewish race and religion. . . . The truth is that a large number of the German refugees are Christians. It is true that many of them have Jewish blood, inherited in most cases from a distant Jewish ancestor; but some are pure-blooded Aryans." Citing Myron C. Taylor's statistics from the Evian Conference, Ritchie contended that roughly 360,000 of the 660,000 people in Germany and Austria who needed to emigrate were Christians. Moreover, he added that 370,000 of the 400,000 people fleeing from the Sudeten region were also Christians, noting that these refugees generally "belong to the cultured and professional classes. Physicians, lawyers, artists, educators and musicians comprise the majority." Clearly hoping to spur new interest in opening American borders to refugees, Ritchie lamented:

> And yet most Christian people in America do not realize the extent of suffering among their own. The Jews, long since aware of the dilemma

with which so many of their people are faced, have made and are making provisions to care for the exiles of their race. The American Committee for Christian German Refugees is trying to do the same thing for Christians. But few people realize the extent of the problem—or, for that matter, fail to realize that there even is a Christian problem.[45]

One other lonely voice in favor of immigration was Rev. Dr. John F. Johnstone, pastor of the First Presbyterian Church of Hartford, who had grand solutions for the refugee crisis. "Merely 'to pray or talk piously' about the brutal persecution of Jews in Germany 'seems naïve and really inexcusable,'" Johnstone declared in a sermon on November 13, 1938. Attacking the passivity of existing responses to Jewish suffering, Johnstone asked:

Would it not be proper that the United States, with its spacious, unoc-cupied territories, such as Texas, might not bring over 100,000 or 150,000 of these sad people?

Or is there any sound reason why Canada, with its present population of 10 or 11 million people, should not welcome 150,000 or 250,000 Jews? Again, why not 100,000 Jews in Australia?

To say that the United States has no human responsibility for the brutal situation in Germany is to speak merely in a narrow, political mood or simply to allow ourselves to be constricted by some economic or social prejudice.

Pointing out that the "Kingdom of God is universal, including Jew and Gentile alike, and every other kindred of people, no matter of what race or color or condition," Johnstone added:

The Christian cannot close his eyes any longer to this type of brutality visited on any group of people in any part of the world without taking severe issue and concretely doing something about it, even to the extent of asking his government to withdraw the ambassador or envoy to that country.

He went on to condemn the Nazi idolatry of race, and declared Christianity to be the only place to find "some source of unifying and clarifying authoritative concept of that way of life which alone can solve the problems of the twentieth century."[46]

A few notable Canadian church leaders spoke in similar terms. From the first signs of persecution, the United Church of Canada's (UCC) national press body exposed and denounced the dark core of Nazism. Both locally and nationally, the UCC was keenly interested in saving Hitler's victims (both Jews and non-Jews), and was arguably the greatest institutional ally of the Canadian National Committee on

Refugees, thanks to the outpouring of editorials, letters, resolutions, and sermons.

Kristallnacht also focused the attention of Canadian Anglicans on the issue of antisemitism, leading to bold headlines in the *Canadian Churchman* a few months later calling on Anglican Christians to pray for the "Jews of all lands," who were the "stunned, desperate, tortured victims of demonic hate," many of whom were being "slowly starved out of existence." Before the end of 1938, the Anglican diocesan synods of Niagara (in Ontario) and Rupert's Land (in Manitoba) restated Anglican sympathy for the Jews, and the Manitoba synod even pledged material as well as moral aid, offering Jews "a place on the earth where they can live in peace and enjoy the freedom which is rightly theirs."

Presbyterians protested against the "stupid," "un-Christian," and "inhumane" Canadian refugee policy, participating in the many large post-Kristallnacht rallies and calling repeatedly for Canada to take in refugees. Similarly, the prominent Baptist minister T. T. Shields railed in a post-Kristallnacht sermon in Toronto about the utterly anti-Christian antisemitism and extreme racialism of the day, identifying Hitler as the devil's chief representative on earth. He and his Baptist colleague Watson Kirkconnell also called for generous quotas for refugees to be allowed to come to Canada.[47]

CONCLUSIONS

In the United States, the liberal Protestant response to Kristallnacht was swift and vocal. It began with the use of Armistice Day services on November 11, and continued through the following two Sundays, during which time Protestants condemned Nazi barbarism and called on Hitler to end his regime's brutalization of Jews. In both the United States and Canada, moreover, church leaders also petitioned their governments to open the doors to Jewish and Christian "non-Aryan" refugees, particularly so, it would seem, in Canada.

Still, this short overview raises at least as many questions as it answers. To what extent did mainline Protestant leaders in the United States and Canada continue to pressure their governments to liberalize refugee policies? How much money was raised on behalf of refugees, and was it only or primarily for Christian "non-Aryans"? Did Christian leaders work alongside their Jewish counterparts? And were there any concrete attempts by mainline Protestants to rescue Jews from Germany between Kristallnacht and the beginning of the war in September 1939?

Perhaps as importantly, we need more understanding about what possibilities existed for American and Canadian churches to give practical aid to refugees. We know there were serious limitations, given the Nazi political and bureaucratic obstacles that hindered Jewish emigration from the German Reich and the North American political and bureaucratic obstacles to immigration there. But what opportunities *did* liberal church leaders have to work practically on behalf of Jews?

Still, in the immediate aftermath of Kristallnacht, it was no small accomplishment that a significant number of mainline Protestant leaders *did* speak out against Nazi atrocities and *did* call for their countries to take in refugees. In light of the limited authority of Christian leaders over either the attitudes of their church members or the policies of their national governments, what they should have been expected to do was to make speeches, mobilize protests, and petition their governments to act. That they did so in spite of wider popular prejudice against Jews was important, and certainly a far cry from silence.

NOTES

1. Irving Abella and Harold Troper, *None Is Too Many: Canada and the Jews of Europe 1933–1948* (Toronto: Lester & Orpen Dennys, 1982), p. 51, 284.

2. While many works on the United States and Canada during the Second World War and Holocaust mention the Christian churches in passing (generally, the assertion is that the Christian response to Nazi atrocities was muted, save for a few noble figures), a handful of authors tackle the subject of Protestant responses more directly. William P. Nawyn, *American Protestantism's Response to Germany's Jews and Refugees 1933–1941* (Ann Arbor: UMI Research Press, 1981) analyzed the American denominational press, and concluded that Protestant Christianity did very little on behalf of Jews and other refugees. He did find, however, slightly more activity among liberal Protestants, ecumenical organizations such as the Federal Council of Churches, and organizations with strong ties to New York City, where the refugee crisis was most deeply felt. In the end, Nawyn argues that only a small core of concerned individuals and organizations understood the significance of the refugee crisis or acted in response to the persecution of the Jews. Around the same time, Robert Ross, *So It Was True: American Protestantism and the Nazi Persecution of the Jews* (Minneapolis: University of Minnesota Press, 1980), condemned the Protestant press for standing by while Hitler and the Nazis persecuted and then annihilated the Jews. Ross's analysis, however, overemphasizes the extent of the church press coverage of the facts of the Holocaust, since the average Christian reader likely only read one or two of the 57 periodicals Ross surveyed. In Canada, Alan Davies and Marilyn F. Nefsky, *How Silent Were the Churches? Canadian Protestantism and the Jewish Plight during the Nazi Era* (Waterloo, ON: Wilfred Laurier University Press, 1997),

responded to the charges of Irving Abella and Harold Troper, *None Is Too Many: Canada and the Jews of Europe 1933–1948* (Toronto: Lester & Orpen Denys, 1982), that the Canadian churches had been silent to the plight of the Jews. Davies and Nefsky found the Protestant response to the Holocaust to be mixed, with some forceful anti-Nazi and (less so) pro-Jewish figures, but much ambivalence and apathy as well. Also, they note that Canadian Protestants, while deeply embedded into the culture, did not have significant political influence. Finally, Haim Genizi, *The Holocaust, Israel, and Canadian Protestant Churches* (Montreal and Kingston: McGill-Queen's University Press, 2002), examines the attitudes of Canadian Protestants in the postwar period, and argues that Protestant responses to the plight of the Jews under Hitler were "few and vague."

3. Hadley Cantril and Mildred Strunk, *Public Opinion 1935–1946* (Princeton: Princeton University Press, 1951), p. 1055.
4. George Gallup, "People Wary of Fuehrer," *Los Angeles Times*, November 12, 1938, p. 8.
5. "Nazi Propaganda," *Chicago Daily Tribune*, November 6, 1938, p. 10.
6. Barnet Nover, "Changes in Europe," *Washington Post*, November 5, 1938, p. 9.
7. Anne O'Hare McCormack, "Europe," *New York Times*, November 5, 1938, p. 18.
8. Demaree Bess, "Germany's Victory," *Christian Science Monitor*, November 9, 1938, sec. WM, p. 1.
9. Samuel T. Williamson, "Armistice Day: The Drama Unfolds," *New York Times*, November 6, 1938, pp. 4–5, 22–23 (special section).
10. "Germany Wipes Out World War Defeat," *New York Times*, November 6, 1938, p. 78.
11. Cantril and Strunk, *Public Opinion 1935–1946*, pp. 381–382.
12. Ibid., p. 382.
13. Ibid., pp. 382–383.
14. Ibid., pp. 383, 385, 1081, 1150.
15. Anson Phelps Stokes, *Church and State in the United States*, vol. 3 (New York: Harper & Brothers, 1950), pp. 274–275.
16. "The Pacifist's Dilemma" (editorial), *Churchman*, October 1, 1938, pp. 7–8.
17. "Nazi Mobs Riot In Wild Orgy," *Los Angeles Times*, November 11, 1938, p. 1; Sigrid Schultz, "Hitler Seizes 20,000 Jews," *Chicago Daily Tribune*, November 11, 1938, p. 1.
18. A good indication of broad American reactions to Kristallnacht can be found in Deborah E. Lipstadt, *Beyond Belief: The American Press and the Coming of the Holocaust, 1933–1945* (New York: Free Press, 1986), pp. 98–111.
19. "British Indignant at Nazi Terrorism," *New York Times*, November 12, 1938, p. 1; "Archbishop of Canterbury Protests Attacks on Jews," *Christian Science Monitor*, November 12, 1938, p. 6.
20. "Nazi Leader Warns Jews in America," *Hartford Courant*, November 12, 1938, pp. 1–2.

21. "D.C. Celebrants Assail 'Armistice of Munich,'" *Washington Post*, November 12, 1938, p. X1, 5.

22. "New Calls to Arm Mark Observance Of Armistice Day," and "Dean Gates Deplores Persecution of Jews," *New York Times*, November 12, 1938, p. 1, 3.

23. "Dewey and Smith Lead Protest Here against Anti-Semitic Riots in Reich," *New York Times*, November 12, 1938, pp. 1, 6; "Dewey and Smith Protest against Nazi War on Jews," *Los Angeles Times*, November 12, 1938, p. 5.

24. "German Consul's New York Home Is Under Guard," *Hartford Courant*, November 12, 1938, p. 1.

25. "Oppression," *Churchman*, November 15, 1938, pp. 24–25.

26. "Prayers Planned for the Oppressed," *New York Times*, November 13, 1938, p. 40. The call to prayer was signed by: Rev. Ralph Atkinson, moderator of the General Assembly of the United Presbyterian Church; Rev. P. O. Bersell, president of the Evangelical Lutheran Augustana Synod of North America; Bishop A. R. Clippinger of the Church of the United Brethren in Christ; Willis M. Everett, moderator of the General Assembly of the Presbyterian Church in the United States; Rev. S. H. Gapp, president of the Provincial Elders Conference of the Moravian Church; Rev. L. W. Goebel, president of the General Synod of the Evangelical and Reformed Church; Arthur J. Hudson, president of the North American Baptist Convention; Bishop Edwin H. Hughes of the Methodist Episcopal Church; Rufus M. Jones, presiding clerk of the Society of Friends; Rev. F. D. Kershner, president of the International Convention of the Disciples of Christ; Bishop L. W. Kyles of the African Methodist Episcopal Zion Church; Rev. Oscar E. Maurer, moderator of the General Council of the Congregational-Christian Churches; Bishop C. H. Phillips of the Colored Methodist Episcopal Church; Bishop John S. Stamm of the Evangelical Church; Rev. James H. Straughn, president of the executive committee, General Conference of the Methodist Protestant Church; Presiding Bishop Henry St. George Tucker of the Protestant Episcopal Church; and Rev. Charles W. Welch, moderator of the General Assembly of the Presbyterian Church in the United States of America.

27. "Wagner Is Elected Methodist Delegate," *New York Times*, November 12, 1938, p. 9.

28. "Methodist Bishops Ask Protest to Reich," *New York Times*, November 13, 1938, p. 37.

29. "Pastors Protest Nazi Persecution," *New York Times*, November 14, 1938, p. 22.

30. "Nazi Cruelties Rouse America," *Los Angeles Times*, November 14, 1938, p. 1.

31. "Hoover Flays Anti-Semites," *Los Angeles Times*, November 14, 1938, p. 6.

32. "Hoover Protests Brutality in Reich," *New York Times*, November 14, 1938, p. 6.

33. Ibid.

34. "Nazi Cruelties Rouse America," *Los Angeles Times*, November 14, 1938, p. 1.
35. Bishop Edwin H. Hughes, "Text of the Protests by Leaders in U.S. against Reich Persecution, *New York Times*, November 15, 1938, p. 4.
36. "5,000 in Detroit Ask Ban on Reich Trade," *New York Times*, November 21, 1938, p. 6.
37. "Christians Join Jewish Mourning," *New York Times*, November 21, 1938, p. 8.
38. "D.C. Pastors Decry Nazi Oppression," *Washington Post*, November 21, 1938, p. X13.
39. "Day of Public Sorrow" (advertisement), *Toronto Daily Star*, Saturday, November 19, 1938.
40. "Canadian Protests Voiced," *Christian Science Monitor*, November 21, 1938, p. 8.
41. "20,000 Told All Religion Threatened," *Globe and Mail*, November 21, 1938, p. 1.
42. "Jews Sob in Sorrow 20,000 Torontonians Protest Persecution," *Toronto Star*, November 21, 1938, pp. 1, 3.
43. Davies and Nefsky, *How Silent Were the Churches?* pp. 132–135.
44. "Way Out Foreseen for Refugees if Nations Assist," *Christian Science Monitor*, November 8, 1938, p. 5.
45. Frank Ritchie, "German Christians Refugees," *Washington Post*, November 10, 1938, p. 10.
46. "Dr. Johnstone Suggests U.S. Admit Jews," *Hartford Courant*, November 14, 1938, p. 1.
47. Davies and Nefsky, *How Silent Were the Churches?* pp. 46, 54, 73, 84–85, 91.

CHAPTER 3

KRISTALLNACHT IN CONTEXT: JEWISH WAR VETERANS IN AMERICA AND BRITAIN AND THE CRISIS OF GERMAN JEWRY

MICHAEL BERKOWITZ

Perhaps due to stereotypes or self-imposed limits of scholarly imagination, veterans' organizations are not thought to be terribly fascinating historical subjects.[1] As voluntary, fraternal bodies, they tend to embrace ideals that informed their members' military service, namely, nationalism and deference to authority. They allow former soldiers a space to socialize, institutionalize nostalgia for wartime duty, and afford men (and sometimes women) opportunities to publicly demonstrate their honor and willingness to sacrifice for a greater good. Organized veterans also engage in admirable, but not necessarily remarkable, types of service. They dress up; attend ceremonies, services, parades, and meetings; provide care to their surviving colleagues; memorialize those who died in battle; and recall the service of members deceased after wartime. As innately conservative groups, self-organized veterans rarely challenge the establishment.[2] Among the few instances when this has occurred, and with far-reaching ramifications, is the rise of Freikorps and Stahlhelm in Weimar Germany, what Peter Fritzsche has termed "rehearsals for fascism."[3] In the history of German Jewry, the Reichsbund jüdischer Frontsoldaten, the Jewish veterans' organization founded in 1919, was one of the most ardently

German-nationalist (and anti-Zionist) among its cohort.[4] The men whom Bryan Rigg misleadingly calls "Hitler's Jewish Soldiers"—mainly those who had no sense of themselves as Jews—have ironically received more attention than perhaps any other Jewish soldiers.[5]

For the purpose of analyzing responses to the event known as Kristallnacht, a closer look at the history of Jewish veterans' organizations in the United States and Britain in the 1930s, however, may prove instructive. I do not wish to argue that these bodies were greatly significant. Yet, as groups that were relatively unwilling to express anything but narrowly circumscribed opinions and mainly exercised ceremonial functions, their actions help to underscore the extent to which the events of November 9 and 10, 1938, spurred the conscience and consciousness of distinctive segments of Jewry and shaped their anti-Nazi endeavors. In sum, I have found that Kristallnacht heightened the feelings and initiatives that had been ignited by Hitler's rise to power—but did not inspire a profound, paradigmatic shift. Among the most practical effects were, in the United States, the Jewish War Veterans' (JWV) intensification of its call for, and attempted enforcement of, the anti-German boycott—which was seen as "the only peaceful weapon which [could] lead Hitlerism to its doom."[6] The boycott is clearly a pivotal event, which recently has been examined in depth by Richard A. Hawkins.[7] The JWV also stepped up its appeal for the admission of Jewish refugees from Germany, including specific plans for large-scale settlement in the United States, and offered support for the emigration of Jewish war veterans from abroad. Of particular significance in the context of the findings in this volume is that among the JWV's attempts at coalition-building there was an interdenominational radio broadcast in the aftermath of Kristallnacht, which reflected a long-term strategy of encouraging and publicizing support from non-Jews to assist in ameliorating the plight of German Jewry. Although the evidence for this is sometimes indirect, it appears that America's Jewish war veterans became increasingly involved in intercommunal and interfaith efforts, a great deal of which focused on relations with Catholics.

Those organized as British Jewish ex-servicemen (AJEX) dedicated themselves more conspicuously, after the events of November 1938, to working with other groups to ward off native fascism, which continued to fester, and tried to intervene in Germany's antisemitic persecution—or at least in the polemics about it in Britain. Similarly to the JWV, AJEX engaged in grassroots efforts to offer a haven to former German-Jewish servicemen.[8] Jewish veterans in the United States took active interest in the work of their British counterparts, as they were keen on apprising themselves of the past and present efforts of Jewish veterans worldwide.

The history of anti-Nazi efforts in both nations gives us a sense of how a self-styled, manly contingent believed it might be able to effect change. Jewish war veterans prided themselves as close to mainstream society in their host country, having earned the respect of the powers that be—yet were aware of their marginal status as well. By revisiting the cases of Britain and America, we also may be able to gain a better understanding of the differences between the two interwar contexts. Homegrown fascism loomed much larger in Britain than in the United States, yet the fact that it existed at all in America was incredibly disturbing to the members of the JWV. As mentioned earlier, the Jewish war veterans of America are often recalled for their part in the declaration of an economic boycott of Nazi Germany as the avant-garde of "anti-Nazi resistance" in 1933.[9] This was combined with a nearly forgotten hands-on policy of intimidating and confronting Nazi sympathizers in the United States. The rough-and-tumble aspect of their activities most likely influenced a rather disparaging characterization of all JWV actions as "strident"[10] and "irresponsible."[11] Jewish organizations that regarded themselves as more respectable protested that the JWV "did not represent American Jewry at large" or "enjoy the support of newsmaking personalities."[12] (AJEX, too, brawled with Nazi sympathizers in England, but its members were apparently careful to do so anonymously.) As much as it is true that the JWV in the 1930s was not a central institution in tune with many major Jewish organizations, its membership of 250,000 was far from insubstantial,[13] and it did have some rather interesting connections in the media and otherwise revealed unusual creativity and open-mindedness in attempting to convey its outrage and strategy to the general public.

At the outset I would like to offer a few caveats, and specify what made Jewish war veterans different from their non-Jewish counterparts. We have few (if any) examples of American and British Jews who followed their fathers in military service or careers—which is more common among Gentiles. Experience in the military tended to be a single-generation phenomenon for Jews, although there was support for a "Sons of the JWV" offshoot.[14] Here I will be focusing primarily on Jewish men who were veterans of the First World War, although in the United States the veterans included those who fought in the Spanish-American War, and in Britain, the Boer War as well as service in Britain's Imperial forces. It seems that American Jewish veterans were not simply cut from the same cloth as veterans at large. Despite their complex but ardent anticommunism, they appeared less reluctant than other veterans' organizations to align themselves with groups that might be defined as left of the political spectrum, particularly those representing the trade union movement and labor unions.

Insight into the weltanschauung of the JWV is revealed by its list of "Big Ten" Jews from January 1933—that is, the coreligionists and countrymen most revered by its membership. Although there is no claim of a scientific sampling, the activities and pronouncements of the body support its pantheon of such idols as "Louis Brandeis, jurist; Felix M. Warburg, banker; Benjamin Cardozo, jurist; Herbert H. Lehman, statesman; Adolph S. Ochs, newspaper publisher; Adolph Lewisohn, author; Felix Frankfurter, jurist; Walter Lippmann, author; Stephen S. Wise, rabbi; and Cyrus Adler, educator."[15] Brandeis (1856–1941), the first Jewish Supreme Court justice of the United States, had earlier won fame as a champion of the common people over corporate interests and close advisor of President Woodrow Wilson. Brandeis was by far the most illustrious American Jew of his time, whose support for Zionism was immeasurably beneficial to the movement's fortunes. Felix M. Warburg (1871–1937) was esteemed for his financial acumen in augmenting not only the strength of his own family's investment bank, but of the United States economy generally through developing the Federal Reserve System. Warburg also was committed to assisting the beleaguered Jews of Europe as a pillar of the American Jewish Joint Distribution Committee (known as "the Joint"). Benjamin Cardozo (1870–1938), perhaps superior to Brandeis as a legal mind, followed Brandeis as the second Jew elevated to the United States Supreme Court. Although appointed by Republican president Hebert Hoover, Cardozo typically sided with the strong liberals on the bench, Brandeis, and Justice Harlan Fiske Stone. Herbert Lehman (1878–1963), who was soon to be elected as a U.S. senator from New York, had been a popular governor of New York State and mainstay of the Democratic Party; Lehman had the added luster of rising to the rank of colonel in the U.S. Army during the First World War. Adolph Ochs (1858–1935), publisher of the *New York Times*, had been largely responsible for his newspaper gaining the reputation as the most unbiased source of news. He also was an effective opponent of American antisemitism through his leadership of the *Times* as well as his activity in the Anti-Defamation League. Of all of these names, Adolph Lewisohn (1849–1938), a banker and philanthropist, would fade from the scene first. He was one of the most prominent Jewish backers of the expansion of Columbia University and the College of the City of New York.[16] Felix Frankfurter (1882–1965), who succeeded Benjamin Cardozo on the United States Supreme Court, was a liberal activist who cofounded the American Civil Liberties Union in 1920. He was second to Brandeis as the most prominent personality in the Zionist Movement in the United States. Walter Lippmann (1889–1974) was respected as one of the most penetrating, popular, and independent-minded of journalists.

Interestingly, only the last two spots are occupied by men who were expressly connected with Judaism, as well as with the Jews. Rabbi Stephen S. Wise (1874–1949) was among the earliest supporters of the Zionist Movement in the Reform rabbinate, and along with Brandeis and Frankfurter, he was identified as a proponent of civil rights for all Americans. Cyrus Adler (1863–1940), a guiding force of the Jewish Theological Seminary of America and the Smithsonian Institution, was not an activist on a par with the likes of Wise, but he was respected for initiating the American Jewish Committee in 1906 and serving as its representative at the Paris peace conference. The Jewish presence in Versailles seems to have made a formidable impression on the JWV.

In addition to these figures, who were mainly on the liberal and progressive side of the religious-political spectrum, the JWV did, additionally, extend its respect to the Chofetz Chaim, a stalwart of Orthodoxy, upon his passing.[17] The organization also offered its good wishes on the fiftieth anniversary of the founding of the Isaac Elkhanan Spector Seminary of Yeshiva College,[18] and later, publicly showed its solidarity with the Union of Orthodox Rabbis of the United States and Canada during the Second World War.[19] The JWV was an enthusiastic proponent of the Zionist project in Palestine, while not expressing a preference for any particular stream of the movement. The JWV revealed next to nothing of its members' ideas about Jewish thought or practice, but was disconcerted that Stalin hindered their Soviet brethren from freely practicing their faith.[20] The orientation was decidedly secular and earthy. JWV members' belief in American democracy and the goodness of the American people was fervent, and a generally optimistic outlook also colored its perspective on Europe. This is poignantly, if sadly, evident in an item in its central organ, the *Jewish Veteran*, entitled "Polish Jewish Vets Challenge Anti-Semites":

> The comradely relations between Polish and Jewish veterans of Poland's war of independence will ultimately wipe out the differences between Poles and Jews and bring about peace and harmony between the two races [*sic*], Senator Kvateczevski, president of the Polish War Veterans, declared in an address at the 20th annual congress of the Jewish Veterans of Poland's War of Independence. The 250 delegates to the congress were greeted by spokesmen for President Moscicki and the minister of war. Declaring their unswerving loyalty to the Polish state, the Jewish veterans adopted a resolution demanding the outlawing of all racialist propaganda and rejected as libellous charges that the Jews are a harmful element to Polish culture. The resolution pointed out that "Jews made and are still making lasting and indestructible contributions" to Polish culture, and vigorously protested against ghetto benches for Jewish college students.[21]

The American Jewish war veterans believed that wherever Jews had proved their mettle as servicemen they could invariably play a role in the development of civil society. Through their choice and style of report-age they demonstrated that the foundation of their secular faith was the possibility of fraternal relations between men, and mutual tolerance, no matter their differences.

In terms of the socioeconomic status, it is crucial to recall that the vast majority of Jewish veterans were distressed, if not wrecked, by the Depression. Most were working-class or small businessmen who did not identify themselves with the upper crust among either Jewish or general society. Along with the JWV's reputation for brazenness, it is possible that the view of the organization as lacking "dignity" also derived from its members' social location as nearer to the working class, as opposed to the middle class.[22] "Fundraising was difficult" for the group in the 1930s, Gloria Mosseson states in a useful official history, "but the needs were greater than ever."[23] In this period there are very few mentions of specific donations on the part of JWV members to their own organization or other causes. Most of the men were of relatively modest backgrounds and circumstances.

According to the JWV's promotional literature, the overarching aim of the Jewish war veterans of the United States is to prove "that Jews were and still are integral components in the defense and maintenance of American security" and to "vividly demonstrate" the service of the Jews in the Armed Forces of the United States in protecting democracy, beginning with "the battles of the Revolutionary War." They also seek recognition for protect-ing the rights of "America's veterans—Jew and non-Jew," and the right to serve as "a defense agency to America's Jews in fighting anti-Semitism and bigotry whenever and wherever it may manifest itself."[24]

The organization germinated in 1896, holding its first meeting in the Lexington Opera House in New York City, with 63 Jewish Civil War veterans recording their presence in a body conceived as "the Hebrew Union Veterans." Supposedly the impetus for the creation of this organi-zation was an allegation by an antisemitic politician that there had been no Jewish servicemen on either side of the Civil War.[25] In 1897, perhaps the single most significant institutional year in modern Jewish history, it held their first memorial service for deceased members, beginning a 50-year tradition. "The recently ordained 24 year-old Rabbi Stephen S. Wise conducted the services,"[26] which might have been a signal that this would not be a typical veterans' organization, as Wise already was identified with progressive causes. In 1900 another Jewish veterans' organization was formed, the "Hebrew Veterans of the War with Spain." These groups worked together in lobbying President Teddy Roosevelt to intervene against the pogroms in Russia, and erected the first national monument "exalting Jewish patriotism at Salem Field Cemetery in Brooklyn." In 1912 these bodies were combined and gained official status in New York State. Their major achievement that year was "in securing passage of legislation removing restrictions against Jews becoming commissioned officers in the State National Guard."[27]

After the United States' entry into First World War, the JWV worked with other groups in creating the Jewish Welfare Board, which facilitated the recruitment of rabbis "to serve as military chaplains and providing staff at military recreation centers at home and abroad." After 1919, upon the influx of Jews who had fought in the First World War, the name of the group was changed to "Hebrew Veterans of the Wars of the Republic." That year some 10,000 Jewish First World War veterans "paraded in New York to protest the pogroms in Poland, Romania, and Galicia." It is significant to recall that tens of thousands of Jews were murdered in the midst of this largely overlooked series of conflicts, killed in the name of anti-Bolshevik fervor. The massacres were also fuelled by reactionary support of Russian, Polish, and Ukrainian right-wing nationalism, to buttress the supposedly Christian and legitimate orders in Eastern Europe. The Minorities Treaties that were a part of the First World War settlement, while constituting an important precedent for recognition in international law of Jewish civil rights, did not stem the flow of blood disproportionately meted out to European Jewry,[28] or guarantee protection for Jews in the successor states of Eastern Europe between the wars.[29] In 1922 Jewish veterans held their first national convention, electing national officers, and established an office in Manhattan. Five years later they again changed their name to the "Jewish War Veterans of the Wars of the Republic." In the wake of the passage of the Johnson Acts, in 1926, the JWV "sought Congressional approval for legislation to give preferential consideration to families and immediate relatives of veterans for immigration to the United States," which was apparently unsuccessful. The next year they requested and secured a law "requiring the American Battlefield Monument Commission to place Star of David markers on the graves of Jewish soldiers buried in war cemeteries in France. Earlier, all markers were crosses. In 1929 the organization's name changed to its current incarnation, the "Jewish War Veterans of the United States of America."[30]

In 1933, the JWV. had pride of place as "the only Jewish organization" to march in "the inaugural parade of President Franklin Roosevelt" on March 4.[31] Some three weeks later around 4,000 JWV members converged on New York (March 23) to take part in a demonstration against the policies of another leader installed in 1933: Adolf Hitler. Assembling

in New York's City Hall, Jewish veterans were said to be "warmly wel-
comed by political leaders," and the "rally captured national and international media attention."[32] The JWV enlisted the support of the American
Legion, which might have been expected to assume a posture of nonin-
terventionism, and that of "other veterans organizations to protest against
the Nazi persecution of German Jews."[33] Immediately they began to
devise a strategy for confronting Nazism, at the forefront of which was
a full economic boycott of German-produced goods and German-based
services. The fact that such a boycott was attempted is common knowledge. What is far less known is the extent to which the JWV was the
instigator, not simply a "supporter."[34] Within a few months this effort
was to be headed by the well-known legal and political figure Samuel
Untermyer.[35] "Untermyer Picked for Fight on Nazis," the *New York
Times* reported, May 22, 1933. "He would represent not only the Jewish
ex-soldier, but all of the United States' veterans—if they consented—
before the League of Nations."[36] The main objective was to assure the
protection of Jews, which had been stated in the Minorities Treaties,
and an attempt to reign in Nazism. "In July [1933], the JWV national
commander went to Amsterdam to join in an international federation to
promote the ant-Nazi boycott. Concurrently, JWV representatives met
in Washington, D.C., with Congressional leaders to secure admission to
the United States of German refugees fleeing Nazism."[37] As a response to
Nazism the organization attempted to forge a comprehensive coalition
of Jewish organizations called "the American League for the Defense of
Jewish Rights."[38] This body achieved at least one notable success, in sponsoring a highly publicized interfaith meeting at the Hotel Astor in which
Democratic leader Al Smith denounced the Nazis as "stupid," in the context of an event pressing for a boycott of German goods.[39]

The organization did not, however, cohere (at least under this name) for
long. It may have appeared as too strident, as Untermyer—noted as one of
great legal figures in developing American civil liberties and protection—
advocated the deportation of Americans who publicly supported Hitler.[40]
Interestingly, although Untermyer was not himself a veteran, he was one
of the leading champions of the JWV cause. Hailing from Virginia, his
father had been a lieutenant in the Army of the Confederacy during the
Civil War. In his stirring "Address at the Annual Memorial Service of the
Jewish War Veterans, New York, May 27, 1933," he stated that like all
other military conflicts in which the United States had been engaged,
"the pages of the Civil War again bear overwhelming witness to the cour-
age, patriotism, and heroism of the American Jew. More than 8,000 were
arrayed on either side. The 1st New York Volunteer Infantry alone was
more than one-half composed of Jews."[41]

Under Untermyer's direction the American League for the Defense of Jewish Rights was subtly converted into the Non-Sectarian Anti-Nazi League to Champion Human Rights. The officers of the association counted some of the best recognized figures in American and Jewish politics: James Gerard, Fiorello La Guardia, Arthur S. Tompkins, Abba Hillel Silver, Theodore Roosevelt, A. Coralnik, J. David Stern, Louis Myers, Mrs. Mark Harris, and Bernard Richards. Its Board of Directors added George Gordon Battle, James M. Beck, John Haynes Holmes, Edward L. Hunt, Frank P. Walsh, Oswald Garrison Villard, Leopold Prince, M. Mardwin Fertig, E.N. Kleinbaum, Abraham Cahan, Jacob Fishman, Benjamin Dubovsky, Allie S. Freed, J. George Fredman, Siegfried F. Hartman, and Ezekiel Rabinowitz.[42] This eclectic group of mainly politicians and journalists was largely non-Jewish with a sprinkling of Jewish notables—such as the editor of the *Vorwarts* (the Jewish Daily Forward), Abraham Cahan, and the up-and-coming Reform rabbi Abba Hillel Silver. It was unmistakeably a nonpartisan effort, comprising Democrats (Gerard, Walsh), Republicans (LaGuardia, Beck, Tompkins), Socialists (Cahan, Kleinbaum), and even a moderate anarchist (Coralnik).

Hitler's rise to power prompted intensified demonstrations of a small but troubling movement in the United States sympathetic to his aims, known as "the German American Bund," as has been addressed by historians such as Donald McKale, Sander Diamond, and Susan Canedy.[43] Despite the fact that there was no official policy condoning such actions, there were a number of instances when Jewish war veterans became involved in attempts to disrupt pro-Nazi meetings and "cells."[44] The closest the official organ of the JWV came to issuing a call for "direct action"[45] was to provide a list of all of the known enclaves of the German American Bund and implore its members to pay them an appropriate social call. "Special Attention! Are you harboring a Nazi cell in your community? Carefully look through the following list and see whether you have a Nazi cell in your community. . . . Posts located in or near cities where the above cities are located, are urged to make note of the existence of such cells."[46] I have written elsewhere that so-called Jewish gangsters tended to assume the lion's share of credit for physically assaulting and intimidating those assembled at gatherings of the German American Bund, but it seems that they played only a bit part compared to groups such as communists, Jewish war veterans, and indignant Gentiles who did not wish to attain notoriety, or possibly be held accountable for their actions.[47]

The JWV focused a great deal of energy, particularly as a reaction to Nazism, on enlisting the support of non-Jewish American veterans' organizations for the trade boycott and anti-Nazi efforts generally. In the mid-1930s, the JWV made deliberate efforts to join forces with other Jewish ex-servicemen's organizations, which was not a typical activity of veterans' organizations generally, as their activities (as opposed to polemics) overwhelmingly focused on the local, as opposed to the international. The JWV sent representatives to "the first International Conference of Jewish war veterans' held in Paris" in 1935. Also unusual for a veterans' organization, it "provided valuable assistance to the formation of the Catholic War Veterans," an alliance that it claims persists to date.[48] (There is, however, no mention of this tie in the Catholic War Veterans of America's official history.)[49] Beginning in 1933 the JWV proposed that the United States and other democracies withdraw from participating in the Olympic Games that were to be held in Berlin in 1936.[50] In 1935 the JWV again officially expressed its opposition to the United States' inclusion in the Berlin Olympics. That year it joined another international gathering of Jewish veterans, this time in Vienna. Much of its energy was apparently directed toward attempting to arrange alternate forums for Jewish athletes, who would most likely either refrain, or be denied from attending the Nazi Olympics.[51] The choice of venue might have been due, at least in part, to the fame of the local Jewish football (that is, soccer) team *Hakoah Wien*, one of the most successful in all of Europe.[52] With their counterparts in Britain and Europe, the JWV sponsored collegiate-level "football" (most likely soccer) matches.

Interestingly, the JWV takes credit for persuading a number of American veterans' groups to join their opposition to the U.S. participation in the Berlin Olympics. The organizations that supported the boycott included the "American Legion, the Veterans of Foreign Wars, and Disabled American Veterans." (It is not known if the Catholics went along.) As is well-known, the JWV did not succeed is keeping the U.S. team out of Berlin.[53] Among those particularly damaged by their exclusion was the Syracuse sprinter Marty Glickman, who consistently outran Jesse Owens[54]—now famed for his reaping of gold medals during the 1936 games—to Hitler's dismay. Regarding the JWV advocacy of a boycott, there were, however, repercussions in the U.S. athletic hierarchy: the combined veterans' organizations, it is claimed, helped to "oust the slate" that upheld American participation and totally replaced the former members of the American Athletic Union.[55] They were unable, however, to dislodge Avery Brundage (1887–1975), an open Nazi sympathizer who persisted as leader of the Olympic movement from 1936 to the "haywire" and tragic Munich Olympics of 1972.[56] Brundage, for decades, made his retrograde mark on the politics of sport through rejecting equality for women athletes, refusing to overturn the withdrawal of medals from Jim Thorpe, an American Indian, and maintaining a double standard concerning professionalism that privileged authoritarian regimes.

Although it is not known if there was opposition initially, by the 1930s it was assumed that JWV members supported the aims of the Zionist movement. In 1937 JWV delegates lobbied British consulate officials in New York City to allow Jewish refugees admission to Palestine, since Britain, as Mandatory power, was ultimately in charge of legal immigration to the *yishuv* (the Jewish settlement in Palestine). In the organization's official timeline, the Nazi November pogrom is not specifically mentioned. It is noted, however, that in 1938—following a failed attempt in 1930—the JWV "proposed the establishment of a federation of all Jewish organizations engaged in fighting anti-Semitism," which was not supported by any other bodies. It also was reported that "many Jewish refugees who served as German soldiers in World War I visited JWV national headquarters in New York for assistance in their resettlement, and that a volunteer staff fluent in German was assembled to handle this assignment."[57] A similar course of action was followed in Britain.[58]

Along with neglecting to mention Kristallnacht, the current official account of JWV activities does not record that the organization redoubled its efforts in calling for an economic boycott of Germany in the wake of the crisis. In an Associated Press item carried by the *New York Times,* November 19, 1938, Isador S. Worth, the commander of the JWV "urged all Americans today to exercise a 'rigid boycott' on all German goods and services." His comments were delivered in the context of a Connecticut JWV "ceremonial program" that centered on Kristallnacht. All of the organizations' national officers were present for "an emergency session to discuss the plight of Europe's Jews."[59] The part of Worth's statement appearing in the AP and *New York Times* article emphasized that the Nazi assault encompassed victims other than Jews:

> If each and every American citizen who feels the present injustice of what is being done to hundreds of thousands of Protestants, Catholics, and Jews in Germany would like to do something toward putting an end to this terrible situation, they can best do so by exercising a rigid boycott on all German goods and services. It is the hope of every Jewish war veteran that every American will join in the boycott to end the tyranny and oppression.

Worth was particularly moved by the statement of support from President Roosevelt, and he also "extended the thanks of the organization" to "the clergymen, men in public life, members of other veterans' organizations and the private citizens 'who have expressed their abhorrence of the recent events in Germany.'"[60]

In addition to the call to reinvigorate the boycott action, in 1938 the JWV had a hand in creating a body termed the "American Jewish

Federation," also known as the "American Jewish Federation to Combat Communism, Fascism, and Nazism," apparently a relatively short-lived amalgamation of organizations. Most likely this was a partially realized body that the JWV hoped would comprise all Jewish organizations. One of their notable activities in 1938 was sponsorship of a multifaith broadcast, which may have been influenced by the post-Kristallnacht Catholic University program of November 16, 1938.[61] It was reported on December 20 that "Protestant, Catholic, and Jewish support of the recently organized American Jewish Federation to Combat Communism, Fascism, and Nazism was urged last night in a broadcast over station WMCA." The *New York Times'* effusive headline "Speakers in Broadcast Ask for Unity of Faiths" probably would have caused some discomfort, if not offense, among the principals. 'Under the auspices' of the newly-mined organization,

> speakers were the Rev. Edward J. Higgins, pastor of the Roman Catholic Church of the Immaculate Conception, Astoria, Queens, and Chaplain of the Catholic War Veterans; the Rev. Dr. Thomas J. Lacey, rector of the Protestant Episcopal Church of the Redeemer, Brooklyn, and Milton Solomon, chairman of the American Jewish Federation. Both Father Higgins and Dr. Lacey attacked communism and all other "isms" and the former pleaded for more cooperation between Catholics and Jews. Mr. Solomon said the federation is pledged to "unite in defense of America from its enemies within as well as without."[62]

Certainly, one of the objectives of the broadcast was to publicize the new organization's staunch anticommunist posture. In large part the speeches restated what the JWV had addressed in its own meeting only six months earlier, accentuating their condemnation of both fascism and communism. That meeting had been notable for the participation of both mainstream and either apolitical or conservative veterans' organizations: the American Legion, Veterans of Foreign Wars, United Spanish War Veterans, and the Disabled Army Veterans.[63] The ecumenical and multifaith character of the radio program was even more pronounced because of the presence and striking message of Edward Higgins, the chaplain of the Catholic War Veterans, who most likely had come to the organizers via the JWV.

It has been contended that "intentional, purposefully, and by communal consent, the public Jewish response to Kristallnacht was repressed. The press spoke loudly, but public action, except for a day of public prayer and a few scattered protests, was virtually nonexistent."[64] A closer look at the response of JWV to the event it called "Black Thursday . . . which shocked the world," shows the very opposite.[65] The reaction was swift, massive, and intended to be far-reaching. "This past month has witnessed the most barbaric pogroms in the world's history of Jewry," wrote Isador S. Worth, in his "Message of the National Commander" column in the *Jewish Veteran*:

> The Spanish Inquisition pales in comparison with the Nazi outrages. They confirmed what the JWV has been warning the world against for the past five and a half years.
>
> There is only one ray of hope and that is the thunderous avalanche of protests against this Nazi barbarism from leading Americans in all walks of life, including the President of the United States. This was followed by the return of our Ambassador to Germany. Undoubtedly this denunciation will make even the ruthless Nazi fanatics pause. It may also result in some form of resettlement for these unfortunate and destitute refugees.
>
> Believing it is a catastrophe of major importance, exceeding the Czarist pogroms and the Turkish atrocities in Armenia, I have telegraphed President Roosevelt urging him to send the American Red Cross to Germany and Czechoslovakia to succor these freezing and starving, homeless human beings. There is ample precedent for this action, and I trust he will accede to our request.
>
> I also convened a National Conference in New Haven on Sunday, November 13th, 1938. There was a large attendance, and some excellent recommendations were made, which are now receiving consideration.
>
> Every one—Jew and Gentile—can help in this world emergency. First, we must contribute to worthy causes, such as the Joint Distribution Committee and the United Palestine Appeals. These funds are of immediate need. Later we will be called on to contribute liberally to some practical program to take the Jews out of Germany and settle them in other lands. We should insist, however, on settling them in a reasonably favorable land. It is far better to contribute voluntarily to such a purpose, than to be compelled to contribute under the lash of a dictator's whip or the threat of concentration camp or worse, as was done in Germany.[66]

The charge of indifference of Jewish organizations also rings hollow in light of the massive public meetings arranged with great speed. On November 21, 1938, a protest in Madison Square Garden vowing to "smash Nazism" drew an audience of 20,000, the capacity of the arena, while "an overflow crowd of perhaps 2,000 listened at loudspeakers in the side streets." The *New York Times* reported that "amid the variety" of the 17 speakers, the unifying feature was "the vigor of the addresses and of the responses of the audience." The rostrum was as star-studded as it was diverse, and included Dorothy Parker, the "poet, essayist, and satirist. . . . Reuben Grainer, former president [*sic*] of the World Zionist Organization . . . Paul Tillich of the Union Theological

Seminary; Dashiell Hammett, writer . . . H.V. Kaltenborn, radio commentator; Michael J. Quill, city councilman and vice president of the
Transport Workers Union; Albert G. Gilbert, Negro lawyer, president of the Harlem Bar Association; Ernst Toller, German writer and
playwright." "Uproarious cheers issued upon the repeated mention of
President Roosevelt as a 'Galahad' and as a man confronted by destiny
in the present crisis with the role of 'leader of democracy and leader of
humanity throughout the world.'" One hour of the meeting was carried
live on the radio station WHOM.[67] There was apparently no direct
representative of the JWV among the speakers, who largely represented
the left-oriented cultural establishment, but the prominence of the resolution to "Ban Trade With Germany" indicated that it was somewhere
in the mix.

In Britain, the December 8 rally and radio address of the former prime
minister Stanley Baldwin in London, then leading the Opposition, was
particularly heartening. Baldwin's remarks initiated the effort to bring
several thousand (mainly) Jewish children to the United Kingdom
for "asylum and transfer" in the event that came to be known as the
Kindertransport.[68] Germany's Jews "might not be our fellow subjects,"
Baldwin asserted, "but they are our fellow men."[69]

At one of the succeeding major demonstrations in New York the role
of the JWV was evident. The Carnegie Hall meeting of December 9,
1938, featured Secretary of Agriculture Henry Wallace as a speaker, was
presided over by Mayor La Guardia and, above all, was championed by
the senior senator of Virginia Carter Glass (1858–1946), a Democrat but
independent-minded Washington insider. "Many civic groups," including numerous Jewish organizations and political bodies with significant
Jewish membership, were among the sponsors. There is little doubt that
individual Jews and Jewish organizations were thrilled with the widespread support for the demonstration, which also was broadcast, in total,
on the radio. It was unmistakable that the event framing this huge occasion was Kristallnacht. "'I have been shocked by the brutal treatment of
the Jews in Germany,' Senator Glass asserted prior to the event, 'and would
sympathetically cooperate with any movement to alleviate the wrongs
perpetrated by this bestial government. I have no doubt that the meeting appointed for Friday will unmistakably reflect the sentiment of all
decent Americans against these beasts abroad.'" Other featured speakers
were U.S. "Senator Theodore F. Green of Rhode Island, Mgr. Fulton J.
Sheen of the Catholic University of Washington, Victor Ridder, publisher
of the New York Staats Zeitung and Herald, and Gertrude Alterton of
the Authors League." The presence of Senator Green (1867–1966) was
probably most striking, as he had a family legacy extending to the nation's

Founding Fathers. The spectrum of organizations officially lending support was also notable, an array including the

> Actors Equity Association, American Association of University Women, American Committee for Christian German Refugees, American Federation of Musicians, American Legion, America's Good Will Union, Association of Catholic Trade Unionists, Association of Christian Youth Movements, Catholic Actors Guild of America, Catholic Benevolent Legion, Catholic Charities of the Archdiocese of New York, Catholic Teachers Association, Catholic War Veterans, Citizens Union, City Affairs Committee, Knights of Columbus, Ladies of Charity of the Archdiocese of New York, League of Nations Association, League of Women Voters, National Association of Social Workers, National Institute of Arts and Letters, National Legion of Decency, New York Federation of Churches, New York Federation of Women's Clubs, New York Country Lawyers Association, New York State Chamber of Commerce, Progressive Educational Association, Protestant Teachers Association, Religious Society of Friends, United Federal Workers of America, Veterans of Foreign Wars.[70]

Again, the mix of organizations would have been received as an unusual coalition, because some were associated with the left or far left (Actors Equity Association, American Federation of Musicians) and some with the center-right (American Legion, Veterans of Foreign Wars). But perhaps most remarkable was the number of American Catholic bodies. The musical portion of the event included the orchestra of Erno Rapee and the choir of the Church of Blessed Sacrament, and "special prayers for the victims of oppression" were delivered by Stephen J. Donahue of the Catholic Diocese of New York and William T. Manning of New York's Episcopal Diocese.[71] The type of social, religious, and institutional breadth was weeks in the making, reflecting an effort that probably began in the immediate aftermath of Kristallnacht. It also is important to recall that priests' appearing with non-Catholics in public was expressly prohibited by the Church.[72]

The new organization associated with the Jewish veterans—although pledged to oppose "all 'isms'"—was one of the more right-leaning organizations, outside of religious bodies, on the Jewish political spectrum.[73] It came into existence less than a month before Kristallnacht. The group's fierce anticommunism and insinuation that if one was not in their orbit, the only other option was to be "for" communism, led to inter-Jewish strife that probably was unexpected. Some six months after its inception, "The American League to Combat Communism and Fascism" was lambasted by none other than Stephen S. Wise, who alleged that the group operated as a means for its members to attain "jobs and judge-ships" through supposed proof of their anticommunist credentials.[74] At this point Untermyer may have been unable, physically, to help guide the Jewish veterans, and Milton Solomon, who had been the commander of the American Legion post of King's County, seemed to be the main animating spirit of the organization.[75]

Consistent with its strategy and sincere desire to build bridges with non-Jewish organizations and individuals, the JWV also utilized Kristallnacht as a way to gauge the impact of the gruesome event on two of the most infa-mous antisemites in the United States: Father Coughlin and Henry Ford. One of the most lauded figures in America, Ford was loathed and feared by Jews because he had published an Americanized version of the notorious forgery *The Protocols of the Elders of Zion* as *The International Jew*. Coughlin was particularly troubling to the JWV, because it had apparently invested a great deal of effort in nurturing good relations with Catholics. The endeav-ors to counteract Henry Ford and Father Coughlin were more pronounced, and more successful, than their outreach to Protestants. The first person described as the chaplain of the JWV, Rabbi Abba Hillel Silver of Cleveland, contrasted Coughlin with Patrick Cardinal Hayes in a detailed survey of American antisemitism in a lengthy *Jewish Veteran* article. Hayes was fre-quently and enthusiastically cited as a friend of the Jews and the JWV.[76] In fact, a brief memorial service for Cardinal Hayes was held at the September 1938 convention of the organization.[77] On a number of occasions Catholic leaders and scholars, such as John A. Ryan and Harry McNeil, were quoted by the JWV as condemning Coughlin[78] and denouncing the ideologies of "Communism and Fascism" as "Anti-Religious."[79] Father Joseph N. Moody's pamphlet "Why Are Jews Persecuted?" was extolled under the banner: "Catholics Fight Anti-Semitism" in the *Jewish Veteran*.[80]

Coughlin reiterated his grotesque worldview even in the wake of Kristallnacht. "Detroit is famous for many things," the *Jewish Veteran* reported.

> Not the least of them are Father Coughlin and Henry Ford. Both were given prominence in the headlines as a result of their expressions on the recent Nazi outrages.
>
> When the entire world was condemning Nazi excesses of the past three weeks—when it appeared as if the expressions of leaders of Catholic, Protestant, and Jewish thought—might tend to stop the spread of hatred and prejudice—Father Coughlin on November 20th, made a nation-wide broadcast which sought to undo much of the good-will created. Through mis-information and distortion of the facts, he sought, under the cloak of expressing sympathy for persecuted Jews, to arouse anti-Semitism in his listeners.

Father Coughlin pays well for his radio hook-up. He likes nothing better than controversy, so that he can get free newspaper publicity and added listeners. Unfortunately, several enlightened and enraged listeners pointed out falsehoods to the Father. This afforded him an opportunity to repeat his broadcast on November 27th and to add other falsifications thereto. The controversy still rages in the press, and Father Coughlin must be happy. We can only guess the purpose of Father Coughlin, but does it become his holy robes in times such as these to incite to racial and religious strife?

The JWV was painfully aware and troubled by Coughlin, as well as the means by which he disseminated his venom—and it sought to provide an alternative through its own programs centering on "Americanism."[81] This effort apparently began in September or October 1938, and sometimes they were able to reach a nationwide audience through the C.B.S. network. Not only did the JWV sponsor a show that featured interfaith speakers, but their members were requested to write or phone in after each program to register that they had listened, and support the broadcast.[82] After Kristallnacht, though, the organization lamented:

We feel it useless to answer Father Coughlin. Were Father Coughlin familiar with the columns of "The Jewish Veteran" he would know that the J.W.V. was among the first to combat communism, and that we have aggressively fought it ever since. Unlike the Father, however, we have not confined our efforts against Communism only, but against all "isms," not the least dangerous of which is Nazism.

Joseph V. Connolly in an address before the National Eucharistic Congress in New Orleans recently said that "Catholics must align themselves on the side of the Jews." He added, "The cries of fleeing Jewish children nineteen hundred years after the time of Herod must, in the name of Christ, be answered NOW by Catholic press and Catholic Action and Catholic force and power of every kind." This should be a sufficient answer unto Fr. Coughlin. [83]

The organization, though meeting Coughlin on their own turf, also revealed that he was best challenged by other Catholics, as they had tremendous faith in the power and goodness of individual Catholic churchmen. The JWV expressed its sorrow at the passing of Pius IX and was nearly ecstatic at the prospect of the papacy of Pius XII. In March 1939 the lead article in the *Jewish Veteran* stated that

we are pleased to receive news of the election of Eugenio Cardinal Pacelli, under the name of Pope Pius XII. Cardinal Pacelli was Papal Secretary of State under the late Pope Pius XI. The new Pope is the only one of the

Popes ever to visit the United States. He was confident and constant advisor of the late Pope, and no doubt agreed with him in his attitude against Nazism, Fascism and Communism.

Our fervent hope is that Pope Pius XII has have a long and successful reign; that he will fill the spiritual vacuum left by the decease of his predecessor, and that he too will be sanctified by the love of his fellow men.[84]

Father Coughlin, however, persisted in the fold of the church, much to consternation of the JWV.

Surprisingly, that other paragon of hate in Detroit, Henry Ford, appeared to have been shaken, if not enlightened, by the events of Kristallnacht. As opposed to Coughlin, it was reported that Henry Ford, who heretofore had been considered unfriendly in his attitude, issued a statement denying sympathy for Nazism by reason of accepting a Nazi medal, expressing revulsion for the hate program of the Nazis, and urging [the] United States to open its doors to oppressed German refugees. He also praised his Jewish employees.[85]

The juxtaposition of the perspectives of Father Coughlin versus Henry Ford was even more deep-seated, complex, and interrelated than the JWV editorialist assumed. Ford had renounced his earlier positions on the Jews as early as July 8, 1927, as a result of two libel suits and growing concern with alienating potential Jewish buyers. Despite an apparent end to his "open hostility," however, Ford was known to articulate and support anti-semitic views.[86] Kristallnacht, as Neil Baldwin notes, was indeed something of a turning point. As mentioned previously, the Madison Square Garden rally of November 21, 1938, was a striking spectacle. In contrast to the repeated and jubilant acclamation of FDR, "[T]he loudest boos of the night were reserved for the roll call of Adolph [sic] Hitler, Joseph Goebbels, Fritz Kuhn [the leader of the German-American Bund]—and last, but not least Henry Ford." [87] The other American industrialist singled out for Nazi sympathies was "Tom Girdler of the Republic Steel Corporation"[88] who was far less illustrious than Henry Ford. Ford claimed that he was unperturbed by the event and his overt association with Nazism. Yet apparently, the reaction to Kristallnacht, and the increasing furor surrounding Father Coughlin's explicit support for the November pogrom, was troubling enough for Henry Ford to approach Moritz Kahn (brother of the architect Albert Kahn, who had a long-standing relationship with Ford) and Rabbi Leo Franklin, a prominent Detroit rabbi, to make a public statement concerning "the German situation."[89]

The possibility exists that the JWV also played a role in Ford's apparent change of heart. In advance of the September 1938 conference of the

JWV in Detroit, the Ford Motor Company announced that it would "put 75 cars and drivers at the disposal of the convention without a penny of cost." Furthermore, "[a]ll of the cars will fly the JWV insignia, which has a Magen David on it." The company also allowed the conventioneers to visit Ford's Greenfield Village "on the same terms as it was given to the American Legion"—meaning they could enter for a dime, instead of the usual quarter.[90] It is likely that the convention chairman, Sam Leve, convinced Ford that it was in the company's interest to treat the JWV as it did the American Legion.

Although there is no reason to assume that the JWV was not profoundly affected by the devastation of Germany's synagogues and the explicit attack on Judaism, the dimension of the Jewish catastrophe it addressed, and attempted to ameliorate, was mainly economic. The JWV was particularly appalled that the aftermath of Kristallnacht would result in the impoverishment of German Jewry, leaving them without resources for survival in or flight from an increasingly hostile environment. The organization felt that the most effective response was increased economic isolation of Nazi Germany.[91] The JWV also believed that it was imperative to continue to collect and analyze as much economic information as possible, in order to facilitate Jews' settlement in other countries. It advanced specific proposals for placing a large number of Jewish refugees in sparsely populated regions of the United States, Australia, and other countries. All of this, however, could be propelled and buttressed by demonstrations of sympathy by non-Jews.[92] Apparently the show of support JWV had helped to coordinate in 1933[93] was revived in the wake of Kristallnacht, as a huge rally was held in early December 1938. The main impression conveyed by the leaders of the JWV was that German Jewry had been catastrophically injured, in an economic sense, which would make their emigration even more difficult. Quite understandably, their fear was that Jews would be trapped in impoverished, wretched circumstances, but there was no indication that this was a signpost on the way to complete annihilation.[94]

Among the significant efforts of the JWV was the attempt to secure the emigration and resettlement of veterans from Germany and elsewhere in Europe. The documentary evidence of this endeavor was apparently lost in the relocation of the JWV Headquarters from New York to Washington, when it was not imagined that such records might be of historical interest. Along with this practical work of relief the organization was keenly interested in diverse aspects of Jewish veterans' experiences abroad, and they were particularly fascinated by the exploits of their brethren in Britain. Some of the most insightful writing on what is now known as AJEX, the Association of Jewish Ex-servicemen and

Women, can, in fact, be found in the journal of the Jewish War Veterans of America. Despite the generally superior attitude of many British and Anglo-Jewish organizations toward all things American, AJEX members frequently saw themselves as "little brothers" compared to their more numerous and better established American counterparts.[95]

Despite the presence of Jews in the British military in the Crimean War (1853–56) and even earlier, Jewish veterans are not known to have organized among themselves until 1928. That year a number of meetings were

> held throughout Britain to protest at Arab anti-Jewish riots in Palestine, then under the British mandate. More than 1,000 Jewish ex-servicemen crowded into the Grand Palais Theatre in the East End of London, with many more, unable to get in, massed outside, and passed a resolution pro-testing "against the massacre of Jewish men, women, and children while under British protection." The resolution also demanded the punishment of those responsible for the riots; "no hindrance to . . . the formation of a Jewish defense corps in Palestine"; "unrestricted Jewish immigration into Palestine"; and the "the granting of preference to Jewish ex-servicemen in the civil and military administration there."
>
> A second resolution called for the formation of a Jewish ex-servicemen's organisation in London. The response was immediate: 90 men enrolled on the spot, forming the nucleus of the Jewish Ex-Servicemen's Legion, and this soon grew to 200. . . . The formation of the Legion was generally well-received, although a small minority of the community believed that there was no need for a separate Jewish ex-servicemen's organisation. As if to refute this view publicly, an impressive Armistice Service, organised jointly by the Legion and the National Remembrance Service Committee, was held at the Great Synagogue, Duke's Place, in the East End of London, in November, 1929, to honour the Jewish men and women of the British Empire who had lost their lives while serving in the Armed and Auxiliary Forces. The service was preceded by a parade of more than 500 ex-servicemen.[96]

This was followed by the effort, announced in London's *Jewish Chronicle*, to create an organization to advance comradeship; to establish close contact with Jewish ex-servicemen abroad; promote friendship and understanding between Jewish and non-Jewish servicemen; to promote the upbuilding of Palestine as the Jewish National Home, especially by assist-ing Jewish ex-Servicemen to settle there; to encourage knowledge of Jewish culture, history, and literature; and to participate fully in all forms of sport. It was to be "a non-party organisation." Despite its embrace of Zionism, it attempted to be as neutral and all-encompassing as possible.[97]

The membership rolls grew substantially throughout the 1930s. Not surprisingly, the organization altered "its order of priorities in accordance with the political situation. While commemoration was still one of the most important facets of its activities, the Legion now had no alternative but to expand and intensify defence and anti-defamation work and give it top priority. Because of the economic situation, growing emphasis was also placed on welfare work."[98] For most of the 1930s the efforts of Jewish veterans in Britain are difficult to disentangle from a complex network of communal bodies involved in joint efforts, mainly under the umbrella of the Trades Advisory Council. They "worked closely" in "anti-defamation activities with the Board of Deputies of British Jews, which had established the Jewish Defence Committee (JDC) to co-ordinate the efforts of Jewish groups to counter the British Union of Fascists propaganda and neutralise its demonstrations."[99] We may take this term "neutralise" to cover a variety of actions, including the use of force, as employed by the Jewish veterans against their pro-Nazi adversaries.[100] In terms of other concrete efforts, the Legion "distributed more than 100,000 leaflets combating the anti-Jewish propaganda of the British Union of Fascists and other Fascist-inspired groups. It also provided speakers, stewards, and observers for public meetings."[101] "Observers" here refers to those who attended fascist meetings for the purpose of both surveillance and direct action. Similar to their American comrades, the British Jewish Legion organized a "German-Jewish Ex-Servicemen's Refugee Aid Committee," which soon went beyond aid to ex-servicemen. Otto Schiff, a (London) City banker in his family's firm and nephew of Jacob Schiff (1847–1920), took a lead role in this work, which resulted in the resettlement in England of some thousands of refugees.[102]

Perhaps the response of Jewish ex-servicemen to Kristallnacht was muted because of its timing. Just days before, AJEX had staged its "Remembrance Service," which was attended by some 7,000 members, and had a larger audience of 100,000—a tremendous crowd.[103] The newsreels of the following week in English cinemas featured the demonstration, and specified that "50,000 Jews had fought for the British Empire."[104] Coordinating another big event so soon afterwards probably would have been difficult.

It is likely that little attention was paid to AJEX in the 1930s, because its reputation declined in the subsequent decade. In addition, the bitterness over the bloody demise of the British Mandate in Palestine surely affected popular attitudes and historiography in many respects. During the Second World War and in its immediate aftermath, the Jewish Defence Committee, under whose auspices the Jewish ex-servicemen operated, "suffered more opprobrium from the community for its seeming inactivity than any other." Even those who wish to underscore the constructive and assertive role of AJEX qualify that their efforts were largely "defensive," as they "had no option. Being a part of the establishment, they could not do otherwise than support the laws of the land even if those laws went against the interests of the Jewish community. Furthermore, they could not condone any action which broke the laws."[105] One may also assume that the lack of publicity is due to the fact that some of its activities were either illegal, or otherwise abrogated the sense of propriety so highly esteemed by Anglo-Jewry. Yet, there is evidence to suggest that as a consequence of efforts by Jewish war veterans and others in Britain to confront native fascism and the German persecution of Jewry, strategies for defending Jews against their opponents, besides nascent explanatory frameworks of the Holocaust—as well as antisemitic justifications of the violence inflicted on Jewish persons and property, some of which continued during the Holocaust and after the war—arose around the events of Kristallnacht.[106] It is evident that even before the Holocaust, diverse ways of conceiving and reacting to Jewish persecution under the Nazis were taking form in both the United States and British contexts.

In the 1930s, organized Jewish war veterans in Britain and the United States were neither cross-sections nor microcosms of the Jewish societies of which they were a part. It is difficult to measure their stake and sway in their own communities and larger bodies they sought to influence. These groups have, nevertheless, been undervalued as components and actors in an order that was very much in flux. In seeking a more nuanced and complex understanding of relations between Jews and Christians, and among Jews themselves, it is helpful to illuminate the attitudes and roles of Jewish veterans—of those who had already experienced what was supposed to have been the war to end all wars. Many among them—although by no means predicting the Holocaust—believed that the Jews already had been drawn into a struggle for survival that required attitudes and behavior transcending the Jews' responses to their earlier struggles. They sought to convey the notion that their efforts for Germany's Jews should not be apprehended as a matter of parochial self-interest, but rather "for sake of humanity itself."[107]

NOTES

1. The treatment is very different and more extensive in the realm of political science; see Ronald R. Krebs, *Fighting for Rights: Military Service and the Politics of Citizenship* (Ithaca, NY: Cornell University Press, 2006), pp. 7–8, n. 40.
2. Bill Bottoms, *The VFW: An Illustrated History of the Veterans of Foreign Wars of the United States,* foreword by Senator Bob Dole (Rockville, MD: Woodbine House, 1991); Thomas A. Rumer, *The American Legion: An Official History,*

1919–1989 (New York: M. Evans, 1990); William Pencak, *For God and Country: The American Legion, 1919–1941* (Boston: Northeastern University Press, 1981); David L. O'Connor, *Defenders of the Faith: American Catholic Lay Organizations and Anticommunism, 1917–1975* (Stony Brook: State University of New York at Stony Brook, 2000); Seymour Weisman, *Jewish War Veterans of the United States of America: A Century of Patriotic Service to the American People, 1896–1996* (Washington, D.C.: Jewish War Veterans of America, 1996); Gloria R. Mosesson, *The Jewish War Veterans Story* (Washington, D.C.: Jewish War Veterans of America, 1971). There is, however, a major book under way about Jews in the military—but excluding the United States—by Derek Penslar, and Zvi Gittelman is in the midst of work on veterans in the USSR.

3. Peter Fritzsche, *Rehearsals for Fascism: Populism and Political Mobilization in Weimar Germany* (New York: Oxford University Press, 1990).

4. R. Pierson, "Embattled Veterans: The Reichsbund jüdischer Frontsoldaten," in *Leo Baeck Institute Year Book* 19 (1974): pp. 139–54; Barbara Welker, "'Ich hatt' einen Kameraden': der Reichsbund jüdischer Frontsoldaten und das Gedenken an die Gefallenen des Ersten Weltkrieges," in *"Bis der Krieg uns lehrt, was der Friede bedeutet": das Ehrenfeld für die jüdischen Gefallenen des Weltkrieges auf dem Friedhof der Berliner jüdischen Gemeinde* (Teetz: Hentrich & Hentrich, 2004), pp. 33–50.

5. Bryan Mark Rigg, *Hitler's Jewish Soldiers: The Untold Story of Nazi Racial Laws and Men of Jewish Descent in the German Military* (Lawrence: University of Kansas Press, 2002). See Geoffrey Giles's excellent critique of this problematic book, *Washington Post Sunday Book Review*, May 26, 2002.

6. Joseph Tenenbaum, "Opening Address," *Hitler a Menace to World Peace. Addresses and Messages Delivered at the Peace and Democracy Rally at Madison Square Garden, March 15th, 1937, Auspices Joint Boycott Council of the American Jewish Congress and Jewish Labor Committee, New York*, p. 9.

7. Richard A. Hawkins, "'Hitler's Bitterest Foe': Samuel Untermyer and the Boycott of Nazi Germany, 1933–1938," in *American Jewish History* 93, 1 (2007): 211–50.

8. See photo of December 1, 1938, AP World Wide: "At a ceremony at the Northwestern Synagogue in the Golders Green section of London, Rabbi M.L. Perlzweig is presented with a Torah scroll from a South German town during Kristallnacht." United States Holocaust Memorial Museum (USHMM) Photo Archives, Desig. No. 525.319, w/s No. 69195. CE no. 0271.

9. Moshe R. Gottlieb, *American Anti-Nazi Resistance, 1933–1941: An Historical Analysis* (New York: KTAV, 1982).

10. Ibid., p. 30.

11. Ibid., p. 47.

12. Ibid., p. 56.

13. Ibid., pp. 97–98.

14. Charles C. Eisenstein, "Sons of J.W.V.," *Jewish Veteran*, January 1933, p. 10.

15. "The Jewish Big Ten," *Jewish Veteran*, January 1933, p. 7.
16. "Adolph Lewisohn Dies at Age of 89. Banker, Donor of the Stadium Named for Him, Aided Great Variety of Charities," *New York Times*, August 19, 1938.
17. J. David Delman, "Jewish News and Views," *Jewish Veteran*, September 1933, p. 28.
18. Ibid., p. 14.
19. Photo of JWV delegation with Orthodox rabbis, 1944, USHMM Photo Archives, Desig. No. 730.1088, w/s no. 60191, CD no. 0271.
20. J. David Delman, "Jewish News and Views," *The Jewish Veteran*, May 1933, p. 14.
21. "Jewish Polish Vets Challenge Anti-Semitism," *The Jewish Veteran*, January 1933, p. 13.
22. Gottlieb, *American Anti-Nazi Resistance*, p. 59.
23. Mosesson, *Jewish War Veterans Story*, p. 39.
24. See www.jwv.org/images/uploads/Jewish%20War%20Veterans%20 Timeline.pdf.
25. J. George Fredman and Louis A. Falk, *Jews in American Wars*, 3rd revised ed. (New York: Jewish War Veterans of the U.S., March 1943).
26. www.jwv.org/images/uploads/Jewish%20War%20Veterans%20Time line.pdf.
27. Ibid.
28. See, for example, Alexander Prusin, *Nationalizing a Borderland: War, Ethnicity, and Anti-Jewish Violence in East Galicia, 1914–1920* (Tuscaloosa: University of Alabama Press, 2005); see also Mark Levene, *War, Jews and the New Europe: The Diplomacy of Lucien Wolf 1914–1919* (Oxford: Littman Library of Jewish Civilization, 1992).
29. See Ezra Mendelsohn, *The Jews of East Central Europe between the World Wars* (Bloomington: Indiana University Press, 1983).
30. www.jwv.org/images/uploads/Jewish%20War%20Veterans%20Time line.pdf.
31. The *Jewish Veteran*, Convention Number, Twelfth National Encampment, Atlantic City, New Jersey, July 1–4, 1933 (unpaginated).
32. www.jwv.org/images/uploads/Jewish%20War%20Veterans%20Time line.pdf.
33. Photograph from March 23, 1933, desig. No. 730.1082, w/s no. 44164, CD no. 0271. Photo Archives, USHMM.
34. Hawkins, "'Hitler's Bitterest Foe,'" 23.
35. Ibid., 211–50.
36. "Untermyer Picked for Fight on Nazis. Will Plead before League on Behalf of Nations Veterans. If They Desire Him to Do So. Jewish Group Names Him. Surprise Move Made at Memorial Services for Action under Minorities Clauses," *New York Times*, May 22, 1933, p. 9.
37. See www.jwv.org/images/uploads/Jewish%20War%20Veterans%20 Timeline.pdf.

38. "Boycott Stamps Issued. Jewish Veterans Begin Sending Out 10,000,000 a Week," *New York Times*, May 22, 1933, p. 10. Gottlieb states that the American League for the Defense of Jewish Rights "followed" the JWV, p. 45.

39. "Smith Denounces Nazis as 'Stupid.' Regime Brings Only Ridicule on Germany, He Tells 1,500 at Untermyer Dinner. Boycott Plan Pressed. Non-Jews Are Exhorted to Stop Trade with Hitlerites," *New York Times*, September 11, 1933, p. 1, 2.

40. "Deportations Urged for Hitlerites Here. Untermyer Declares Federal Officials Are Investigating Nazi Propagandists," *New York Times*, September 25, 1933, p. 3.

41. *Nazis against the World. The Counter-Boycott is the Only Defensive Weapon against Hitlerism's World Threat to Civilization. Selected Speeches from World Leaders of Public Opinion* (New York: Non-Sectarian Anti-Nazi League to Champion Human Rights, 1934), p. 78.

42. Ibid., frontispiece.

43. Donard McKale, *The Swastika Outside Germany* (Kent, OH: Kent State University Press, 1977); Sander A. Diamond, *The Nazi Movement in the United States 1924–1941* (Ithaca, NY: Cornell University Press, 1974); Susan Canedy, *America's Nazis: A Democratic Dilemma. A History of the German American Bund* (Menlo Park, CA: Markgraf, 1990).

44. See, for example, "Violence at Rally Laid to Nazi Group. Jewish War Veterans Charge Fighting at Queens Meeting Was Incited by Hitlerites. Illegal Actions Alleged. But Counter-Boycott Leaders Deny Blackjacks Were Used or Laws Disregarded," *New York Times*, April 10, 1934, p. 10.

45. Mosesson, *Jewish War Veterans Story*, p. 51.

46. Edgar H. Burman, "On the Boycott Front," *The Jewish Veteran*, January 1933, p. 15.

47. See Michael Berkowitz, "Crime and Redemption? American Jewish Gangsters and the Fight against Nazism," in *Studies in Contemporary Jewry* (New York: Oxford University Press, 2004), pp. 95–108.

48. See www.jwv.org/images/uploads/Jewish%20War%20Veterans%20Timeline.pdf.

49. See www.cwv.org/history/history.htm.

50. "AAU Threatens German Olympics Ban," *The Jewish Veteran*, November 1933, p. 32.

51. See www.jwv.org/images/uploads/Jewish%20War%20Veterans%20Timeline.pdf.

52. See John Bunzl, "Hakoah Vienna: Reflections on a Legend," in *Emancipation through Muscles: Jews and Sports in Europe*, eds. Michael Brenner and Gideon Reuveni (Lincoln: University of Nebraska Press, 2006), pp. 106–115; John Bunzl, *ha-Koah=Hakaoah: ein jüdischer Sportverein in Wien, 1909–1995*, ed. Jüdischen Museum Wien (Vienna: Der Apfel, 1995).

53. *1936, die Olympischen Spiele und der Nationalsozialismus: eine Dokumentation*,
    ed. Reinhard Rürup, with Marcus Funck, Helga Woggon, and English
    translation by Pamela E. Selwyn (Berlin: Argon, 1996).
54. Marty Glickman with Stan Isaacs, *The Fastest Kid on the Block: The Marty
    Glickman Story* (Syracuse, NY: Syracuse University Press, 1996).
55. See www.jwv.org/images/uploads/Jewish%20War%20Veterans%20Tim
    eline.pdf.
56. See Allen Guttmann, *The Games Must Go On: Avery Brundage and
    the Olympic Movement* (New York: Columbia University Press, 1984);
    John M. Hoberman, *The Olympic Crisis: Sport, Politics and the Moral
    Order* (New Rochelle, NY: A. D. Caratzas, 1986); Hoberman, *Sport and
    Political Ideology* (Austin: University of Texas Press, 1984).
57. Ibid.
58. See photo of December 1, 1938, AP World Wide: "At a ceremony at the
    Northwestern Synagogue in the Golders Green section of London, Rabbi
    M.L. Perlzweig is presented with a Torah scroll from a South German
    town during Kristallnacht." United States Holocaust Memorial Museum
    (USHMM) Photo Archives, Desig. No. 525.319, w/s No. 69195. CE
    no. 0271.
59. "Asks of 'Rigid Boycott.' Commander and Jewish Veterans Officers Meet
    on German Action," (AP, New Haven), *New York Times*, November 19,
    1938.
60. Ibid.
61. See Maria Mazzenga, "Toward an American Catholic Response to the
    Holocaust: Catholic Americanism and Kristallnacht," chapter 4, this
    volume.
62. "Fight on 'Isms' Urged. Speakers in Broadcast Ask Unity of Faiths," *New
    York Times*, December 20, 1938, p. 16.
63. "Jewish Veterans Vote War on 'Isms': Communism and Fascism Are
    Condemned in Resolution of State Convention," *New York Times*, May
    23, 1938.
64. Haskel Lookstein, *Were We Our Brothers' Keepers? The Public Response
    of American Jews to the Holocaust* (New York: An [e-reads] Book,
    1988), p. 49.
65. J. David Delman, "Black Sunday" in "Jewish News and Views," *The
    Jewish Veteran*, p. 12.
66. Isador A. Worth, "Message of the National Commander," *The Jewish
    Veteran*, December 1938, p. 10.
67. "20,000 Jam Garden in Reich Protest. Varied Groups Hear Pleas to
    'Smash Nazism' to End Its Persecutions. Fund of $4,655 Is Raised.
    Resolutions Ask Roosevelt to Call World Parley and to Ban Trade With
    Germany," *New York Times*, November 22, 1938.
68. See Mark Jonathan Harris and Deborah Oppenheimer, *Into the Arms of
    Strangers: Stories of the Kindertransport* (New York: MJF, 2000).
69. I wish to thank Kyle Jantzen for this reference. See www.archives.cbc.
    ca/IDC-1-109-1257-7062/1930s/1938/clip4.

70. "Protest Assembly Endorsed by Glass. Mayor Will Preside Tonight at Carnegie Hall Meeting to Oppose Oppression. Wallace to be a Speaker. Many Civic Groups Join Forces to Register Disapproval of European Policies," *New York Times*, December 9, 1938, p. 16.

71. Ibid.

72. I wish to thank Patrick Hayes for this important point.

73. "Heads New Jewish Group. J.W. Smith Says Aim Will Be to Combat Foreign 'Isms'," November 7, 1938, *New York Times*, p. 19.

74. "Federation Answers Attack by S.S. Wise. Anti-'Ism' Group Denies It is Hunting Political Jobs," *New York Times*, May 9, 1939, p. 10.

75. "Jewish Group Formed to Combat 'Isms.' Milton Solomon Seeks Adherents in Americanism Program," *New York Times*, October 17, 1938, p. 3.

76. Abba Hillel Silver, "Jews Don't Have to Apologize! Let Us Not Permit Ourselves To Be Put on the Defensive!" *The Jewish Veteran*, October 1938, pp. 6–7.

77. "J.W.V. Pays Dual Tribute to Cardinal Hayes," *The Jewish Veteran*, October 1939, p. 5.

78. John R. Ryan, "Catholic Scholar Condemns Father Coughlin," *The Jewish Veteran*, February 1939, p. 3.

79. Harry McNeill, "Communism and Fascism are Anti-Religious," *The Jewish Veteran*, March 1939, p. 7.

80. Allen Lesser, "Catholics Fight Anti-Semitism: A Priest Looks at Race Hatred," *The Jewish Veteran*, December 1938, p. 7.

81. "J.W.V. Americanism Program," *The Jewish Veteran*, November 1938, p. 6.

82. "Jews in America," *The Jewish Veteran*, February 1939, p. 4.

83. "Out of Detroit," *The Jewish Veteran*, December 1938, p. 4.

84. "Hail Pope Pius XII!" *The Jewish Veteran*, March 1939, p. 4.

85. "Out of Detroit," *The Jewish Veteran*, December 1938, p. 4.

86. Albert Lee, *Henry Ford and the Jews* (New York: Stein and Day, 1980), p. 85.

87. Neil Baldwin, *Henry Ford and the Jews: The Mass Production of Hate* (New York: Public Affairs, 2001), pp. 293ff, 298–300.

88. "20,000 Jam Garden In Reich Protest. Varied Groups Hear Pleas to 'Smash Nazism' to End Its Persecutions. Fund Of $4,655 Is Raised. Resolutions Ask Roosevelt to Call World Parley and to Ban Trade With Germany," *New York Times*, November 22, 1938.

89. Baldwin, *Henry Ford and the Jews*, pp. 293ff, 298–300.

90. "Ford Lend 75 Cars to J.W.V. Convention," *Jewish War Veteran*, August 1938, p. 11.

91. "Protest on Hitler Growing in Nation. Christian and Non-Sectarian Groups Voice Indignation Over Anti-Jewish Drive. Urge Washington to Act. Catholic Truth Society Wants Berlin Chided—Green Speaks for the A.F. of L.—Boycott Move Spreads. Merchants Cancelling Orders for German Goods—Day of Fasting Ordered for Monday," *New York Times*, December 10, 1938.

92. "An Inter-Faith Group Is Important," *The Jewish Veteran*, May 1939, p. 6.

93. "Protest on Hitler Growing in Nation," *New York Times*, March 23, 1933.

94. "Protest on Hitler Growing in Nation. Christian and Non-Sectarian Groups Voice Indignation Over Anti-Jewish Drive. Urge Washington to Act. Catholic Truth Society Wants Berlin Chided—Green Speaks for the A.F. of L.—Boycott Move Spreads. Merchants Cancelling Orders for German Goods—Day or Fasting Ordered for Monday," *New York Times*, December 10, 1938.

95. Interview with Gabriel Kaufman, vice-president of AJEX, who graciously guided me through the AJEX Museum in Hendon, North London, July 17, 2007.

96. Henry Morris, *The AJEX Chronicles: The Association of Jewish Ex-Servicemen and Women: A Brief History* (London: AJEX, 1999), pp. 15–6.

97. Ibid., p. 17.

98. Ibid., pp. 17–8.

99. Ibid., p. 19.

100. "Anti-Fascist Meeting Scenes. Man Fined for Hitting Chairman in The Face. Iron Bolts Thrown," *E. London Advertiser*, May 29, 1937.

101. *AJEX Chronicles*, p. 19.

102. Ibid., p. 20. See Vivian D. Lipman, "Anglo-Jewish Attitudes to the Refugees from Central Europe, 1933–1939, in *Second Chance: Two Centuries of German-Speaking Jews in the United Kingdom*, ed. Werner E. Mosse (Tübingen: J. C. B. Mohr (Paul Siebeck, 1991), pp. 520–22; *Advocate for the Doomed: The Diaries and Papers of James G. McDonald, 1932–1935*, eds. Richard Breitman, Barbara McDonald Stewart, and Severin Hochberg (Bloomington and Indianapolis: Indiana University Press, 2007), pp. 525–6, 530–44.

103. "Record Attendance at the Remembrance Service," in *Jewish Chronicle*, November 11, 1938, p. 26.

104. Letter of Mrs. S. Sharpe in *Jewish Chronicle*, November 11, 1938, p. 27.

105. Morris Beckman, *The 43 Group* (London: Centerprise, 1992), p. 15.

106. See Fascism (cuttings), Volume II, GB 0103, Trades Advisory Council, 1936–1983, University College London archives.

107. "Poster issued by the Jewish War Veterans of the United States calling for a boycott of German goods" (undated), USHMM Photo Archive, desig. No. 730.25, w/s no. 89404, CD 0271.

CHAPTER 4

TOWARD AN AMERICAN CATHOLIC RESPONSE TO THE HOLOCAUST: CATHOLIC AMERICANISM AND KRISTALLNACHT

MARIA MAZZENGA

Most scholarly works that address the question of Catholic responses to the Nazi persecution of Europe's Jews focus on the attitudes and actions of the Vatican and the European Catholic churches.[1] While this focus is appropriate given European Catholic institutional proximity to the Nazi regime, these works do not offer us anything close to a comprehensive view of how the U.S. Catholic Church responded to what today is known as the Holocaust.[2] Here, I take a very preliminary step in that direction, focusing primarily on how American Catholic leaders responded to Kristallnacht, the anti-Jewish pogrom that took place in Germany and German-occupied territory on November 9–10, 1938. Widely and accurately reported in the United States, Kristallnacht generated extensive and emotional responses within the American Catholic community. These responses reflect the existence of two distinct strains of thought within the institutional American Catholic Church—two Catholic Americanisms that were clearly articulated in the context of the intensifying Nazi brutality against Europe's Jews. My focus here is on the immediate and institutional responses: those articulated in late 1938 and early 1939 by representatives of American Catholic institutions, particularly bishops and prominent priests who held special influence in American Catholic affairs. This scope, while limited, enables a fuller exposition on a pivotal moment in American Catholic and Jewish relations as well as a more detailed discussion on how the Church leadership grappled with the thorny problem of the immensely popular and increasingly antisemitic Father Charles Coughlin.

A closer look at American Catholic institutional responses to the Nazi treatment of Europe's Jews is long overdue. The seat of the Church's authority may have been in Rome, but the American Church possessed characteristics all its own, a fact that alternately fascinated and frustrated Roman Catholic authorities. By 1938, there were over 20 million Catholics in the American Church. Institutional life had stabilized and flourished by the late 1920s, particularly in the cities, where Catholics would remain concentrated until after the Second World War. New parishes, schools, colleges, orphanages, seminaries, and hospitals were built throughout the United States, particularly during the economically flush 1920s. By the 1930s the infrastructural growth trend slowed because of the Depression, but local Catholic life, rooted in a uniquely American combination of ethno-racial and territorial parishes, continued to thrive. Persistent anti-Catholicism often meant that Catholics of a range of classes and ethnic origins felt less comfortable in public institutions than within their own. It also meant, however, that the U.S. Catholic Church, while managed by a predominantly Irish- and German-American hierarchy, was ethnically diverse. Public respect for ethnic diversity became an ideal of the American Church, necessitated in part by the need to manage a multiethnic flock, and in part because it was central to the national imagination. Ethnic diversity in the United States renders study of distinctly American responses to the persecution of Europe's Jews absolutely essential. In contrast with the ethnically based political systems of European countries is the American reality of an ethnically plural nation united by civic ideals, which in turn shaped the evolution of the Church in the United States.[3]

Another element distinguishing an American Catholic response to the Nazi persecution of Europe's Jews is the fact of *religious* pluralism and the ideal of religious liberty in the United States. Though the Vatican found the ideal of religious liberty unacceptable (Catholicism being, for the Holy See's representatives, unquestionably the one and only true faith), it could not ignore what Gerald P. Fogarty calls the "United States with its peculiar religious situation," because the United States was an emerging world power with expanding global influence that could benefit Catholic authorities in Rome. The debate over the acceptability of religious liberty would not come to a head until after the Second World

War, but it emerged earlier, during the 1890s Americanist controversy. The controversy, which entailed several prominent bishops lining up in opposition over the question of how fully the U.S. Church should embrace American institutions and ideals as it grew with the new nation, had been temporarily mitigated with the issuance of the papal encyclical *Testem Benevolentiae Nostrae*. This 1899 letter from Pope Pius XIII to the Americanist Cardinal James Gibbons of Baltimore (though intended for the entire American hierarchy) amounted to a condemnation of the liberal position that sought rapport between American institutions and the Church.[4] Though the controversy possessed many elements, the component wherein the liberals felt church-state separation and religious liberty were national ideals acceptable to Catholics is of special relevance here. The American Church authorities took the formal position that religious liberty was unacceptable, but there was ambivalence among many Catholic leaders, who were compelled to grapple with the fact of the plurality of faiths in American life throughout the first decades of the twentieth century despite the doctrinal position. The fact of religious pluralism and the concept of religious liberty must, then, be factored into the American Catholic response to the Nazi treatment of Jews in the 1930s. Two basic attitudes toward the Jewish situation were discernable within the U.S. Church. More conservative American Catholics viewed any formal defense of Jews as associated with the officially unacceptable position that Judaism was religiously equal to Catholicism, and therefore rejected any public display in support of Jews as a transgression against their own faith. However, some Catholic clerical leaders, in the tradition of the Americanists of the late nineteenth century, drew from American ideals of religious liberty to fashion an alternative American Catholic response to the persecution of Jews. These Catholics publicly condemned Nazi antisemitism and engaged in public, if limited, expressions of inter-faith support.

This situating of Catholicism in the American setting is not, alas, an attempt to absolve the U.S. Church of the long history of antisemitism embedded in Catholicism itself from its earliest days. As Frank J. Coppa shows, the popes oscillated "between paternal protection and overt per-secution" in their position toward Jews since early Christianity. Indeed, opposition to Judaism is present in the New Testament and is rooted in the early Christian assertion that Jews "killed" Christ. Coppa writes that the "anti-Judaism of the New Testament reflects more than simple retali-ation for the Jewish 'persecution'; it appears motivated by the need for the new religion to differentiate itself from its parent." Catholics, unlike, for example, the Christian fundamentalists discussed by Matthew Bowman in the last chapter of this volume, believed (and some continue to believe) that Christianity superseded Judaism, justifying the exclusion and violence committed against Jews in Catholic-dominated Europe. David I. Kertzer connects the historic Catholic anti-Judaism of the Church to the race-based antisemitism of the Nazis.[5] The immensely popular Father Charles Coughlin, as we will see, combined historic anti-Judaism with modern antisemitism. At the core of Coughlin's late-1930s Catholic Americanism was an anti-Jewishness that drew from both American populism and Catholic theology. However, several American Church leaders, many of whom found Fr. Coughlin's late-1930s demagoguery repulsive, had internalized ideals of religious liberty and freedom of worship, and combined these with traditional ideals of Christian love and tolerance to fashion a more inclusive attitude toward Jews. Sometimes these leaders exhibited a kind of institutional pragmatism, ignoring the Vatican position that defense of the rights of members of a faith other than one's own suggested that all religions were equal. Others deliberately found ways of circumventing restrictions on public expression of support for the rights of other faiths out of a personal sense of moral and civic duty. Some of these church leaders were compelled to embrace a contradiction: defend the rights of non-Catholics to practice their own religions while maintaining a belief in Catholicism as the one true faith. When faced with the tragedy of the plight of German Jews in the late 1930s, prelates that spoke out against the atrocities sometimes used their American ideals—which could make room for acceptance of the truth of several religions at once—to mediate this contradiction.

Also relevant in understanding the American Church's response to Jewish persecution is the trend toward romanization of the hierarchy in the late nineteenth and early twentieth centuries. The Americanist controversy, Fogarty writes, caused the Vatican to emphasize "a more vertical concept of authority with each bishop autonomous in his own diocese and not only dependent upon but directly responsible to the Holy See alone, or more specifically a Roman patron."[6] This caused a range of local expressions of Catholicism to develop on the diocesan and archdiocesan levels, with local authorities dependent on highly placed contacts made in Rome. In the 1920s and after, moreover, regionalization increased, and the once all-powerful eastern sees had to share power with expanding midwestern ones. Regionalization meant local sees developed local power. In 1938, as we will see, for example, many local bishops embraced a multidenominational national day of prayer for the Jewish victims of Nazi persecution, while others did not, suggesting participation was optional rather than controlled by a central authority.

If American religious liberty presented, from the Vatican's perspective, dangerous temptations to reduce all religions to equal status, American national citizenship itself could also threaten to diminish one's faith. For Vatican officials, Catholicism demanded a loyalty that transcended national boundaries, individualism, and the authority of the nation. National loyalty does not necessarily have to get in the way of this religious loyalty, but the two could conflict, and sometimes both Catholic leaders and Vatican representatives were uncertain as to how these two sets of loyalties could be reconciled.[7] Anticommunism could function as a mediator of the relationship between American citizenship and Catholicism—for the vast majority of American Catholics of the 1930s, being Catholic meant being anticommunist in no uncertain terms, and the Vatican found this brand of American citizenship acceptable. Fr. Charles Coughlin would take full advantage of this Catholic predisposition, using the charge of communism against just about anyone who disagreed with him toward augmenting his personal popularity. Global events reinforced Catholic anticommunism. The Spanish Civil War of 1936–1939, widely reported in the U.S. Catholic press, reinforced anticommunist feeling among U.S. Catholics. Leftist anticlericalism in Mexico, too, received heavy coverage in the American Catholic press. In both cases, Catholics were victims of atrocities committed by forces associated with socialism and communism. These circumstances caused some Catholics to sympathize with fascists (concordats had been reached between the Vatican and fascist Italy in 1929 and fascist Germany in 1933), who, at least initially, were more supportive of Catholic institutions than were communists or socialists. American Catholic outrage against anti-Catholic socialist reforms in Mexico, and approval of the concordats in Italy and Germany, as John McGreevy points out, were expressions of belief that Catholic religious liberties should be protected.[8]

Reflecting these circumstances, two strains of American Catholicism bearing special relevance for the reception of the news of Hitler's treatment of Jews in Germany are discernable. One strain tended toward a defensive anticommunist posture and sympathy with European fascism, while a second exhibited a compatibility with American religious liberty and ethnic pluralist ideals. Fr. Charles Coughlin was the chief architect of the defensive Catholicism of the later 1930s, adopting a siege mentality, emphasizing Catholic persecution by leftists, and espousing radical anticommunism. Coughlin's strain of American Catholicism, moreover, drew from Catholic theological and cultural antisemitism, subscribing to a view of Judaism as an illegitimate religion superseded by Catholicism, suspicious of a wealthy Jewish economic conspiracy against non-Jews, and certain of Jewish control of global communism. The Catholic diocesan newspaper *The Brooklyn Tablet* and its editor, Patrick Scanlon, also reflected this defensive strain, as would the Christian Front, a violently antisemitic organization founded by Coughlin.[9] Of those who sought to reconcile American ideals of religious liberty and ethnic pluralism with their Catholicism, Fr. John A. Ryan and Fr. Maurice S. Sheehy, among others, were key figures. Their Americanism was critical of Coughlin's radical anticommunism because they saw it as constricting American individualism and political liberty, and they sought to see commonalities rather than differences between Judaism and Catholicism—both emphasized, for example, Christ's Jewishness and saw Catholic prejudice against Jews as inherently contradictory. Both strains represent the American Catholic Church of the 1930s and would shape responses to the events of November 1938 and beyond.

On November 20, 1938, Fr. Charles Coughlin, the hugely popular Catholic "radio priest" from Michigan, went on the air to deliver one of his most notorious broadcasts: "Persecution—Jewish and Christian." Claiming he would add his voice to those protesting the brutal Nazi pogrom of several days earlier against Germany's Jewish population, Coughlin instead offered a convoluted justification of the Nazi atrocities as a natural defense against a Jewish-dominated communist movement. "Let us pause to inquire why Nazism is so hostile to Jewry in particular and how the Nazi policy of persecution can be liquidated," Coughlin began with an air of learned authority that convinced so many of his followers that his words were fact. "It is the belief, be it well or ill-founded, of the present German government, not mine, that Jews not as religionists, but as nationals only, were responsible for the economic and social ills suffered by the Fatherland since the Treaty of Versailles." Without pausing to debunk this position supposedly not his own, Coughlin then launched into his familiar practice of linking Jews with communism: "Imbued with this idea, be it right or wrong, an idea that spread rapidly, particularly since 1923 when communism was beginning to make substantial advances throughout Germany, a group of rebel Germans under the leadership of an Austrian born war veteran, Adolf Hitler by name, organized for two purposes. First, to overthrow the existing German government under whose jurisdiction communism was waxing strong, and second, to rid the fatherland of communists whose leaders, unfortunately, they identified with the Jewish race." "Thus," he concluded, "Nazism was conceived as a political defense mechanism against communism, and was ushered into existence as a result of communism, and communism itself was regarded by the rising generation of Germans as a product not of Russia, but of a group of Jews who dominated the destinies of Russia."[10]

The concept articulated here—Nazism arose as a reaction to Jewish-dominated communism—formed the core of the broadcast, and while the narrative went on for some time after these initial comments, Coughlin's talk ultimately reinforced the idea that the Nazis were justified in their persecution, rather than condemning it. The broadcast was also peppered with insinuations that communist "atheistic" Jews "appropriated" Christian property, and that wealthy Jewish bankers had financed "the Russian Revolution and Communism."[11] The twisted reasoning and insinuation were classic Coughlin. Charged with overseeing Coughlin's speeches and writings as his superior in the Archdiocese of Detroit, a frustrated Archbishop Edward Mooney once said that Coughlin's articles on Jewish matters "are so cleverly gotten up and so contrived to say and unsay a thing in almost the same breath that it is almost impossible for a censor to do much deleting."[12] The strands of thought embedded in this broadcast, as contradictory as they may seem (wealthy capitalist Jews bankrolling the founding of a theoretically classless society, for example), also drew from the darker strains of both American populism and Catholic theology. As Michael Kazin has shown, Coughlin's antisemitism could also be found within the American populist tradition of the late nineteenth century, where antisemites like Tom Watson "identified Jews as both nonproductive manipulators of 'other people's money' and the carriers of decadent, radical doctrines from abroad."[13] Coughlin's populist antisemitism was also informed by his Catholicism: Mary Athans definitively links the radical antisemitism Coughlin began expressing in the fall of 1938 to his reading of the works of the Irish priest Denis Fahey, a correspondent of Coughlin's who shaped his view that Jews were part of a "mystical body of Satan" out to destroy Christianity.[14]

Coughlin's November 20 broadcast, which actually marked his most intense on-air antisemitism to that date, is all the more stunning because Kristallnacht had the opposite effect on much of the rest of the world. It illustrated beyond doubt that Hitler's regime intended to enforce its racist doctrines in an overt, systematic, and brutal way. This realization was as evident among American Catholics as it was among the rest of the population, and emboldened Coughlin's opponents within the Church to undermine his inflammatory agenda. Archbishop Mooney, Coughlin's superior, once fearful that he would alienate millions of Catholics if he silenced the priest, grew increasingly aggressive in curtailing Coughlin's activities after 1938, as Leslie Tentler shows. For similar reasons, we might surmise, the priests charged with censoring Coughlin's work were more likely to delete antisemitic text from his broadcasts after this time. Coughlin was so irate at the deletions of one 1940 text that he responded with a "silent broadcast," during which music interspersed with announcements to tune in the following week replaced his usual monologue. Coughlin then submitted the same antisemitic text to the censors for a subsequent broadcast, who then decided to pass the text on to the archbishop. Archbishop Mooney made so many deletions that Coughlin changed the topic of the broadcast. So many stations had failed to renew contracts with Coughlin by then that he was compelled to cancel his 1940–1941 broadcast season. The openly antisemitic *Social Justice*, officially edited by the layman E. Perrin Schwartz, but actually controlled by Coughlin, also came under closer scrutiny by Archbishop Mooney. After several tussles over the content of the publication, Coughlin was forced to remove his name from all of its articles, though, as Mooney knew, Coughlin continued to influence the paper editorially. In 1942, the U.S. government intervened, threatening to bring sedition charges against the magazine, and when Mooney threatened Coughlin with suspension, the priest was forced to end his association with the publication.[15]

The story of Fr. Coughlin's late-1930s antisemitism is not new; it has been told elsewhere. I recount the basic elements here, however, because it has deeply shaped our understanding of American Catholics and anti-semitism in the late 1930s and early 1940s. Coughlin was a lead actor in creating the "extra-ordinary antisemitism" of this period. The mid to late 1930s was a period in which, as David Gerber writes, "quasi-fascist and anti-communist antisemitism which blamed Jews for the Great Depression and the international crises in Europe appeared and threatened for a time to become the basis of a mass political movement."[16] Because the American political system emphasizes ideals of religious liberty and individual expression, antisemitism usually remains "ordinary," practiced privately and generally without government sanction on an everyday level, in social, economic, and educational institutions, through random verbal and physical harassment, and through the promotion of negative stereotypes in art and media.[17] In seeking to build a movement around antisemitic ideas through broadcasts, speeches, writings, and the Christian Front, however, Coughlin was practicing the former variety, and in building it partially around Catholic ideas, he was fashioning an American Catholic antisemitism. However, he ultimately failed to sustain the movement he helped generate, and while his Kristallnacht speech marks the height of the power of his extraordinary anti-Jewish prejudice, it also marks the start of the decline of his influence among all but extreme right-wing Catholics.

Coughlin's public antisemitism was out of step with the attitudes emerging from the rest of the institutional American Church, which was moving away from such prejudice in favor of a Catholic Americanism exhibiting a new openness to religious pluralism as well as an inter-faith cooperation that would gain fuller expression during the Second

World War. Fr. John A. Ryan, the foremost progressive American Catholic thinker of the first half of the twentieth century expressed the newer approach in a 1938 denunciation of Nazism. Ryan wrote that Nazism "deprives the Church of necessary freedom of worship and freedom of education." Excessively nationalistic, it "adheres to a theory of racial superiority and racial purity which are without foundation in fact, and which have been used as a pretext for an enormous amount of injustice and uncharity toward the Jewish race."[18] While most scholars of American Catholicism would date the Church's de facto acceptance of religious pluralism and embrace of interfaith cooperation at the start of the Second World War, I would argue that this history extends further back in time, and for a more complex range of reasons than has previously been acknowledged. Kristallnacht was a key moment in this history. Fr. Coughlin's November 20 broadcast marked a dramatic decline in his popularity, precisely because most of the Catholic Church interpreted Kristallnacht as a call to oppose Nazi brutality against Jews, not justify it.[19]

Both Ryan and Coughlin exhibited populist sympathies, emphasizing the rights of working people over elites. Both drew heavily from the papal encyclicals, particularly *Rerum Novarum* and *Quadragesimo Anno*, in their expositions on social justice in American life. Not a talented public speaker himself but more academically inclined than Coughlin, Ryan had originally admired the Michigan priest's tremendous ability to get ideas he advocated through books, articles, and university lectures on Catholic social teaching and reform out to millions of Americans with little inclination toward academia. As Coughlin began his outright criticism of Roosevelt, his convoluted and unsound discourses into monetary theory, and his insinuations of global Jewish conspiracies, however, Ryan quickly turned against him. As a highly respected social justice thinker whose views influenced many New Deal figures, Ryan came to believe that Coughlin's monetary proposals were quackery, and that the Michigan priest's allegations that the president was a communist were ridiculous.[20] The Ryan-Coughlin rift became overt in 1936, when Ryan delivered a national public broadcast supportive of the candidacy of Franklin Roosevelt and critical of Coughlin and his Union Party program for economic recovery. Ryan received well over a thousand letters from individuals across the country responding to the broadcast, only 200 of them approving. Many of the critical letters contained antisemitic remarks, overt extrapolations from Coughlin's writings and speeches containing thinly veiled anti-Jewish commentary related to international money changers and communist conspiracies. Echoing the theme, J. E. Barnhart, the author of one of these letters, asked Ryan, "How much did you get from Roosevelt to attack Fr. Coughlin, you are like the Jews in Christs [*sic*] time crucified [*sic*] him for 30 pieces of Silver."[21] Coughlin retained his popularity, but, as George Flynn shows, much of the American hierarchy and clergy began to turn against the radio priest as his discourses became more slanderous and intemperate in 1936.[22] As Coughlin's broadcasts and writings became increasingly antisemitic, Ryan publicly criticized the Michigan priest. "Antisemitism is contrary to Christianity and violates the basic principles of American democracy," he told a Jewish Community Center audience in early 1939. "Followers of Christ cannot believe He would hate the race from which he sprang, or any other people." "Constitutional guarantees" Ryan went on, ensured that antisemitism could not bring practical political results, suggesting that Coughlin was attempting to gather political support, but that such efforts were fruitless in America. As Coughlin drew his ideas from an antisemitic blend of Catholic teaching and American populism, Ryan drew his from national political ideals overtly expressed in American political documents, his own understanding of populism, and Catholic teaching in his attacks on Coughlin. As the *Washington Post* recognized in its reporting on this Ryan speech of early 1939, "Though the name of Rev. Charles E. Coughlin was not mentioned in the address, the entire speech was considered to be a condemnation of the Michigan priest's recent antisemitic pronouncements."[23] Ryan had been earlier criticized by his superiors for singling out Coughlin for criticism by name, as it made the Church, sensitive to non-Catholic American opinion, appear divided, so Ryan tried to limit his criticism to the content of Coughlin's speeches. Ryan's membership, along with that of the Catholic University sociologist Father Paul Hanley Furfey, on the executive board of the "Committee of Catholics for Human Rights (Committee of Catholics to Fight Antisemitism)" was also doubtless aimed at combating Coughlin-style antisemitism. At the same time, Ryan also denounced the Nazi program separately from his criticism of Coughlin.[24] As the Ryan-Coughlin conflict suggests, New Deal politics and antisemitism became intertwined among Catholics of the 1930s, largely due to Coughlin's tendency to mingle attacks on FDR, who Coughlin implied was a Jew and a communist, with assertions that Jews were part of a communist conspiracy to take over the world.

The Ryan-Coughlin conflict provides some context for understanding the responses of other prominent Catholic leaders to Nazi antisemitism in 1938. Ryan's critique of Coughlin began in the realm of politics and expanded to include denunciations of Coughlin's antisemitism. Fr. Maurice Sheehy, assistant professor in the Department of Religious Education at Catholic University and assistant to the University Rector, was also a New Dealer and staunch supporter of FDR. Less well known than Ryan, Sheehy was nonetheless strongly committed to combating religious prejudice, and recognized that Coughlin's pronouncements were making it appear that the entire Catholic Church was antisemitic. As was the case with Ryan, Sheehy's post at the Catholic University in Washington, D.C., enabled him to cultivate contacts within the FDR administration and other circles of power, and he pursued such contacts relentlessly. Sheehy worked with James A. Farley, head of the Democratic National Committee, to bring FDR to the university's 1933 commencement ceremony to speak and to receive an honorary degree. He also used his friendship with FDR's secretary, Marguerite "Missy" LeHand, to get messages to the president promptly with her support. Reflective of the growing embarrassment among Catholic clerical leaders over Coughlin's speeches, Sheehy wrote LeHand in October 1936: "I made a trip through the west recently at the suggestion of Senator [Joseph] O'Mahoney [of Wyoming]. Among the people I visited, which included four bishops and several score of priests, President Roosevelt is stronger than ever before. There is a feeling prevalent among the priests that the priesthood, through Father Coughlin, has betrayed the President, and some extraordinary things are being attempted to offset this betrayal."[25] Sheehy was extremely active in his private campaigning for the president, both in 1936 and in 1940.[26]

When the Nazi pogrom against the Jews occurred in early November 1938, a chance to clarify a Catholic position in opposition to Coughlin's increasingly antisemitic speeches and writings presented itself. In this respect, a Catholic University anti-Nazi broadcast organized by Sheehy served two purposes. It would present an authoritative Catholic position on the Nazi persecution of Jews, and an opposing Catholic position to Coughlin's growing antisemitism within the United States context. Sheehy was an ideal person to organize such an event quickly. An avid traveler with a genius for organizing who held influence with several key priests and bishops through positions such as assistant to the rector and assistant professor in the Department of Religious Education at Catholic University, Sheehy had managed the Catholic University radio station for years and had cultivated many media contacts. Early in his career at Catholic University, Sheehy published "National Attitudes in Children" (1932), an essay recounting with alarm instances of young American Catholics committing acts of violence against Jews.[27] He deeply disliked the Nazis, a disposition that would take him on a government-sanctioned tour to combat Hitler's influence in South America in 1939 and to favor early advocacy of entry into the Second World War, when he would serve as a military chaplain in the Pacific theater. Sheehy, moreover, was enthusiastically ecumenical, and would serve as the Catholic representative at the National Conference of Christians and Jews (NCCJ) in the early 1950s. Finally, as a priest rather than a bishop, he could avoid the institutional restraints that governed the membership and staff of the National Catholic Welfare Conference (NCWC)—several bishops lent their authority to the broadcast but could not be charged with encroaching on the authority of their fellow bishops by organizing it.[28]

The broadcast exhibits the emerging strain of Catholic Americanism also being articulated by Ryan. "The world is witnessing a great tragedy in Europe today," Sheehy told listeners, "and after sober, calm reflection, various groups and leaders of the Catholic Church have sought permission to raise their voices, not in mad hysteria, but in firm indignation against the atrocities visited upon the Jews in Germany." Sheehy continued, "The Catholic loves his Jewish brother, because, as Pope Pius XI has pointed out, we are all spiritual Semites." The phrase used by Sheehy in the recorded broadcast and in an early Catholic University press release of Sheehy's remarks, "the Catholic loves his Jewish brother," has a fascinating genealogy. Sheehy uses the word "loves," as does the university press release of the broadcast, dated November 16, 1938. An NCWC press release on the broadcast dated November 21, 1938, however, substitutes the word "likes" in place of "loves." This second press release by the NCWC, which was a single release of the collective remarks of all involved in the broadcast, was issued on the day following Charles Coughlin's antisemitic Kristallnacht speech. As will be discussed further shortly, the second press release was probably issued to assert the hierarchy's opposition to Coughlinite antisemitism, but also with an altered terminology so as not to aggravate Coughlin's followers. Sheehy himself was surely aware of the use of the term "loves" versus "likes" with regard to Catholic sentiment toward Jews. In a 1941 volume of selected broadcasts in which the anti-Nazi broadcast is reprinted, the priest notes that the broadcast was "reprinted as transcribed by the *New York Times*." The *Times'* reprint of November 17, 1938, however, uses the word "likes" while Sheehy uses the word "loves" in his version. If he did use the *Times* as the source for the reprint, he took care to return to the stronger emotion later on—he clearly wanted to use the stronger word to express his sympathy for Germany's Jews. In this same vein, Sheehy titles his reprint of the broadcast "Persecution of the Jews in Germany." The Catholic University November 16 press release on the broadcast, moreover, used Sheehy's terminology in its subtitle, asserting that his remarks dealt "with the Jewish persecution." The later NCWC press release, however, titles the address "Texts of Catholic Protest Broadcast," not mentioning Jews at all in its introductory comments. The use of language here reveals the delicate context in which the broadcast was received. The NCWC press department exhibited more caution than Sheehy and the university's public relations department, probably altering the broadcast and calling it "Catholic Protest Broadcast" in order to avoid antagonizing Catholic antisemites, and especially antisemitic followers of Coughlin.[29] The various word changes, in short, suggest that attitudes toward Jews in 1938 were complex and highly contested within the Church.

Sheehy's comments commenced the broadcast by six American Catholic leaders and carried nationally by the Columbia Broadcasting System and the National Broadcasting Company. Sheehy was joined by Archbishop John J. Mitty of San Francisco, California; Bishop John M. Gannon of Erie, Pennsylvania; Bishop Peter L. Ireton of Richmond, Virginia; the former Democratic presidential Candidate and Governor of New York Alfred E. Smith; and the Catholic University Rector Monsignor Joseph M. Corrigan. The participants were selected to represent both lay Catholics' (hence Smith's inclusion) and clerical leaders' unified view that the violence unleashed on Jews and Jewish property in Germany was immoral, contrary to Christian teaching, but also against their own developing ideas of religious and civic freedom.[30]

From a twenty-first century perspective, the content of the Catholic University anti-Nazi broadcast might seem odd for the indirectness with which it approaches its main topic. In the address following Sheehy's, Archbishop John J. Mitty of San Francisco notes that Catholics "have a deep and immediate sympathy with the Jewish men and women who are being lashed by the cruelty of fierce persecution." He then continues with a seemingly outsized explanation as to why that is the case, detailing the persecutions of Catholics in both Spain and Mexico. Mitty notes, for example, that "for more than two years our fellow Catholics have suffered a parallel crucifixion in Spain, and our sympathy for them has largely been in silence," continuing, "the Mexican story of the long persecution of Catholics is a similar story of the persistent silence of our press and of our singular indifference as a neighboring people." Today, of course, such comparisons seem ridiculous, given the extent of the systematic mass killings of Jews that occurred during the Second World War, but I would suggest that such comparisons were Mitty's way of situating Jews and Catholics near enough to each other to create a context for a civic Catholic empathy, and of course, the systematized mass killings of the Holocaust hadn't yet occurred, so Kristallnacht seemed more comparable to the Spanish and Mexican atrocities. American Catholics, moreover, were genuinely chagrined at the treatment of their coreligionists in not only Mexico and Spain, but Nazi Germany as well and wanted to bring attention to the plight of their coreligionists as well as condemn the treatment of the Jews in Germany and Nazi-occupied territories.

Finally, Mitty and the others involved in the broadcast knew that they would be attacked, particularly by Coughlin's followers, if they did not mention the "parallel persecutions" of Catholics. In other words, Mitty's talk anticipates Coughlin's defensive American Catholicism. After his discussion of the "parallel" atrocities committed against Catholics in Mexico, Mitty brings his comments full circle by focusing on persecution of Catholics within the United States: "We have had the experience of Know Nothingism, the A.P.A. and the Ku Klux Klan." Mitty concludes that "only by a more even justice, only by a wider sense of fellowship, only by a fuller life of brotherhood, can we integrate all our people into a nation that shall realize the vision of our founding fathers, a nation resting in security and peace on the eternal principles of immortality and religion." For Mitty, American ideals allow for the transcendence of anti-Catholicism and, by implication, anti-Jewish persecution as well. Bishop John Gannon of Erie, Pennsylvania, followed Mitty with an anti-Communist counternarrative to Coughlin's, taking note of persecution of Catholics in Mexico, then Spain, seeing the "advent of Lenin in Russia" as the first instance of "this horrible specter of persecution." Conflating fascism and communism, Gannon continued, "and now the horrible thing has broken loose in Germany where the Jewish people, a small helpless minority, less than 1 percent of the population, are subjected to the fierce passions of the mobs, the harsh, unjust decrees of dictators, and the almost total loss of civic and moral rights. In the face of such injustice toward the Jews of Germany, I express my revulsion, disgust and grief." For Gannon, antireligious sentiment, embedded in both communism and fascism, was responsible for the "almost total loss of civic and moral rights" suffered by Jews under Nazism. Jews, he advised, should "turn to God." Yet, he found it "a privilege and an honor" to share their grief and advised "fellow citizens to stand with them in protest." Bishop Peter Ireton began "not with bitterness but with sadness. The world is shocked. Our sense of justice is outraged by the persecution of the Jew in Germany." Ireton emphasized in his part of the broadcast, however, the perils of racist nationalism: "The exaltation of racism to near deification begins its usual course. Destruction of its fancied enemies before it develops its own destruction. There has been an ascending grade of injustices, political reprisal, concentration camps, religious persecution, calumny, purges, obliteration of speech and press, exile and expropriation." Countering defensive American Catholicism, Ireton made a call for unity against German anti-Jewish prejudice:

> My individual protest, your individual protest, our mutual feeling of sympathy for those persecuted and outraged by the autocrats of Europe, will

not change instantly the present issue, but the combined condemnation of all of those whose love freedom and justice throughout the world will channel itself into a righteous flood of indignation that will sweep away the barriers of censorship and will reach the minds and consciences of the rank and file of the German nation.[31]

Al Smith, for his part, echoed President Roosevelt's comment that he "could scarcely believe that such things could occur in a twentieth century civilization" and wondered if Germany had returned to the "dark ages." While it shocked him that the German people were engaging in "outrageous assaults on persons and property," he also believed that the "German officials can stop this cruel assault on their own people and on civilization at large at any time that they want to do it. Thank God for the United States of America." In his concluding address, Monsignor Joseph Corrigan quoted a statement made by Pius XI at the Catholic University, "The Catholic is necessarily the champion of true human rights and the defender of human liberties." After approving of President Roosevelt's statement of the previous day condemning the atrocities in Germany, Corrigan asked that "the world should not forget nor cease to protest with earnest sincerity and growing vigor until it be cleansed of the poisonous cancer even now gnawing at the very vitals of organized society and just government."[32] The support for persecuted Jews was conducted as much through use of American political language as by appeals to Christian love and charity and Catholic social teaching.

Responses to the broadcast point toward its perceived importance in the national press, and doubtless the shadow of Father Coughlin and his increasing antisemitism made the broadcast sensational as far as news went. Hundreds of articles from across the country reported on the broadcast; the *New York Times* ran a front-page article the day after, "Catholics of U.S. Score 'Atrocities'; Nazi 'Cancer' Denounced by Prelates—Smith Joins in Praising Roosevelt Stand," and reprinted the entire address. Stories on the broadcast ran across the country.[33] Indeed, the non-Catholic public was probably surprised to hear a collection of Catholic prelates denouncing antisemitism after listening week after week to Fr. Coughlin's increasingly angry and prejudiced harangues. Unnoted in previous analyses of Coughlin's November 20 broadcast, moreover, is its reference to the Catholic University broadcast, which suggests that the Michigan priest saw the earlier address as a challenge to his power. In reference to the comments of Archbishop Mitty, Coughlin responded with sarcasm and coded language:

> I was thrilled to hear the Most intellectual Archbishop of San Francisco remind his compatriots that this universal surge of sympathy whose waters are now about to wash clean the impure emotions of a materialistic

America, I was thrilled and so were you to hear him state that at long last the press and the radio of this nation are beginning to play their part in arousing a dormant people to the other injustices and persecutions besmirching our civilization.[34]

Most of Coughlin's followers were not intellectuals; the priest had a large number of economically discontented followers, among whom, as Sheldon Marcus writes, he "succeeded in galvanizing a feeling of class discrimination, which evolved into class and eventually religious hatred."[35] This comment appeals precisely to this group of followers. The designation of Mitty as the "Most intellectual Archbishop" was a way of tapping into the suspicion that upper-level hierarchy was overly privileged and not to be trusted. "Compatriots . . . surge of sympathy . . . cleanse the impure emotions of materialistic America" do not make complete logical sense if Coughlin is talking, as he wants to appear, about Mitty's sympathy for the persecuted; instead, these words are symbols of communism Coughlin had been sowing among his followers for years, implying that Mitty and by association the others in the broadcast are sympathizing with the communist Jews. Finally, the comment that Coughlin was thrilled (and intimately, "so were you") that the press was finally paying attention to "the other injustices and persecutions besmirching our civilization" was clearly sarcastic—why else would he add the word "other" than to suggest that the press (and by extension Mitty, et al.) only cared about the persecution of Jews? The obscure symbolism of Coughlin's language here, then, is an elaborate response to the careful construction of the Catholic University broadcast, which was itself designed to counter anticipated criticism by Coughlin that these Catholic leaders were exhibiting disproportionate sympathy for Jews, and second, to prevent accusations that they were communist sympathizers. The two texts, in fact, can be seen as representative of two competing strains of thought within the Church at the time: The Catholic University broadcast as representative of a strain aiming toward an expanded notion of American Catholic idealism, and Coughlin's speech as an increasingly paranoid and defensive American Catholicism that saw Jews as treated better than other groups (thanks to their alleged conspiratorial machinations).

Monsignor Joseph Corrigan, as university rector, received several dozen revealing letters in response to the Catholic University broadcast. Some of these letter writers took their cues from Coughlin and said that they had a difficult time seeing Jews and Catholics as equally worthy of defense by Catholic leaders. Corrigan's response is reflective of the ascendant strain of American Catholicism, however. James T. Kyne wrote, "It seems strange to me that few seem to remember that when Catholics were being slaughtered in Spain, for instance, no voice was raised; there were no indignation meetings or recalling of Ambassadors. How much help did Catholics get from our Jewish Brethren? On those occasions?" Henry Brady wrote, "Now the Jews deserve our sympathy and help; we owe it to them as Americans with the ideals of the Constitution in mind as well as Catholics with the words of Christ on the Cross . . . and yet, in this practical world, should we forget ourselves? Should we forget the oppressions of our own people, of both clergy and laity of the True Faith?" Corrigan responded to Brady that "cases where Catholics have been and are being persecuted furnish a very real basis for us to show the practical workings of Christian charity when another minority group becomes the victim of such cruel and savage treatment as was accorded the Jews in Germany after the assassination of the secretary of the German Embassy in Paris." Corrigan added that Catholics and Jews, while distinct, could not act alone to prevent their own oppression, and that "we are all aware of the possibility of co-operation between the portions of each of these groups concerned in a given time and place with the same issue."[36] Corrigan was clearly adhering to the more expansive religiously and ethnically pluralist American Catholic view as opposed to the Coughlin variety, which saw the separations between Catholics and Jews as more essential than the commonalities.

Other letters to Corrigan, including one that enclosed a copy of Fr. Charles Coughlin's publication *Social Justice*, are clearly motivated more by overt antisemitism than anything else, although they are in the same family of ideas expressed by Kyne and Brady. Rose Scholey wrote, "When you and the other Priests and Bishops broadcasted recently in protest of the persecution of the jews [sic] in Germany, I wondered why?" Fr. Coughlin was the only one that knew why [the author never explained this, but referenced a particular *Social Justice* article—which Corrigan returned to the woman], yet he was tormented by the press, and the "jealous" Catholic clergy. She wondered why the clergy didn't defend Fr. Coughlin, yet "when the jews [sic] get into trouble, what does Catholic U. do, get a broadcast together, in sympathy for the jews [sic]." The majority of letters, from Christians and Jews, praised the effort. "After listening to your radio address," wrote one person, "I have come to the conclusion that you are truly a disciple of God, to be immortalized, for the wisdom you have used." A telegram from "an American Jewess" said she had "just finished listening to your broadcast / our heartfelt thanks for your fine words and sympathy may peace and happiness reign again in the near future." Myron Blum wrote that "more of such enlightening facts over the air would do much to eliminate any growth of ill feeling among the three great religions in our own country.[37]

Another letter to Corrigan from Irving Sherman, a Jewish man from New York, following Coughlin's November 20 speech, asked why members of the Church didn't do more to prevent Coughlin's broadcast, wherein the radio priest "deliberately quoted Nazi sources as his information for the false statistics that he gave against his fellow men and women? How can you reconcile the teaching of democracy in this beloved land when you have such a trouble maker preaching for the church?" To which Corrigan responded, "If earlier action had been taken by his ecclesiastical superiors, there would have been a loud outcry against the Church preventing a citizen from using his treasured right of free speech." Then he continued, "You are surely aware that his present attitude has been unexpected and has put him in open antagonism with the views expressed by the national broadcast of this University . . . it is a very difficult position for his religious superiors," and the "Church moves very slowly in such problems and uses every effort of conciliatory admonition before any final action."[38] This comment suggests that Corrigan saw the broadcast as the response of the American Catholic hierarchy to Coughlin's intensifying antisemitism.

Indeed, other actions were being taken in the wake of Kristallnacht by Catholic leaders in opposition to Coughlin's increasingly prejudiced pronouncements and writings. Other clerical leaders also engaged in the denunciation of the events of November 9–10 at the same time as the Catholic University broadcast. On November 16, 1938, Monsignor Michael J. Ready, general secretary of the NCWC, the representative organization of the American bishops, delivered a speech to the Holy Name Lecture Bureau in Milwaukee asking them "to unite to drive the forces of intolerance and untruth from the land." He told the group of 100 members, "The hysteria which drives out defenseless Jews and vilifies Catholic prelates in Europe is the same which makes our own loud-mouthed defenders of a Soviet brand of democracy dangerous to the institutions decent Americans love." Sensitive to possible charges of sympathy with "Jewish Communists," which, in fact, Coughlin would employ later on, Ready denounced both leftist and rightist political "extremism." George Johnson, the director of the Department of Education of the NCWC, and secretary general of the National Catholic Educational Association, in a national radio broadcast of November 18, 1938, also denounced "the horror of what is happening in Nazi Germany."[39]

An examination of the local Catholic press in the weeks following Kristallnacht also reveals a range of responses, most of them sympathetic toward the Jewish situation, though certainly not all. An article in the November 20, 1938, issue of Indiana's *Our Sunday Visitor* titled "Day of

Prayer for Racial Victims Is Asked by Prelates" reported that day as one "of prayer for all refugees from political tyranny and all victims of religious and racial persecution." According to the article, though the announcement for the day of prayer was made by the National Conference of Jews and Christians, eight U.S. Catholic bishops heeded the call and made the day one of support for victims of religious discrimination as well.[40] The editors of the antisemitic *Brooklyn Tablet*, however, were offended by the announcement of participation by several dioceses in the November 20 day of prayer. "We Pray for ALL Victims of Persecution," the November 19, 1938, issue editorialized, implying that the emphasis on the Jewish situation excluded Catholics. Challenging what they believed was an excess of attention placed on Jewish persecution, the editors wrote that "we are opposed to the persecution of Jews, Protestants, and Catholics on racial or religious grounds." But they believed not enough attention was being given to anti-Catholicism in Germany, Spain, and Mexico. The editorial asserted that "in Germany today the Catholic victims of the carnival of hate out-number all others as ten to one." Moreover, "while the press and public officials bitterly denounce the attack on ten synagogues in Germany, the breaking of Jewish shop windows, and the brutal dispersal of Jews, unfortunately the protest has not been widened to include the far worse crimes committed against the Catholics of Spain." The second part of the editorial, however, revealed an additional agenda on the part of the authors. Claiming that there were "designing men and women who want to involve our country in European strife" and "sacrifice the youth of our country on the rock of internationalism," it expressed a "determination to keep out of war." In other words, those denouncing persecution of Germany's Jews earlier that November were plotting to bring the country into a war to defend Jews—an illegitimate reason, in their eyes, to go to war. Apparently, the authors didn't see going to war to aid persecuted Catholics as justified. The *Tablet*'s reporting of the Catholic University broadcast took a similar approach to the question. "Prelates Mention All Persecutions" the headline ran. At no point did the article on the broadcast mention that it was undertaken to denounce the Jewish pogroms.[41] This belief that defending Jews somehow crowded out defense of Catholics is epitomized in Coughlin's defensive Catholic Americanism. A question for future research is why and under what circumstances some Catholics were unable to envision Catholics and Jews as religiously equal, while others were.

Other articles indicate further varieties of response to the situation of Germany's Jews. The *Monitor* of San Francisco reported on the bishops' broadcast on November 19: "Catholic U. Broadcasts in Defense of Jews."[42] Chicago's *New World* reported that the "rising tide of indignation of American Catholics over religious and racial persecution continued to swell this week. It found expression in a great number of denunciatory addresses delivered by distinguished prelates, clergy, educators, statesmen and professional men throughout the land." The article went on to report that all over the country "bishops issued pastoral letters calling for the prayers of the Faithful for the peoples lashed with the thong of despotic persecution. Especially, prayers were requested for the bitterly oppressed Jewish minority in Nazi Germany."[43]

This local response is particularly interesting given the fact that institutional restraints were placed by Church law and the Vatican on Catholic participation in interfaith expression in general.[44] Because of these restrictions, the American Catholic response to the Jewish persecution will look quite different than the Protestant and Jewish responses toward the affairs of the day, hence the need for further analysis and comparison. Invitations issued in the 1930s by members of the NCCJ to the leadership of the NCWC were nearly always rejected, a situation that the war altered dramatically (in spite of the continued existence of the restrictions).[45] Formal exchanges among upper-level clergy and non-Catholics throughout the 1930s reflect the reluctance on the part of church leaders to violate institutional church rules. What I have suggested here, however, is that a response to Coughlin and to Kristallnacht took place through less formal channels and not necessarily with the Vatican's blessing, even as Coughlin was permitted to continue expressing his own antisemitism. The anti-Nazi protest of 1938 can be seen as a moment of expansion in American Catholic notions of religious pluralism and liberty, transpiring as it did on behalf of a non-Catholic religious group during a period in which the Church was extremely cautious about such activities. On the other hand, the protest was generated in part by Catholic self-interest. Speakers emphasized Catholic persecution in Spain and Mexico as well as anti-Jewish activities in Germany, feeling that the American public had neglected prejudice against their own coreligionists in other countries. The protest was, moreover, intended to distance American Catholic institutional leadership from the powerful antisemitic strain of American Catholicism articulated most influentially by Coughlin, though without actually saying so outright.

NOTES

1. Representative are: Michael Phayer, *The Catholic Church and the Holocaust, 1930–1965* (Indianapolis: Indiana University Press, 2001); *David I. Kertzer, The Popes Against the Jews* (New York: Knopf, 2001); John Cornwell, *Hitler's Pope: The Secret History of Pius XII* (New York: Penguin, 2000); Frank J. Coppa, *The Papacy, The Jews, and the Holocaust*

(Washington, D.C.: Catholic University Press, 2006); Guenter Lewy, *The Catholic Church and Nazi Germany* (Cambridge, MA: Da Capo, 2000).

2. There are several works that address the response of the United States to the Holocaust, but none that address specifically American Catholic responses. Suzanne Brown-Fleming's *The Holocaust and Catholic Conscience: Cardinal Aloisius Muench and the Guilt Question in Germany* (Notre Dame, IN: Notre Dame University Press, 2006) does address the question because it includes analysis of American Catholicism, antisemitism, and the Holocaust, but it focuses on the postwar years and German and German-American Catholicism. Gerald P. Fogarty's essay "Roosevelt and the American Catholic Hierarchy" is useful in its discussion of diplomatic relations between members of the U.S. hierarchy, the Roosevelt administration, and the Vatican during the war, but there is no direct discussion of American Catholic institutional responses to the Holocaust. See Fogarty's essay in David B. Woolner and Richard G. Kurial, eds., *FDR, The Vatican, and the Roman Catholic Church in America, 1933–1945,* (New York: Palgrave Macmillan, 2003), 11–43. Fogarty discusses the now famous 1937 "Mundelein-Hitler paper hanger" comment, which is very relevant, in his *The Vatican and the American Hierarchy from 1870 to 1965* (Collegeville, MN: Liturgical Press, 1985), 249. Cardinal Mundelein branded Hitler "an inept paper hanger," a comment that found its way into the press and caused Germany to withdraw its ambassador to the Holy See. While Fogarty's essay implies a critique of Nazi antisemitism, it is, however, not a direct analysis of Mundelein's views on anti-Jewish prejudice and Nazi persecution of Jews. Gershon Greenberg's essay "American Catholics during the Holocaust" is an excellent overview of the American Catholic Church's response, covering U.S. Catholics and refugee policy; attitudes toward a Jewish state; Catholic protest against antisemitism; the efforts of Apostolic Delegate to Washington, D.C., Amleto Cicognani, on behalf of Jews in Europe; and antisemitism in the United States. See essay (undated) online at the Simon Wiesenthal Center's Museum of Tolerance, http://motlc.wiesenthal.com/site/pp.asp?c=gvKVLcMVIuG&b=395083. See also Patrick Hayes' essay "J. Elliot Ross and the National Conference of Christians and Jews," *Journal of Ecumenical Studies 37,* Issue 3/4 (Summer/Fall 2000): 321–333. This essay describes the efforts of the Paulist J. Elliot Ross to forge bonds with Jews and Protestants, as well as the institutional obstacles to the formation of such bonds (specifically the bans on interfaith gatherings issued by the Vatican).

3. James Hennesey, *American Catholics, A History of the Roman Catholic Community in the United States* (New York: Oxford University Press, 1981), 237, 283; on parish life and ethnic identity, see Joseph E. Ciesluk, *National Parishes in the United States* (Washington, D.C., Catholic University of America Press, 1947); John T. McGreevy, *Parish Boundaries: The Catholic Encounter with Race in the Twentieth-Century Urban North* (Chicago: University of Chicago Press, 1996); on Catholics and American identity, see David O'Brien, *Public Catholicism* (New York: Macmillan, 1989)

and John T. McGreevy, *Catholicism and American Freedom* (New York: W. W. Norton and Co., 2003).

4. Literally, *Testem Benevolentiae Nostrae* means, *"Witness to Our Goodwill."* On the encyclical and its impact, see Fogarty, *Vatican and the American Hierarchy*, xvii.

5. Frank J. Coppa, *The Papacy, the Jews, and the Holocaust* (Washington, D.C.: Catholic University of America Press, 2007), chapter 1 and passim, quote on p. 6; Kertzer, *The Popes Against the Jews*. On American Catholic antisemitism, see Leonard Dinnerstein, *Antisemitism in America* (New York: Oxford University Press, 1994), chapter 7.

6. Fogarty, *Vatican and American Hierarchy*, xviii, 228–229. For a look at how Romanization shaped the careers of individual prelates, see James O'Toole, *Militant and Triumphant; William Henry O'Connell and the Catholic Church in Boston* (South Bend, IN: Notre Dame University Press, 1993) and John Cooney, *The American Pope; The Life and Times of Francis Cardinal Spellman* (New York: Times Books, 1984).

7. Fogarty, *Vatican and American Hierarchy*, xviii–xix.

8. McGreevy, *Catholicism and American Freedom*, 173. American liberals, McGreevy notes, tended to side with socialist reformers, in Mexico and in Spain. And most were extremely critical of Hitler, as well as the later Mussolini. Hence, McGreevy writes, the "cumulative effect of the divide between Catholics and liberals over Mexico, Italy, and, especially, Spain, meant that extended analysis of connections between Catholicism and fascism appeared throughout the liberal press." Fr. Coughlin's popularity confirmed such beliefs. Such analyses meshed with an already existing belief that Catholic institutional life was incompatible with democratic institutions.

9. On the Christian Front in New York, see Gene Fein, "For Christ and Country: The Christian Front in New York City, 1938–1951" (PhD dissertation, City University of New York, 2006).

10. "Address By Father C E Coughlin," November 20, 1938, transcript, 4–5, Folder 1, Box 16, National Catholic Welfare Conference/United States Conference of Catholic Bishops/Office of the General Secretary (NCWC/USCCB/OGS) Papers, General Administrative Files, American Catholic History Research Center and University of America Archives (ACUA).

11. "Address By Father C E Coughlin," November 20, 1938, Folder 1, Box 16, 7–9. NCWC/USCCB/OGS, ACUA. For a thoughtful discussion on how Nazis interpreted Jewish involvement in a range of organizations while belonging to separate nations, see Henry Feingold, *Bearing Witness: How America and its Jews Responded to the Holocaust* (Syracuse, NY: Syracuse University Press, 1995) 33–36.

12. Mooney quote in Leslie Tentler, *Seasons of Grace: A History of the Catholic Archdiocese of Detroit* (Detroit: Wayne State University Press, 1990), 337.

13. Michael Kazin, *The Populist Persuasion: An American History* (New York: Basic Books, 1995), 131. On populist antisemitism see also David Gerber,

ed., *Antisemitism in American History* (Urbana: University of Illinois Press, 1986), 30, itself based on John Higham, "Ideological Antisemitism in the Gilded Age" in *Send These to Me: Immigrants in Urban America* (Baltimore: Johns Hopkins University Press, 1984).

14. Mary Christine Athans, "A New Perspective on Father Coughlin," *Church History* 56, no. 2 (June 1987): 224–235, and Mary Christine Athans, *The Coughlin-Fahey Connection: Father Charles E. Coughlin, Father Denis Fahey, C.S.Sp. and Religious Antisemitism in the United States, 1938–1954* (New York: Peter Lang, 1991). Fahey, like Coughlin, insisted he was not antisemitic, 232. See also Rev. Denis Fahey, *The Mystical Body of Christ in the Modern World* (Dublin, Ireland: Browne and Nolan Limited, 1939, first edition, 1935), esp. chapter XI, "The Struggle of the Jewish Nation against the True Messias," 259–287. On Coughlin's antisemitism, see Athans, *The Coughlin-Fahey Connection*, and Tentler, *Seasons of Grace*, 336–342.

15. Tentler, *Seasons of Grace*, 338–342.

16. Gerber, *Antisemitism in American History*, 29.

17. Ibid., 20; see also Dinnerstein, *Antisemitism in America*, and the concise overview of American antisemitism by Jonathan Sarna, "American Antisemitism" in *History and Hate: The Dimensions of Antisemitism*, David Berger, ed. (Philadelphia: Jewish Publication Society, 1986), 115–128.

18. John A. Ryan, "Relation of Catholicism to Fascism, Communism and Democracy" (Washington, D.C.: National Catholic Welfare Conference, 1938) 9–10. For a discussion of both Ryan and Coughlin, and how they fit into a broader 1930s "Social Catholicism," see O'Brien, *Public Catholicism*, chapter 7.

19. See, for example, O'Brien, *Public Catholicism*, chapter 7–8.

20. See, for example, John A. Ryan, "Quack Remedies for the Depression Malady," where Ryan criticizes proposals for currency speculation to remedy the Depression of the type proposed by Coughlin, reprinted in *Seven Troubled Years, 1930–1936; A Collection of Papers on the Depression and on the Problems of Recovery and Reform* (Ann Arbor, MI: Edwards Brothers, 1937), see especially 189–190. On Ryan's countering of criticism that FDR was a communist, see George Q. Flynn, *American Catholics and the Roosevelt Presidency, 1932–1936* (Lexington: University of Kentucky Press, 1968), 224–226.

21. Flynn, *American Catholics and the Roosevelt Presidency*, 230; J. E. Barnhart to John A. Ryan, October 30, 1936, Box 42, Folder 13, John A Ryan Papers, ACUA.

22. Flynn, *American Catholics and the Roosevelt Presidency*, 208.

23. "Mgr. Ryan Asks Race Tolerance; Priest Quotes Late Pope in Attack on Antisemitism" *Washington Post*, March 4, 1938; "Race Theories Anti-Christian, Says Mgr. Ryan, Constitution Makes Hatred Futile in U.S., Professor Declares" *Washington Post*, March 29, 1939; John A. Ryan and George N. Shuster. "Antisemitism: Facts of History, Fr. Coughlin Facts," *Commonweal*, December 30, 1938, 260–262.

24. See letterhead, Dr. Emmanuel Chapman to Stephen Early, July 24, 1940, requesting presidential approval of the new organization. FDR endorses letter to the group, July 27, 1940, reel 3, FDR Papers, ACUA.
25. Maurice Sheehy to Marguerite LeHand, October 5, 1936, reel 3, microfilm, FDR Papers, ACUA.
26. See these letters: Sheehy to Stephen Early, September 29, 1936; Sheehy to LeHand, July 14, 1937; LeHand to Sheehy, July 19, 1937; Sheehy to LeHand, May 3, 1940, reel 3, microfilm, FDR papers, ACUA.
27. Pamphlet, Rev. Maurice S. Sheehy, "National Attitudes in Children" (Washington, D.C.: Catholic Association for International Peace, 1932), 4, 17, NCWC Social Action Department records, Box 49, folder 10, ACUA.
28. See files on Sheehy, Rector Files, ACUA; on Sheehy's activities, also, Sheehy to FDR, December 3, 1938, reel 3, microfilm, FDR Papers, ACUA; "Latins Cool to Naziism, Sheehy Finds," *Washington Post*, January 31, 1939; "New Catholic Leader Named to NCCJ Unit," *Washington Post*, May 13, 1952.
29. Recorded Catholic University of America anti-Nazi protest, November 16, 1938, CUA Public Affairs Audio/Visual Collection, ACUA. Press Releases on Broadcast, for each individual speaker, Catholic University of America Bureau of Public Relations, 11/16/38, CUA Public Affairs Files, ACUA. "Texts of Catholic Protest Broadcast," 11/21/38, News Release, N.C.W.C. News Service, Chronological Files; "Catholics Register Strong Protest On Jewish Persecution," 11/17/38, News Release, Catholic University of America Bureau of Public Relations, Reference File, NCWC, NCWC/USCCB, ACUA; "Catholics of U.S. Score Atrocities; Nazi 'Cancer' Denounced by Prelates—Smith Joins in Praising Roosevelt Stand," *New York Times*, November 17, 1938; "Persecution of the Jews in Germany" in Maurice S. Sheehy, *Selected Broadcasts* (Silver Spring, MD: Council for Democracy, 1941), 45–52.
30. "Texts of Catholic Protest Broadcast," 11/21/38, News Release, N.C.W.C News Service, Chronological Files, NCWC/USCCB, ACUA; "Catholics Register Strong Protest On Jewish Persecution," 11/17/38, News Release, Catholic University of America Bureau of Public Relations, Reference File, NCWC/USCCB, ACUA.
31. NCWC Press Release containing CUA Broadcast Transcript, November 21, 1938.
32. Ibid.
33. "Catholics of U.S. Score Atrocities; Nazi 'Cancer" Denounced by Prelates—Smith Joins in Praising Roosevelt Stand," *New York Times*, November 17, 1938. The Catholic University Archives has a scrapbook with clippings of articles on the broadcast from newspapers across the country.
34. "Address By Father C E Coughlin," November 20, 1938, Folder 1, Box 16, 6, NCWC/USCCB/OGS, ACUA.

35. Sheldon Marcus, *Father Coughlin: The Tumultuous Life of the Priest of the Little Flower* (Boston: Little, Brown and Company, 1973), 37.

36. James T. Kyne to Rev. Joseph Corrigan, November 17, 1938; Henry J. Brady to Rev. Joseph Corrigan, November 20, 1938; Rev. Joseph Corrigan to Henry J. Brady, December 1, 1938; Rector-President Files, Box 28, Folder 36, ACUA.

37. Rose Scholey to Father Joseph Corrigan, November 27, 1938; Unsigned letter to Joseph Corrigan, postmarked January 18, 1939; Telegram from "An American Jewess" to Joseph Corrigan, November 17, 1938; Myron L. Blum to Joseph Corrigan, November 21, 1938; all in Box 40, Folder 37, Rector-President Files, ACUA.

38. Irving Sherman to Joseph Corrigan, November 25, 1938; Joseph Corrigan to Irving Sherman, December 1, 1938; Rector-President files, Box 28, Folder 36, ACUA.

39. "Msgr. Ready Scores Brutalitarianism of Europe's Tyrants," "Persecutors Most Pitiful Figures Says Dr. Johnson," 11/21/38, News Release, N.C.W.C News Service, Chronological Files, NCWC/USCCB/OGS, ACUA.

40. "Day of Prayer for Racial Victims Is Asked by Prelates," *Our Sunday Visitor*, November 20, 1938, 14.

41. "We Pray for All Victims of Persecution," "Prelates Mention All Persecutions," see also "Many Persecuted Catholics Found" November 19, 1938, 1.

42. "Catholic U. Broadcasts in Defense of Jews" *Monitor*, November 19, 1938, 12.

43. "Germany," *New World*, November 25, 1938, 2.

44. On restrictions placed on interfaith expression, Hayes, "J. Elliot Ross," and John Cornwell, *Hitler's Pope: The Secret History of Pius XII* (New York: Viking, 1999). Cornwell writes in his analysis of the revision of the Code of Canon law in the early twentieth century: "While tightening up assent to centralized Roman authority, the code also curbed peer-group ecumenical discussion in Canon 1325: 'Catholics are to avoid disputations or conferences about matters of faith with non-Catholics, especially in public, unless the Holy See, or in case of emergency the [bishop of the] place, has given permission,'" 43.

45. For example, when asked by the NCCJ director, Everett R. Clinchy to sign a social justice statement condemning poverty and referencing the papal encyclical *Quadragesimo Anno* (the statement had the support of several Catholic priests), the assistant general secretary of the NCWC, Michael Ready, responded, "By reason of my position, I must decline to sign the statement," adding, "I regret the necessity of this decision because I think the statement is excellent and timely and I am sure it will have a great influence in pointing the way to sane programs of social reconstruction." The Statement, on "basic spiritual, moral and social issues underlying the economic problems which face our country," had

the support of Fr. Francis Haas, Fr. Edwin Walsh, and Fr. Philip Furlong, among others, dated March 8, 1933; letter to Michael Ready from Everett R. Clinchy, March 13, 1933; response from Ready to Clinchy, March 20, 1933; the exchange is one of the many that can be found in the NCWC Papers, "Church: Intercredal Cooperation, National Conference of Christians and Jews, 1927–1938," Box 19, Folder 5, NCWC/USCCB/OGS, ACUA.

Chapter 5

American Catholics Respond to Kristallnacht: NCWC Refugee Policy and the Plight of Non-Aryans

Patrick J. Hayes

The received wisdom on religious responses to Kristallnacht leaves an impression of lackadaisical interest or outright complicity in the Nazi machinery that ratcheted up a program of mass genocide.[1] This is perhaps no more evident than on the question of refusing assistance to the swarms of refugees flooding out of European countries between 1933 and 1945. Given the outcomes of this period, when so many suffered and perished, it seems altogether natural to judge churches or governments as acting in far too passive a manner in the face of the Nazi aggression. Recognition of the lack of assistance provided to those who wished to escape, and to whom it became a matter of life or death, can often lead to the conclusion that refugees did not count. The callousness evinced by institutions like religious bodies or governments—which ordinarily enjoy moral cover—is, in view of the subsequent tragedy, blameworthy.

This perception has sometimes been attached to the Catholic Church. Two decades ago, the historian of immigration Haim Genizi wrote that the responses of religious Americans to the refugee crisis in Germany during the Nazi years were marked by widespread "Christian apathy" and that this attitude—or lack of one—was an incontrovertible fact.[2]

His previous book on the subject of Christian refugees laid out similar charges. The Catholic response to their coreligionists, he said, was "muted," and what protests were raised over the treatment of German Jews were "sparse and uninfluential."[3] The logical instrument to provide a moral voice and practical relief was the National Catholic Welfare Conference (NCWC), an agency founded by American bishops in 1919. But Genizi suggested that the refugee issue—both for German Catholics and for German Jews—was something that the staff of the NCWC's Bureau of Immigration Affairs was taking too lightly, in part because their own antisemitism was blinding them to the real possibility of mass immigration.[4]

Genizi's interpretation is considered rather normative, but I want to challenge these claims by examining some of the context surrounding the decisions made at the Bureau, together with some of its allies, during the years leading up to and immediately following Kristallnacht in November 1938. Thus the aim of this essay is rather modest. I merely wish to complicate the current picture that we now have on rescue efforts by American Catholics and to expand a paltry literature on the subject of Catholic involvement with this refugee crisis.[5] By doing so, I hope to reduce some of the tensions and suspicions that this period in Christian-Jewish relations has tended to foster.

TRACKING SHIFTS IN LEGAL NOMENCLATURE

An examination of the internal correspondence of the Bureau, as well as outside documentation, reveals that the impression of institutional inertia might be attributed to new realities created by the German government's Nuremberg Laws of 1935. A new category of human being, "non-Aryans," flew in the face of all known standards of personhood, as well as their human rights, depriving whole classes of people of their personal identity and reclassifying them along supposed racial lines.[6] According to these statutes, the law distinguished between "those of German blood, Jews, *Mischlinge* [so-called mixed-breeds] of the 2nd degree, [and] *Mischlinge* of the 1st degree."[7] People with three or four Jewish grandparents were considered under German statute to be Jews, but others with only two Jewish grandparents, as well as those with one, were considered "non-Aryans." As David Wyman has noted, "In theory, non-Aryans had fewer legal disabilities than full Jews. In practice, non-Aryans were hardly less oppressed."[8] Anyone who had a Jewish grandparent was denied citizenship rights, and restrictions on marriage were put into place that ordered a general prohibition against anyone who would enter into a union where "it is expected that offspring will jeopardize maintaining the purity of the German blood."[9] These laws blurred the distinctions between race, ethnicity, and religion and frequently disregarded—and often voided—what an individual considered their own identity.[10] Any claim for rights as a citizen of the Reich, no matter how assimilated one might be, was abrogated by the Nuremberg Laws. Non-Aryans could be Catholic converts from Judaism or children or grandchildren of Jewish converts or Jewish individuals who intermarried with Christians of the Reich. According to Nazi policy, one could be a non-Aryan through a bloodline that included at least one Jewish grandparent, and in many instances, assimilated or even atheistic Jews, had their identities replaced. After September 1935, one's self-understanding needed to conform to these new ordinances.

For German Catholics, non-Aryans represented a new category of individual that ran counter to the natural-law tradition by which all Catholics felt bound. Indeed, the papal encyclical of Pius XI, *Mit Brennender Sorge*, had reminded the German Catholic faithful that the natural law was inviolable.[11] The presentation of this new type of individual created diffidence within German intellectual circles, a group that became split over the traditional norm of loyalty to the state as it clashed with traditional German personalism, a philosophical movement that lionized the intrinsic value of every individual.[12] Nazi lawmakers effectively ended this strain of thought when they made the personalistic aspect of the natural law applicable only to the Aryan members of the German citizenry. As one of the central pillars of Catholic natural law theory in interwar Europe, intrinsic personality and its accompanying set of rights evaporated with the special designation of Aryan and non-Aryan.[13] What the Nuremberg Laws hoped to accomplish was a reinvigoration of the German *völk* through a perversion of the natural law by an unbridled acceptance of positivism. Deimut Majer explains this ideological quest with precision:

> According to this doctrine, community could only consist in a community of the same race; people of different races could have no part in it. The essential feature, peculiar to Nazi ideology, can be defined as the racial principle or, more precisely, as the principle of racial or *völkisch* inequality among humans. . . . The dominant role of the race concept in National Socialist doctrine originates with Hitler himself, who during his time in Vienna absorbed the purely biologically based teachings of such radical anti-Semites as Jörg von Liebenfels, Georg Ritter von Schönerer, and Hans Leuger; these muddled notions he then combined in an abstruse mix with the politically and economically motivated anti-Semitism that had been widespread in the nations of Europe since the end of the nineteenth century. According to this doctrine, whatever race was stronger was therefore

the better one, and the weaker therefore the worse; the stronger race's rule over the weaker was a necessity ordained by nature (a 'basic aristocratic idea of nature'). The most valuable race was that of the Aryans; it alone was capable of creative labor and was therefore 'called' to rule (the entire world). The essential feature of Nazi racial dogma was not the assertion of racial differences or the enumeration of unscientific racial terminology or the doctrine calling for the suppression of people of other races, but rather the inference drawn from this teaching: that the stronger race had the right to rule by virtue of destiny or natural law.[14]

This new category of individual defied established norms, but then, that was precisely the point.[15] One pro-Nazi publication put it this way: "For nearly two thousand years the German people have been brought up in the belief that moral principles are not fundamentally derived from blood and racial characteristics, but from a revealed religion alone which claims to be valid for all nations and all races. Consequently the German personality was outrageously raped in its spiritual and racial elements."[16] Pastoral care of non-Aryans was especially difficult. How should the parish priest, for instance, treat a Jewish person who is married to a Catholic or a Jewish convert whom the civil law said was nevertheless a Jew by blood or racial distinction, a heritage blackened by accident of birth? Roman Catholic canon law given in the Pio-Benedictine Code of 1917 recognized the status of the baptized as possessing both natural rights and all rights accredited to Christians (cc. 12 and 87). In Germany, as elsewhere, the Catholicism of the non-Aryan was canonically valid and binding through the fact of baptism. While they may have been considered racially Semitic, they were religiously Catholic and a member of the Church. No civil law could say otherwise without being considered unjust—both for the individual Catholic and for the Church into whose membership she or he was engrafted. But the Code says nothing about the pastoral outreach owed to non-Catholics who find themselves in a marriage with Catholics. Indeed, the Code supplies a number of canons urging prudential striving toward the conversion of the non-Catholic and generally takes a negative view of those who would create an impediment for the Catholic party.

It perhaps goes without saying that the Nazi officials who promulgated and enforced the Nuremberg Laws did not consider the pastoral needs of parish priests in the formulation of these decrees. "To repeat the pithy formula uttered by [Hans] Kerrl (appointed by Hitler as Reich Minister for Church Affairs) on October 16, 1935, in Berlin: 'It [religion] has nothing to do with the practical affairs of life' and, since, it threatens to split the Germans into various denominations, it must be thrust into the background by great national, unifying, experiences."[17] Indeed, all too often pastoral care was only as effective as the law permitted; also, for many German priests who considered themselves citizens of the Reich, personal observance of the nation's laws remained equally important.[18]

Hitler's government forced the Church's leaders to come to terms with the new situation. Kevin Spicer has traced the significance of the non-Aryan group as one of the central pastoral concerns of many German dioceses, including Berlin, which took up the issue repeatedly in the Catholic press:

> The first article concerning non-Aryans appeared in the diocesan *Amtsblatt* on December 5, 1933—during the tenure of Bishop [Christian] Schreiber—under the title "Care for Catholic non-Aryans." In this brief article, the anonymous author publicly informed the clergy of the work of the St. Raphael Association, whose central office was in Hamburg. The Church had founded this organization to assist Catholic non-Aryans with emigration. In February 1937, under Bishop [Konrad] Preysing, a second article, "Catholic Non-Aryans," appeared in the same publication, offering similar information concerning the St. Raphael Association. This time, however, the article stressed that the work of the association was being conducted under the authority of the German bishops. Then, on May 29, 1938, a significant article appeared in the Berlin diocesan newspaper under the title "Responsibility of Christians for Non-Christians." This article contained an excerpt from the work of Austrian theologian Michael Pfliegler, whose *The Living Christian Before the Actual World* reminded Christians of their vocation to live out their baptismal call in the world by practicing good works for lapsed Christians and for non-Christians alike.[19]

Even though these articles received the attention of scores of clergy throughout Germany, the rest of the world was struck dumb by the passage of the Nuremberg Laws, as well as subsequent measures, which contributed to the persecution of the Church. The Laws presented one of the most significant stumbling blocks to those American Catholics disposed to aid refugees, in part because of the struggle to understand a group designation that was largely alien to their thought. Further, they were often caught second-guessing their abilities in light of the legal obligations presented by the governments of Europe and the American Department of State, as well as the moral obligations framed by the Holy See, the American bishops, and the Church tradition. Additionally, a general disinclination to coordinate and cooperate in relief efforts of those religious agencies in the United States—Catholic, Protestant, and Jewish—fueled an already confusing situation. This contributed to the perception that the response that actually came was slow and ineffective. But Catholic agencies in America did not remain idle, nor was their reaction tepid, particularly in light of the circumstances on the ground.[20] Moreover, it is important to realize that this disinclination to cooperate was not due to ill will, but a deeply held sentiment to protect the boundaries established through centuries of missionary activity and ecclesial domination. In fact, as I argue below, this crisis occasioned a radical shift in the attitudes of American Catholics toward interfaith cooperation. In the remainder of this essay, I want to explore the ramifications of the Nuremberg Laws on non-Aryans, who quickly became the object of the American Church's reaction to the ensuing refugee crisis.

SOURCES FOR THE AMERICAN CATHOLIC RESPONSE

A considerable archival repository on the Church's response may be found at the Center for Migration Studies in Staten Island, New York. The Center holds the collections of the old National Catholic Welfare Conference's Bureau of Immigration Affairs, a former agency of the American Catholic bishops that produced thousands of pages of memoranda and correspondence, official reports, and white papers on matters related to refugees from around the globe. Among the files that are open to researchers, one can see how Hitler's edicts are tracked and assessed: Nazi legislation forced over half a million Jews into continuously progressive hardship, pushing them out into foreign lands. Many went to Poland or Austria or Czechoslovakia, only to be uprooted once more when the Nazis stormed into those territories.[21] Some Catholic families, too, wished to leave Germany. From a humanitarian standpoint, the burden placed upon them was equally distressing. The Church hierarchy found that many of these Catholics were considered "non-Aryan" by the Hitler government because they were converts from Judaism or there was Jewish heritage in the lineage going back to at least one grandparent.

This did not seem to sway the stalwarts of the National Socialist Party, who sought to codify an irrational racial logic and promote a perception of Jews or non-Aryans as genetically and racially tainted. Both by definition and status, the German Jew and non-Aryan were demoted to inferior rank. The German government proceeded carefully, timing its repressive measures to avert negative publicity and maximize effect. Indeed, as John Fox has remarked,

> It was one thing to state that the Jew was the enemy of the German people; the Nazis found it was quite another to legislate against such a person or race until 'they' had been properly and legally defined. From April 7, 1933, until September 15, 1935, the euphemism 'non-Aryan' was adopted, although there were continual demands that the word Jew

should be used in legislation. . . . Various compromises on the Jewish question within Germany and in its diplomatic handling appeared during 1935–36 for the simple reason that Germany did not want anything to prevent the 1936 Olympics from being held in Berlin. Thus, the assassination by a Jew on February 4, 1936, in Switzerland of a National Socialist official, Wilhelm Gustloff, did not lead to any Kristallnacht as did that of vom Rath in Paris in November 1938.[22]

Since many Jews had intermarried into Catholic families or had simply converted, the Nazis merely took such arrangements as decidedly unfavorable to the Reich and held reprisals against these Jews or confiscated their property with the same vehemence they did with full-fledged Jews. Catholics as such were already under strain almost immediately after the signing of the Concordat between the Holy See and the Reich in 1933, but the fate of non-Aryan Catholics—numbers of whom have been notoriously hard to pin down—was precarious without outside assistance.[23] The German bishops looked to America for help.

The NCWC had heard about the plight of Catholic non-Aryans and responded to their German brother bishops by establishing the episcopal Committee for Catholic Refugees from Germany (CCRG) in November 1936. The CCRG set an ambitious agenda: if émigrés could get out, every last one placed in the care of the committee would be resettled. Archbishop Joseph Rummel of New Orleans chaired the committee.[24] Rummel would be associated with this issue from then on, serving not only as chairman of the CCRG, but also on the President's Advisory Committee for Political Refugees from Germany—a role he took up during Holy Week in March 1938. The CCRG was to work in tandem with the Bureau of Immigration Affairs, which was a department put in place less than a year after the creation of the NCWC itself. It had an able director in Bruce Mohler in Washington, and the director of the New York field office on Whitehall Street was Thomas Mulholland, who spent countless hours on the docks receiving new immigrants from Ellis Island. Mohler was the sometime stand-in for episcopal members who sat on various advisory boards and committees in Washington and was frequently called to testify before Congress on immigration affairs. Eventually, in September 1940, Archbishop Rummel would ask Mulholland to extend his expertise to the International Catholic Office for Refugee Affairs, which was forced to relocate from Europe. It was headed by an Austrian Dr. Frederick Hess.[25]

The paper trail that Mohler and Mulholland left behind is an extraordinary compilation. The two wrote memoranda to one another, typed up their synopses of conversations that they had with staff and

representatives of government and other private agencies, and logged
thousands of documents related to refugee matters nearly every day,
day after day, for over three decades. So close was their affiliation that
Mulholland was best man at Mohler's wedding.

INTERNAL LIMITATIONS AND THE CATHOLIC ANALYSIS OF THE PROBLEM

Several months before the CCRG was established, the staff at the Bureau
of Immigration Affairs was taking cognizance of new shifts in domestic
and foreign policies. Several of the memoranda that passed between
Mohler and Mulholland anticipate—correctly, I might add—the policy
directions taken by the U.S. government as well as the efforts of various
secular and religious agencies in response to the crisis of Kristallnacht.
As early as March 1936, when the secular newspapers were announcing plans to raise millions of dollars to evacuate thousands of Jews from
Germany, the NCWC staff was taking note of how to approach the
influx of Jews and Christians into America. An interoffice memorandum
suggests that because Jewish groups were going to shoulder the financial
responsibilities, a boundary was set up over which the NCWC dared not
cross. Jews would take care of themselves; Catholics would do likewise.
What is interesting about this memorandum is that it displays an awareness of the situation in Palestine, where so many of the Jewish refugees,
it was thought, would be directed.[26] However, the NCWC did not think
that the direction of these refugees would be toward Palestine, as the
news reports claimed, but toward the United States and Britain. Looking
back, this assessment proved to be true.

On October 7, 1937, the Board of Directors of the National
Coordinating Committee for Aid to Refugees and Emigrants Coming
from Germany (NCCARECG) voted to invite the NCWC's CCRG to
affiliate, but it did so with some hesitation.[27] According to the board
minutes,

> There was some discussion as to why it is necessary to have a separate
> committee to handle the cases of Catholic refugees in view of the fact that
> the American Committee for Christian German Refugees, affiliated with
> the National Coordinating Committee, is handling the cases of Christian
> refugees. Professor Chamberlain [Joseph Chamberlain of Columbia
> University] expressed the feeling that the principal object in setting up
> a separate group is that it is difficult to get money from Catholic groups
> unless the funds are used solely for Catholics. It was voted that the newly
> organized Episcopal Catholic Committee should be invited to join the
> National Coordinating Committee as one of its affiliates.[28]

The NCWC did join, but found the group to be more adept at spinning its wheels, having meeting after meeting, with little practical effect. Both Mohler and Mulholland found their participation in these meetings something to be dreaded, though they doggedly attended them for years.

There were many logistical hurdles to be surmounted in securing passage for those about to flee Germany, not least of which were governmental regulations and protocols erected between other religious and secular aid agencies. But within the Bureau and the adjunct CCRG, there were also ecclesiological and philosophical limitations whose boundaries on intercredal cooperation could not be transgressed. Anything leading to religious mixing was to be avoided. Catholics who went beyond both written and unwritten directives against intercredal cooperation were risking their reputation and could be disciplined accordingly by their bishop or ecclesiastical superior.

Elsewhere I have discussed the extent of the problem of intercredal cooperation from the perspective of Catholics struggling to achieve in principle what they could not obtain in practice, namely, the appreciation of tolerance and understanding among Catholics, Jews, and Protestants.[29] Some Catholics latched on to a progressive movement that sought to bridge religious divides—the National Conference for Christians and Jews (NCCJ), which was founded in 1927 in New York City. Its work in promoting tolerance and amity in every corner of the United States had shown some success, though the task was daunting given the rise in Klan activity and the near simultaneous foundation of nativist political groups. And yet the NCCJ, as well as the Institute for Religious and Social Studies at the Jewish Theological Seminary in New York, which formed several years later, were enterprises that were not fully embraced by the American hierarchy, precisely because the bishops wished to avoid the appearance of indifferentism. The kernel of this ideology and practice was the visible manifestation of the Church's humiliation. A conscious effort was made, for the sake of ecumenical or interreligious parity, to place the Catholic Church on a par with other religious bodies, as if to suggest that one way to God is as good as another.[30] Pope Pius IX had condemned the practice of indifferentism in the *Syllabus of Errors* of 1864, and his successors Leo XIII and Pius X, had regarded it as loathsome to the faith.[31] In the practical realm, the mixing of programs and personnel was generally to be avoided altogether, though of course common social interests could be explored.[32] Moreover, if one willfully refused to subscribe to the doctrines of the Catholic faith, one was *de facto* in error and, by extension, error had no rights.[33] Anyone in such a state was liable to be shunned by those who held the orthodox faith. Interreligious mixing with apostates and heretics may have been a holdover from post-Reformation Europe, but the pastoral context in the United

States suggested a certain rationale for the prohibition. American Catholics had known attacks on their faith, sometimes violent, in the shaping of their identity in this country, and so the consistent episcopal instructions forbidding religious interchange were meant to protect the Catholic population from both outside ideas and physical threats. One sees this on a more intimate level in the Church's canonical prohibitions or restrictions on "mixed marriages" or on those unions that suffered under "disparity of cult."[34]

The crisis occasioned by the Hitler government, including its continuous disregard for its Concordat with the Holy See, forced a new interpretation of this prohibition against religious mixing. The NCWC and its related committees recognized the primacy of charity toward those overseas, particularly toward the plight of non-Aryans. The Catholic Church in the United States would make these non-Aryans the targeted group for assistance, and this was conveyed to the U.S. State Department early in the planning stages of the Evian Conference, which took place in July 1938. Monsignor Michael Ready, the NCWC General Secretary, attended Evian as an observer and proxy for Archbishop Rummel.[35] But already in April of 1938, Ready was in touch with the State Department to communicate the NCWC's willingness to cooperate in the national "effort to give asylum to persecuted nationals in other countries."[36] In May, Ready contacted Sumner Welles, then Under-Secretary of State, to bring him the Church's policy recommendations for Evian.[37] The recommendations were well received, and Ready would continue to participate in discussions with Welles on the refugee issue and other foreign policy matters.

In June, Archbishop Rummel received a communiqué from Cardinal Eugenio Pacelli, then the Vatican's Secretary of State, instructing the American hierarchy to cooperate with the bishops of Germany for refugee relief. Pacelli's letter was merely an official approbation for work already under way, but he urged Rummel to continue contact specifically with Bishop Wilhelm Berning of Osnabrück who was then working with other European nations to absorb tens of thousands of non-Aryan refugees from Germany and Austria.[38] Just prior to his participation in the Evian Conference, Ready met with Pacelli, who expressed to him personally the Holy See's desire to assist Catholic refugees through "strong national committees," such as the ones being established in the United States and some European countries.[39] What that meant in terms of material assistance was an open question.

JAMES MCDONALD: A LAY CATHOLIC HUMANITARIAN

Quite apart from Ready's own observations and contacts, which were shared with the Apostolic Nunciature in Washington, the Holy See's interests at Evian were well informed. Not only were all the European

Catholic organizations and the NCWC in constant touch (to the extent possible and at times through the diplomatic pouch), but also James G. McDonald, the special advisor to Myron Taylor, who headed the American delegation at Evian, made a point of visiting with Pacelli after the conference in order to discuss non-Jewish refugees.[40] He did so through the offices of Count Enrico Galeazzi, who was close to Pacelli and a confidant of the pontifical household.[41] McDonald, a Catholic, was formerly the League of Nations High Commissioner for Refugees (Jewish and Other) Coming from Germany—a position he resigned in protest in 1935. He later became the chairman of President Roosevelt's Advisory Committee on Refugees. By the summer of 1938, McDonald was president of the Brooklyn Institute of Arts and Sciences—a position he sought and enjoyed, but which ultimately served as a distraction from his work on refugee matters.[42] In the months before and after Kristallnacht, however, no other lay Catholic outside the NCWC would serve the cause of refugee relief more diligently.

McDonald's relationship to the Holy See was understood not merely as that of an interested American Catholic, but as one who represented the government of the United States at a high level, one who had a distinguished record of humanitarian work, one who was willing to share information, and one who understood the mission and interests of the Church in Germany. McDonald had been meeting with Pacelli since 1935, principally over issues of religious persecution in Latin America, but also to see which of the numerous Catholic countries might be in a position to accept German refugees. Usually these meetings were arranged through Galeazzi, too. Through the efforts of these laymen, a gradual relaxation of the prohibitions against interreligious cooperation occurred, as it became more apparent that affected religious groups could seek common cause against totalitarian statism.[43]

The trust garnered by McDonald abroad was replicated at home. The NCWC and specifically McDonald's comember on the President's Advisory Committee for Political Refugees from Germany, Archbishop Rummel, was in frequent contact with him by letter and in person, and McDonald periodically acted as a go-between for Rummel and Myron Taylor.[44] This was especially true in the days following Kristallnacht. In meetings of the President's Advisory Committee in New York on November 11 and 21, 1938, Rummel and McDonald had specific conversations on issues touching non-Catholic refugees, among other items, but all parties recognized the need to raise awareness of the crisis in Germany.

McDonald and Rummel, with Rummel's proxy Monsignor Ready, were joined by Frederick Baerwald on the President's Advisory Committee on Political Refugees from Germany. Baerwald was a noted financier and honorary chairman of the American Jewish Joint Distribution Committee. With both Catholic and Jewish interests represented, the minutes of their meetings display frank interchange. About a month before Kristallnacht, the President's Advisory Committee met, and Monsignor Ready quickly wrote up a report to the NCWC Administrative Board, dated October 10, 1938, detailing some of the proposals they were then working out. One of these was to work "toward the organization of a united national drive to care for refugees." Ready wrote, "The Jewish organizations are not especially interested in this united drive idea, since they have built up in the past five years an extensive organization and have collected from Jewish people large sums to take care of Jewish refugees. These Jewish agencies have helped, both in the United States and countries of Europe, numerous Catholic refugees, with money as well as technical help."[45] From this report, it would seem that one of the barriers to intercredal cooperation on the refugee issue was the tacit acknowledgment that each group would take care of its own.

A further problem arose over the merits of beginning a national campaign initiated and sponsored by the President. In the fall and winter of that year, Rummel often relied on McDonald for information on the status of a proposed plan to raise the necessary funds to insure that the multitudes of refugees would be able to meet the quota fees demanded by many countries in the Western hemisphere.[46] But Baerwald, it seems, had reservations, as evident in a memorandum from McDonald to Myron Taylor. In describing a meeting he had with Rummel on November 10, 1938, McDonald told Taylor that "the Bishop was most anxious to have full information . . . [on] the possibility of the President issuing a general appeal for refugees. He felt that such an appeal would not only help materially to raise funds but would serve an important educational purpose. He is anxious to know whether the President is or is not likely to move in the near future because the Bishops' Committee has about exhausted its present resources and must consider the possibility of making a new appeal of its own if there is to be no comprehensive effort by all the groups." McDonald also explained that Rummel's interest in a general appeal by the President was something that he had mentioned also to Baerwald. "Mr. Baerwald's reaction," wrote McDonald, "was that while it would be desirable to discuss this possibility further, he did not think that now was the time to ask either our committee or the President to sponsor an appeal."[47] Although a plan for a general appeal never came to fruition, the cooperative spirit engendered by McDonald signified his importance.

Notwithstanding Baerwald's resistance, McDonald was also trusted by many other Jewish Americans at a time when prominent Jews were under attack by Father Charles Coughlin, the vituperative radio priest. If Catholics supported an isolationist stance, they did so in part at Coughlin's suggestion. As one of the dominant cultural forces within American Catholicism, Coughlin further riled his listeners by making antisemitic broadcasts in November 1938, which were but a postlude to private overtures he made to Benito Mussolini earlier in September. The radio priest offered space in the pages of his *Social Justice* periodical to promote Italian fascism, and Coughlin must have been further energized by a string of racist legislation emerging from Il Duce's pen within hours of the Kristallnacht pogroms.[48] But the November tirades found the important investment banking concern of Kuhn, Loeb in Coughlin's crosshairs. Founded by two Jews (Abraham Kuhn and Solomon Loeb) in 1867, it grew under the direction of Jacob Schiff, who guided it in its heyday, when it backed extensive railroad projects around the country and helped clients like Westinghouse and the Rockefeller and Rothschild families. By the time of Coughlin's remarks, Lewis Strauss, a noted member of the executive boards of the American Jewish Committee (AJC) and the American Jewish Joint Distribution Committee, was the chief executive of Kuhn, Loeb. Like Frederick Baerwald, Strauss was a major philanthropic force in the Jewish community. When Coughlin unleashed his antisemitic ramblings in the aftermath of Kristallnacht, he specifically mentioned the name of Kuhn, Loeb's Jacob Schiff as the one responsible for underwriting the Bolshevik Revolution. Connecting Jews to the communist menace was an old canard, but this particular fabrication also served to distract from and foment opposition to any effort at assisting those suffering in Germany. Worse still, it suggested that the world ought to blame the victim for its own misfortune. Strauss was incensed.

In a letter to Strauss, McDonald relayed some of the embarrassment felt by Catholics over Coughlin's remarks.[49] At the time, Strauss was weighing the possibility of launching a lawsuit and was in consultation with the firm of Cravath, de Gersdorff, Swaine, and Wood over the next several months about it.[50] McDonald managed to dissuade Strauss from suing, in part because of assurances that men like Archbishop Rummel, with whom McDonald had conversed, would work to disavow Coughlin's speeches. "On the basis of this talk," he wrote Strauss, "I am venturing to suggest that you do nothing about the Detroit matter," adding that he would personally see Archbishop Mooney in Detroit in the coming days to pressure Coughlin's ordinary to discipline him.[51]

In the weeks and months following Kristallnacht, McDonald carried on several other working friendships that cut across denominational lines, making him one of the bridge builders between faiths.[52] His many Jewish contacts helped him professionally from his days as the League of Nations

High Commissioner, including Frederick Baerwald. It is perhaps a testament of the trust placed in McDonald that Baerwald gladly facilitated
a request by Rabbi Morris Lazaron of Baltimore—a leader in interfaith
cooperation—to have McDonald alert media outlets that any references
made to the refugee catastrophe stirred up in the wake of Kristallnacht
should phrase the problem as concerning "Christian and Jewish refugees."
McDonald gladly complied with the request and wrote Lazaron directly,
thanking him for the suggestion.[53] Soon the press began to make this a
stock phrase, which doubtless had an impact on public opinion.

PROVIDING PERSONNEL FOR PRACTICAL AID

The focus on non-Aryan refugees by American Catholics was a limited
success, enabling over 3,500 to emigrate by the end of July 1939.[54]
Attention to non-Aryans became a preoccupation in the days leading
up to Kristallnacht. At the practical level, preparations by the NCWC
had been made against the impending influx of refugees. The CCRG
established a New York office under the direction of Father Joseph
Ostermann on January 1, 1937. Ostermann was then director of Leo
House, which at the time was a haven on 23rd Street in Manhattan
for newly arrived German Catholic immigrants, serving as a hostelry,
food pantry, and legal aid society.[55] Leo House was established in the
nineteenth century in conjunction with the St. Raphaelsverein, a social
service group in Germany that assisted travelers without regard to social
status. Ostermann was nearly always informed about new developments
in immigration regulations by the NCWC's Mohler and Mulholland, on
whom he came to rely in dealing with dozens of cases.

Ostermann informed Mohler a week before Kristallnacht that reports
from Germany suggested that some non-Aryans were being overlooked
for visas, which were instead being given to Jews exclusively.[56] On
November 5, Mohler received notice that Archbishop Rummel was
displeased that so little was known about the refugee problem among
the American population generally and among Catholic Americans in
particular. The organization was in place in terms of personnel. What was
needed now, the Archbishop said, was a massive infusion of funds on the
lines of the charitable campaigns run by Jews (not tens or even hundreds
of thousands of dollars, but millions).[57] But even after the news of the
destruction of Germany's Jewish religious landmarks and businesses,
the arrests, the beatings, and the deaths, that came the following week,
Catholics were not moved to contribute.

Within two weeks, the news from Germany grew worse for Catholics,
too. Twenty-five Catholic religious orders of women and men had their

property confiscated. If there was Catholic outrage at German aggression toward Jews, there was assuredly the rising of Catholic ire in the wake of the injurious actions toward priests and nuns.[58] Shortly thereafter, the CCRG's subscription stubs began showing up in parishes across the country, headlined with the following words: "The Mystical Body of Christ today lies torn and bleeding along the pagan roads of Nazi Germany. Are you the good Samaritan whom Christ called the good neighbor because his good deeds proved he was a man of good will toward all men?"[59] There followed a list of nine coupons that promised monetary relief, scholarship assistance for college, transportation funds for those wishing to migrate, and the promise of gratis medical services.

The appeals for large amounts of Catholic donations never really materialized, though many good families wrote to the NCWC offering space in their homes for displaced children. Nothing approaching the millions Rummel called for ever came about, partly because the appeal seemed so utterly misplaced. It had become abundantly clear that it was not European Catholics who needed rescuing. As anyone who picked up an American newspaper on November 11 knew, it was the Jews.

ADDITIONAL BARRIERS TO INTERCREDAL COOPERATION

The November pogroms certainly intensified attention to the plight of Germany's immigrants, but if they served to raise public consciousness and executive action abroad, they were preceded by the hardness of months of hesitation in preparing for the magnitude of the catastrophe. Political inertia thus presents itself as a further barrier to intercredal cooperation. In late March 1938, Maurice Bisgyer, Executive Secretary of B'nai Brith, met with Bruce Mohler over the then Secretary of State Cordell Hull's policy recommendations to grant asylum to political, religious, and racial refugees from Germany and Austria. Mohler notified Monsignor Ready on April 2, detailing the meeting, the upshot of which was that both men agreed about the hopelessness of introducing a bill to increase or pool immigration quotas, which at the time was 153,000 for all countries (though only 50,244 of these were used in 1936–1937).[60] If these two, who were in a position to pressure government and religious groups to alter national policy, did not act, it was because the isolationist view was so entrenched. It also signaled a harsh reality, namely, that all these denominations could do was to agree to do nothing.

This type of foot dragging was hard to dispel. A short time after the Kristallnacht pogroms, Jewish philanthropists were openly wondering to themselves about the wisdom of enlisting Catholic financiers for their cause or of sharing funds already obtained with Christian aid agencies.

Lewis L. Strauss, the noted financier, had been mulling this problem with several of his contemporaries. He prompted correspondence, dated November 26, 1938, between Henry Ittleson, founder of CIT Financial Services, and James Rosenberg, a New York lawyer with close ties to government. Ittleson circulated his opinion as follows: "I seriously question the expediency of using Catholic and Protestant sources as co-beneficiaries in your Emergency Campaign:- 1. I think it unwise to use that angle now, when it will be necessary for the big programme. 2. The task to get money from contributors to JDC and UP and Co-ordinating (on the scale outlined even in our 'Emergency' campaign) is difficult enough without having at this moment to defend and explain the non-Jewish angle."[61]

Others, however, told Strauss the opposite. Referring to the work of the AJC's "Survey Committee"—a group of wealthy Jews concerned with assisting European Jews specifically and defeating antisemitism generally—Rosenberg wrote to Strauss:

"I think that the Survey Committee should devote very special consideration at this time to do everything it can to rallying the forces of liberal minded Catholics and Protestants. Dr. Cavert of the Federal Council of Churches of Christ is one of them. . . . I am not suggesting specific things but I am trying to throw out some thoughts to you, which thoughts I know you already have. The argument with the Christians that the fight against anti-Semitism is their fight also against anti-Christianism at this moment in the flux of world events, has a good deal of weight."[62]

To buttress this suggestion, Rosenberg had highlighted some events printed in the *JTA News*, including how, on October 18, 1938, the bishops' CCRG petitioned the wider conference to adopt a resolution to oppose antisemitism "as an un-Godly, uncharitable and un-Christian" scourge. The NCWC did so at its annual fall meeting. Within a week, another prominent Catholic made headlines and Rosenberg brought this to Strauss' attention as well. On October 23, Joseph Connolly, general manager of the Hearst Newspapers, addressed the journalists' session of the Eucharistic Congress in New Orleans. Connolly urged a Catholic fight against the persecution of Jews. The *JTA News* quoted Connolly as saying: "A battle must begin now against the destructive movements in the Old World, which, if not checked, are certain to break the dikes of Germany, Italy and Russia and drench the other frontiers of the civilized world."[63]

Connolly was not reading tea leaves, but his own newspapers. He was, unfortunately, speaking in the teeth of contrary winds among his coreligionists. Most of Catholic America did not have the Jewish refugee problem on their list of foreign policy priorities. Indeed, for years, the Hearst papers had advocated an isolationist stance and, by extension, had helped American nonintervention "become the hand-maiden of European appeasement."[64] This was reflected in the numbers of German émigrés to the United States. In 1936, only 6,000 were permitted to enter; in 1937, the number had climbed to 11,000—still far short of the estimated number of those who needed refuge.[65] Even after repeated attempts by some congressional leaders to modify the quota system went down in defeat, and the news from Germany continued its grim course, when by mid-1939 a *Fortune* poll asked whether one would, if they were a member of Congress, vote yes or no to open the nation to these European refugees, "85 percent of Protestants, 84 percent of Catholics, and an astonishing 25.8 percent of Jews answered no."[66]

Notwithstanding the popular opinion, many Jews who recognized the gravity of the situation also knew the stakes in consolidating their efforts with Catholics. Frustration often accompanied their outreach. This may be attributed in part to their own lack of unanimity in the face of the impending calamity in Germany, the urgency of the cause, and the absence of a definite plan. In New York, Samuel Untermyer, a prominent Jewish Wall Street attorney, had been campaigning to bring economic pressure on Germany since Hitler came to power in 1933. But Untermyer, who died in 1940, could not get past all of the inertia in the face of such grievous disaster, eventually blaming fellow Jews for the impasse. In a December 1937 radio broadcast on the Mutual Broadcasting System, he puzzled:

> I cannot understand why Catholics, Protestants, Organized Labor, Rotarians, Masons, and Americans generally have been so indolent, callous, and shortsighted as to have failed long since to effect a mutual protective organization to safeguard civilization, or why they permit this perilous situation aimlessly to drift, when they have within easy reach the means of self-protection for themselves and their brethren in Germany— by the simple expedient of the boycott of German goods and services. . . . The wave of world-wide anti-Semitism, led and encouraged by Germany, that is inundating our country should serve only to make us more race conscious, tie us closer together and confirm us in our determination to combat and overcome by every means in our power the vast propaganda of this world-bully and braggart and the forces of evil that inspire it. There are still too many turn-coats, hyphenated Jews and apostates in our ranks. The sooner we expose them and rout them out, the better it will be for our welfare and self-respect. They are an undiluted liability.[67]

This sounds shrill, but it is expressive of the agony of individuals of high moral principle who attempted to do the good in the face of evil. Boycotts were seen as a bit too radical for most Catholics, though other types of confrontation and consciousness-raising were not unknown. For instance, Father Coughlin's reach into the American Catholic psyche was tempered only slightly, but with considerable verve, by the Catholic Worker movement. Led by Dorothy Day, the movement offered an important intellectual and moral voice against Nazism and Italian fascism, which it recounted in its own print organ, *The Catholic Worker*. Among other efforts, Catholic Workers picketed outside the German embassy in New York and protested with thousands of other "Reds" at Pier 86 where the German liner *The Bremen* was docked.[68]

The magnitude of the calamity, however, spiraled out of the control of those who hoped to do the right thing. They tried to achieve their objectives, but often failed. Catholics and Jews who did cooperate were often foiled by the Byzantine immigration policies between nations, which were not streamlined, as many expected, after the Evian Conference.[69] Although many of the participants, including McDonald and Taylor, were somewhat self-congratulatory in the days following, the meeting did little to alleviate the disarray caused by the capricious changes in Nazi emigration law.[70] While it set out to obtain the agreement of the 32 participant nations to a nonbinding, voluntary revision of their respective refugee policies to admit vulnerable populations fleeing Germany, the challenges proved insurmountable.

For Catholics, information was considered the best weapon against inertia. For his part, Father Ostermann tried to relay cases he heard about to Mulholland, who was of great assistance, but whose workload nearly doubled in the process. Ostermann, Mulholland, and Mohler each had their own network of contacts, many of which overlapped. That included Cecelia Razovsky.[71] As head of the National Coordinating Committee, which soon changed its name to the National Refugee Service, Razovsky was often in Washington consulting with government agencies, but also with religious organizations like the NCWC. Days before Kristallnacht, she was at the State Department for a briefing on the situation in Cuba, whose quota numbers were becoming exhausted. Ostermann alerted Bruce Mohler to her presence in the capital and suggested a meeting while she was in Washington.[72] By this time, Razovsky was well-known in the refugee assistance community, and she would be the most constant Jewish presence available to NCWC staffers as America lurched toward war.

COOPERATING WITH RELIEF AGENCIES ABROAD

There was another facet to the problem of assisting in the refugee effort and that was the coordination between the Church in America and in Europe. National Catholic relief agencies, as they were able, followed the lead of the Holy See with respect to non-Aryans. The Jesuit Pierre Blet has written that some of the lessons learned in the First World War carried over into the troubles created by Germany's National Socialist government, but this "new category of people . . . were appealing to the Holy See for assistance in a manner unknown during 1914–1918." Blet notes how Kristallnacht added to "increasingly oppressive measures" already occurring in Germany against the Jewish population. "And just as the state of war, far from bringing about a holy union, merely aggravated the hardships facing the church, so too did it give signs that there would be more and more violent persecutions against the Jews."[73] Non-Aryan Catholics who were Jewish by heritage became the object of the Holy See's humanitarian interventions in Germany because, says Blet, "this group was in very great need since Jewish relief organizations were often unaware of them."[74]

German bishops recognized the great ally they had in the American episcopate. Bishop Wilhelm Berning of Osnabrück wrote the NCWC Administrative Board Chairman Archbishop Edward Mooney of Detroit that the German bishops were grateful for the assistance lent to their people and that he had informed Cardinal Pacelli at the Secretariat of State of the American bishops' cooperation through its CCRG.[75] The CCRG's European contact was Pallottine Father Max Groesser, PSM, executive director of the German St. Raphaelsverein, founded in 1871 and based in Hamburg, which was busy providing material and pastoral aid to travelers exiting Germany. Before St. Raphaelsverein was suppressed in 1941, it had a ready-made organizational structure to assist the newly formed Relief Committee for Non-Aryan Catholics (*Hilfsausschuss für katholische Nichtarier*), which it joined in March 1935.

In March 1937 Groesser visited the NCWC with 300 cases in hand. Work on their resettlement began almost immediately.[76] It was advised, for his protection and that of his clients, that Groesser's name be left entirely out of the press.[77] At that time he met with Bruce Mohler at the NCWC offices in New York in order to establish future policies for their collaborative work and to discuss where potential refugees could flee, including South America, the Caribbean islands, and the Philippines. As the principal immigration aid agency for Catholic Germany, Groesser knew his organization would be the vehicle for the departure of non-Aryans. It was a good thing that the plans were set in place while he was in America. Groesser would be jailed by the Nazis later in December of that year.[78]

The key elements of this relationship were that the St. Raphaelsverein would obtain the necessary travel documents and book passage, while the NCWC would provide financial, housing, and employment assistance—as well as pastoral care—to needy cases once they arrived.

The work of the St. Raphaelsverein enlisted local service agencies, such as the *Hilfswerk beim Bischöpflichen Ordinariat Berlin*, which began under Bishop Konrad Graf von Preysing in July 1938. Funding was supplied by every diocese in the country, together with smaller grants from individuals and societies. Again, the focus was on non-Aryans. The *Hilfswerk*, according to Kevin Spicer, was "specifically designed to stand beside persecuted Christians of Jewish descent."[79] Several area bishops gave assistance, as well as Heinrich Krone, the director of Caritas Emergency Services—Germany's equivalent to America's present-day Catholic Relief Services. Although he founded the *Hilfswerk* primarily as a pastoral agency in an attempt to meet the spiritual and material needs of Christians of Jewish descent, von Preysing had every intention of opening the gates of relief to everyone of Jewish extraction and creed. One of his principal advisors who was given charge of the *Hilfswerk*, Monsignor Bernard Lichtenberg, served in this capacity until his arrest in fall 1941, after which time von Preysing himself took over the reins.[80] Lichtenberg—who was beatified by the Church in 1996—was the provost of St. Hedwig Cathedral in Berlin. The day after Kristallnacht, he took to the pulpit excoriating the authorities for allowing it and saying that the synagogue was just as much a house of God as the cathedral. Lichtenberg would continually pray publicly for the welfare of Jews and Christians until his arrest for "subversive activities." He was imprisoned for over two years and died in a cattle car on his way to Dachau in November 1943.

The *Hilfswerk* began during the same month as the Evian Conference. While in France, the NCWC made contact with members of the six Catholic delegations sent to Evian from across Europe. Rummel was supposed to attend as a member of the President's Advisory Committee on Refugees but, as noted above, the Archbishop sent the NCWC General Secretary Monsignor Michael J. Ready instead. Ready was active in nearly every major aspect of the Church's social welfare programs in America. He relied on Mohler and Mulholland's advice for this meeting, and Rummel felt comfortable having him as his representative. Ready not only provided his observations, but established protocols with the Dutch and the Swiss Catholic representatives, who had begun their work some months prior. All coordinated with German agencies like the *Hilfswerk*. In addition to the *Hilfswerk* and the St. Raphaelsverein, in the aftermath of Evian, the NCWC's CCRG formed relationships with other American aid agencies, including those sponsored by Protestant and Jewish organizations.

By December 1938, Jews became the objects of charity along with German Catholics. The Bureau of Immigration Affairs sought to physically extract German Catholics and Jews for resettlement, particularly south of the American border. One gets the sense from reading the internal memoranda that the Bureau sought out every loophole and site to obtain safe haven for the refugees. For example, on December 30, 1938, Mohler drafted a memorandum to Monsignor Ready, the NCWC General Secretary, about rumors of the possibility of large numbers of Jews entering the United States through Cuba, which he subsequently copied to Ostermann on January 3, 1939. The rumors proved false, because Cuban citizenship, which would have enabled unfettered travel to the United States, could only be earned after five years of permanent residency. But the necessary inquiries were made about this entrance through the "back door." Not only did Mohler personally check on this with the Cuban consulate, he called his contacts in the U.S. State Department who confirmed that the State had "no knowledge of Jews entering in large numbers after having acquired Cuban citizenship," a matter that would have been reported by the American consul in Havana. On the other end of the line was Edward Shaughnessy, Deputy Commissioner of Immigration at the U.S. Department of Labor. He had not heard about a Jewish influx from Cuba and told Mohler that "if it did exist their undercover man in Havana and the inspectors in Miami would certainly have reported it to headquarters."[81]

CONCLUSION

By Mulholland's count, 78 percent of German refugees came to America, and so it is somewhat staggering to think about the accompanying hardship and workload for each individual and each family.[82] It should be stated that at no point in the documentation do we find Mulholland or Mohler capitulating to public opinion polls or otherwise lessening their efforts. Unfortunately, there was never a direct strategy on how to assist this surge of refugees, in part because the NCWC had not yet realized the magnitude of the problem. Rather, the Bureau sought to use its numerous contacts and prestige to pave the way for the care and transition of these immigrants as they came to its attention. By July 31, 1939, the number of refugees who were taken in was 3,520, a number that appears in a statistical summary of activities in the first three fiscal years of the CCRG's existence, though there is no accompanying analysis.[83] We do not know the breakdown in the number of "non-Aryans" to "Aryans," nor of those who were fully Jewish. We do know that of those who immigrated by 1939, the Committee counted only half of its applicants that were actually from the *Altreich*. The other half came from other European nations, whence they had fled, and from where their contemporaries would be victimized further through later deportation. It might also be said that of the 3,250 individuals who obtained assistance under Catholic auspices, several were priests and religious.[84]

It does not seem possible, given the record presented in this essay, to affirm the efforts of the Church in America as either a success or a failure. Seen in hindsight, the numbers who received aid seem woefully small. But they are not negligible, and all the more impressive considering the circumstances surrounding their entrance into this country. One German official, in surveying all his government had wrought, gave a disingenuous summary. After the Kristallnacht of November 9, 1938, the German Ambassador to the Court of St. James, Herbert von Dirksen, wrote, "I should now like to state how pleased I am at our decision to play an active part in transporting as many Jews as possible out of Germany in an orderly manner."[85] Between popular American will, intergovernmental inertia, bureaucratic red tape, German arrogance, and—we must acknowledge it—a malignant antsemitism at home and abroad, well-intentioned Catholics had considerable forces working against them.[86] That American Catholics accomplished as much as they did in the period before America's formal entrance into the European conflict certainly warrants an alternative to criticisms of their legacy.

NOTES

1. A survey of the historiography on this point is available in Frank Brecher, "David Wyman and the Historiography of America's Response to the Holocaust: Counter-Considerations," *Holocaust and Genocide Studies* 5:4 (1990): 423–446.

2. Haim Genizi, "Christian Charity: The Unitarian Service Committee's Relief Activities on Behalf of Refugees from Nazism, 1940–1945," *Holocaust and Genocide Studies* 2:2 (1987): 261–278.

3. Haim Genizi, *American Apathy: The Plight of the Christian Refugees from Nazism* (Ramat-Gan: Bar-Ilan University Press, 1983), 141, 144.

4. Ibid., 146. This charge of antisemitism within the staff of the Bureau is echoed by Gershon Greenberg, who cites Genizi approvingly, in his "American Catholics During the Holocaust," available online at http://motlc.wiesenthal.com/site/pp.asp?c=gvKVLcMVIuG&b=395083, accessed August 9, 2008. Oddly, in a later book, Genizi switches tack even further and, lapsing into hyperbole, claims that when it came to non-Aryans, "no Christian relief organization took care of them." Cf. Haim Genizi, *America's Fair Share: The Admission and Resettlement of Displaced Persons, 1945–1952* (Detroit: Wayne State University Press, 1993), 2.

5. There are two unpublished dissertations on the NCWC and refugees, though these works touch on the subject only briefly. Cf., George V. Murry, *Welcoming the Stranger: The American Catholic Church and*

Refugee Newcomers, 1936–1980 (Ph.D. diss., Washington, D.C.: George Washington University, 1995), esp. chapter 2; Earl Boyea, *The National Catholic Welfare Conference: An Experience of Episcopal Leadership, 1935–1945* (Ph.D. diss., Washington, D.C.: Catholic University of America, 1987). See also George N. Shuster, "The Conflict Among Catholics," *American Scholar* 10 (Winter 1940–1941): 5–16. Shuster was an important voice in American Catholicism, having been an editor at *Commonweal* magazine and later president of City College in New York.

6. On non-Aryans, see especially James Tent, *In the Shadow of the Holocaust: Nazi Persecution of Jewish-Christian Germans* (Lawrence: University of Kansas Press, 2003); Ursula Bütner and Martin Greschat, *Die verlassenen Kinder der Kirche: Der Umgang mit Christen jüdischer Herkunft im "Dritten Reich"* (Göttingen: Vandenhoeck und Ruprecht, 1998); Aleksander-Sasa Vuletić, *Christen jüdischer Herkunft im Dritten Reich: Verfolgung und organisierte Selbsthilfe, 1933–1939* (Mainz: Verlag Philipp von Zabern, 1999); Jeremy Noakes, "Nazi Policy towards German-Jewish 'Mischlinge' 1933–1945," *Leo Baeck Institute Yearbook* 34 (1989): 291–354, reprinted in eds. David Cesarini and Sarah Kavanaugh, *Holocaust: Critical Concepts in Historical Studies* (New York: Routledge, 2004), 239–311.

7. A useful visual aid that charts the intricacies of the Nuremberg Racial Laws of 1935 has been developed and translated by the United States Holocaust Memorial Museum through a contribution of The Hirsh and Braine Raskin Foundation. It is reprinted in the exhibition catalogue *Deadly Medicine: Creating the Master Race* (Washington, D.C.: United States Holocaust Memorial Museum, 2004). Translations of the Laws themselves may be found in *Documents on the Holocaust: Selected Sources on the Destruction of the Jews of Germany and Austria, Poland, and the Soviet Union,* ed. Yitzhak Arad, Israel Gutman, and Abraham Margolit, trans. Lea Ben Dor (Lincoln: University of Nebraska Press, and Jerusalem: Yad Vashem, 1999), 76–79.

8. David Wyman, *Paper Walls: America and the Refugee Crisis, 1938–1941* (Amherst: University of Massachusetts Press, 1968), xiv.

9. Ibid. Such unions included also "a *Mischling* coming from forbidden extramarital relations with a Jew and who was born out of wedlock after July 31, 1936."

10. Cf. Michael Burleigh and Wolfgang Wippermann, *The Racial State: Germany 1933–1945* (New York: Cambridge University Press, 1992); Uwe D. Adam, "An Overall Plan for Anti-Jewish Legislation in the Third Reich," *Yad Vashem Studies* 11 (1976): 33–55; Jacob Boas, "The Shrinking World of German Jewry, 1933–1938," *Leo Baeck Institute Year Book* 31 (1986): 241–266; Abraham Margaliot, "The Reaction of the Jewish Public in Germany to the Nuremberg Laws," *Yad Vashem Studies* 12 (1977): 75–107.

11. Cf. Encyclical letter of Pius XI, *Mit Brennender Sorge* (March 14, 1937), accessed via Internet at http://www.vatican.va/holy_father/pius_xi/encyclicals/documents/hf_p-xi_enc_14031937_mit-brennender-sorge_en.html,

August 15, 2008. The Pope issued the document in German, and it was smuggled into Germany, copied, and read out in its entirety from the pulpits of Catholic churches during Holy Week. The Pope wrote: "Such is the rush of present-day life that it severs from the divine foundation of Revelation, not only morality, but also the theoretical and practical rights. We are especially referring to what is called the natural law, written by the Creator's hand on the tablet of the heart (*Rom.* ii. 14) and which reason, not blinded by sin or passion, can easily read. It is in the light of the commands of this natural law, that all positive law, whoever be the lawgiver, can be gauged in its moral content, and hence, in the authority it wields over conscience. Human laws in flagrant contradiction with the natural law are vitiated with a taint which no force, no power can mend . . . . To overlook this truth is to forget that the real common good ultimately takes its measure from man's nature, which balances personal rights and social obligations, and from the purpose of society, established for the benefit of human nature." (30)

12. While this is not the place to enter into the question of the German *Bildung*, or cultivation, of authentic human personhood, the philosophical capitulation of the German intelligentsia to the National Socialist State undoubtedly influenced and mutually reinforced the wider cultural rejection of Jews and their kin within German society. See further, Jan Olof Bengtsson, *The Worldview of Personalism: Origins and Early Development* (New York: Oxford University Press, 2006).

13. Perhaps as testament to their importance, the tenets encompassed by the natural law were rehabilitated in the aftermath of the Second World War, particularly in the prosecution of Nazi war criminals. Cf. Michael S. Bryant, "Prosecuting the Cheerful Murderer: *Natural Law* and National Socialist Crimes in West German Courts, 1945–1950," *Human Rights Review* 5:4 (2004): 86–103. It might be added that intrinsic personal rights included the right to protest and resist unjust laws, which German theologians of the period had advocated and which were part of Catholic social teaching at least since Pope Leo XIII's Encyclical *Immortale Dei* (1885), though rooted as far back as John of Salisbury (d. 1180). For discussion, cf. Mary Alice Gallin, *German Resistence to Hitler: Ethical and Religious Factors* (Washington, D.C.: Catholic University of America Press, 1961).

14. Cf. Diemut Majer, *"Non-Germans" Under the Third Reich: The Nazi Judicial and Administrative System in Germany and Occupied Eastern Europe with Special Regard to Occupied Poland, 1939–1945*, trans. Peter Thomas Hill, Edward Vance Humphrey, and Brian Levin (Baltimore: Johns Hopkins University Press, 2003), 36–37.

15. Incredibly, there were non-Aryan Christians of Jewish descent who happily and actively sought association precisely on account of their loyalties to the National Socialist State. Cf. Werner Cohn, "Bearers of a Common Fate? The 'Non-Aryan Christian Fate-Comrades' of the Paulus Bund, 1933–1939," *Leo Baeck Institute Yearbook* 33 (1988): 327–366.

16. *Schwarze Korps* (May 6, 1937), 6, quoted in n.a., *The Persecution of the Catholic Church in the Third Reich: Facts and Documents Translated from the German* (London: Burns and Oates, 1940), 459.

17. Waldemar Gurian, *Hitler and the Christians*, trans. E. F. Peeler (New York: Sheed and Ward, 1935), 47.

18. Indeed, the work of Gordon Zahn and Donald Dietrich shows that not only was there loyalty to the Fatherland among Catholic clergy, there were frequent links between expressions that may be seen as jingoistic and overtly antsemitic. See Gordon Zahn, *German Catholics and Hitler's Wars: A Study in Social Control* (New York: Sheed and Ward, 1962) and Donald Dietrich, *Catholic Citizens in the Third Reich: Psycho-Social Principles and Moral Reasoning* (New Brunswick, NJ Transaction Publishers, 1988).

19. Kevin P. Spicer, *Resisting the Third Reich: The Catholic Clergy in Hitler's Berlin* (DeKalb: Northern Illinois University Press, 2004), 127, citing the *Amtsblatt des Bischöpflichen Ordinariats Berlin*, December 5, 1933, 106–107. The St. Raphaelsverein, a traveler's aid society, is discussed below.

20. The situation of German emigration has been comprehensively described by Sir John Hope Simpson, who helped the world understand the tremendous difficulties faced by German émigrés in a report issued initially in 1938 and supplemented over the next few years. John Hope Simpson, *The Refugee Problem* (Oxford: Oxford University Press, 1939). Sir John's detailed analysis of the problem was typically measured, but it did not hide the tremendous hurdles to be surmounted, especially in moving half a million from Germany. It takes a historical view, beginning to analyze the refugee problem in the aftermath of the First World War. The journalist Dorothy Thompson's *Refugees: Anarchy or Organization* (New York: Random House, 1938) gives a far more impassioned account.

21. Consider the Jews of the Sudetenland. In 1930 their numbers were around 25,000, but in 1938 there were 28,000. But a precipitous decline ensued, so that by November 1938, 12,000 had left. On this transformation, see especially Jörg Osterloh, *Nationalsozialistische Judenverfolgung im Reichsgau Sudetenland 1938–1945* (Munich: Oldenbourg, 2006).

22. John P. Fox, review of *The Twisted Road to Auschwitz: Nazi Policy Toward German Jews 1933–1939* by Karl A. Schleunes, and *La Diplomatie du IIIe Reich et les Juifs (1933–1939)* by Eliahu Ben Elissar in *International Affairs* 47:4 (October 1971): 771–773. Fox cites von Dirksen's comment from *Documents on German Foreign Policy*, Series D, v. 5, p. 908.

23. On the estimated numbers of non-Aryans in Germany prior to November 1938, cf. Jeremy Noakes, "Nazi Policy towards German-Jewish '*Mischlinge*' 1933–1945," *Leo Baeck Institute Yearbook* 34 (1989): 291–354. Noakes puts the figure at 69,000 "half Jews" in Germany and Austria. It is impossible to say whether they had any religious affiliation. Ernst Christian Helmreich puts the number of conversions by Jews to Catholicism between 1930 and 1939 at 3,546 and indicates that "the number was never above 100 a year until 1933, when it jumped to 304."

See Helmreich, *The German Churches Under Hitler: Background, Struggle, and Epilogue* (Detroit: Wayne State University Press 1979), 522 n. 105. Helmreich obtained his statistics from the Bundesarchiv in Koblenz, Reichministerium für kirch, Angelegenheiten R79/19. Guenter Lewy follows Raul Hilberg in estimating the number of "half Jews" and "quarter Jews" at 150,000 by 1942. Cf. Guenter Lewy, *The Catholic Church and Nazi Germany* (New York: McGraw-Hill, 1964), 288, citing Hilberg, *The Destruction of the European Jews* (Chicago: Quadrangle Books, 1961), 267. A broad analysis of the disparity of these numbers may be found in William D. Rubenstein, *The Myth of Rescue: Why Democracies Could Not Have Saved More Jews from the Nazis* (New York: Routlege, 1997), especially chapter 2, "The Myth of Closed Doors, 1933–1939."

24. Center for Migration Studies, Staten Island, New York: National Catholic Welfare Conference Bureau of Immigration Affairs, Collection 023, Box 9: "The Committee for Catholic Refugees from Germany," n.d. Citations referring to collections housed at the Center for Migration Studies will hereinafter be designated "CMS, NCWC, BIA, Collection 023, box #." Others on the Committee included Archbishop Samuel Stritch of Milwaukee, Bishops John Noll of Fort Wayne, Stephen Donahue of New York, Archbishop John Glennon of St. Louis, Archbishop Maurice McAuliffe of Hartford, and Bishops Bernard Sheil of Chicago, Aloysius Muench of Fargo, John Duffy of Buffalo, Francis Beckan of Dubuque, and John Cantwell of Los Angeles.

25. Rummel to Mulholland, September 10, 1940, in CMS, NCWC, BIA, Collection 023, Box 82.

26. Cf., Mulholland to Mohler, March 13, 1936, in CMS, NCWC BIA, General Correspondence, Box 37: Jews/Jewish. The memorandum was generated by and accompanied a short article in *The New York Herald Tribune* of March 13, "Jews to Raise 15 Million for Reich Emigres."

27. American Jewish History Society Collection; the Admiral Lewis L. Strauss Papers (P-632): Box 41: (1935–1937). Hereafter "Strauss Papers." Most of the documentation in this box relates to the National Coordinating Committee for Aid to Refugees and Emigrants Coming from Germany, based on 57th Street in New York.

28. Cf. Strauss Papers (P-632): Box 41: (1935–1937), letter of Cecilia Razovsky to Lewis Strauss, with enclosed Board Minutes, October 30, 1937. Cecilia Razovsky became secretary/executive director of the German-Jewish Children's Aid as well as the secretary and executive director of the NCCARECG, the latter group having been founded in 1934 with Joseph Chamberlain as chairman. Chamberlain was a professor of public law at Columbia and author of the "New York City Charter Plan."

29. Cf. Patrick J. Hayes, "J. Elliot Ross and the National Conference of Jews and Christians: A Catholic Contribution to Tolerance in America," *Journal of Ecumenical Studies* 37:3/4 (2000): 321–332, and idem., "Elite Catholic Isolationism in the United States: Impediment or Failure in the

Fight against Nazi Genocide?" in *The Genocidal Mind: Selected Papers of the 32nd Annual Scholar's Conference on the Holocaust and the Churches*, ed. Dennis B. Klein, et al. (St. Paul: Paragon House, 2005), 139–155.

30. Cf. s.v., "Indifferentism," in *New Catholic Encyclopedia*, 2nd ed. (Detroit: Gale Press, 2003), VII:421–422; N. Molinski, "Indifferentism," in *Sacramentum Mundi*, ed. Karl Rahner et al. (New York: Herder and Herder, 1968), III:120–121.

31. The theological analysis and ensuing debate over intercredal cooperation was carried on most prominently in a series of essays beginning in the 1940s. Cf. John LaFarge, "Some Questions as to Interdenominational Cooperation," *Theological Studies* 3:3 (1942), 315–332; John Courtney Murray, "Current Theology: Christian Co-operation," *Theological Studies* 3:3 (1942): 413–431; idem., "Current Theology: Co-operation: Some Further Views," *Theological Studies* 4:1 (1943): 100–111; Wilfrid Parsons, "Intercredal Co-operation in the Papal Documents," *Theological Studies* 4:2 (1943): 159–182; Francis M. Connell, "Catholics and 'Interfaith' Groups," *American Ecclesiastical Review* 105 (1941): 336–353. Connell cites several decisions of the Holy Office condemning or prohibiting inter-credal cooperation: in 1864, 1865, and 1919; related to the prohibition on Catholics participating in the "Society for the Union of Christendom," as well as to similar prohibitions against Catholics participating in the Lausanne Conference in 1927; to *Mortalium Animos* (which condemned *communio in sacris*); and to the letter of Leo XIII to Archbishop Satolli, *Coetus in Federatis*, September 18, 1895. Such participation of Catholics in these kinds of intergroup projects is, according to Connell, "a grave menace to the faith of our people." See also Jacques Maritain, "The Achievement of Co-operation among Men of Different Creeds," *Journal of Religion* 21 (1941): 332–364; and idem., *Ransoming the Time* (New York: Scribner's, 1941), esp. chapter 5: "Who is My Neighbor?" But Pius XII in his letter *Sertum Laetitiae* notes that cooperation with all people of goodwill is something desired by the Holy See—"not indeed for the purpose of seeking agreement on a minimum of fundamental revealed doctrine, nor with the idea of communicating with them in religious worship as the outcome of basic agreement, *but purely within the sphere of the natural law*, particularly in its social applications." *Sertum Laetitiae*, *AAS* 31 (1939): 635–644. On the canonical implications, cf., T. Lincoln Bouscaren, "Co-operation with Non-Catholics: Canonical Legislation," *Theological Studies* 3:4 (1942): 475–512.

32. I have found only a couple of references of public involvement of the Bureau of Immigration staff with members of other faiths on joint panels, such as the one which took place on February 17, 1937, at the 92nd Street Young Men's Hebrew Association in Manhattan on the subject "The Threat to Deport Aliens." On the dais was Congressman Celler, Cecelia Razovsky, and Bureau representative Thomas Mulholland.

33. Cf., Eric D'Arcy, "The Logic and Meaning of the Dictum: 'Error Has No Rights,'" in *Thomistica Morum Principia: Communicationes v. Congressus*

Thomistici Internationalis, v. 3, ed. Charles Boyer (Rome: Catholic Book Agency, 1960), 287–297.

34. This is not the place to go into the particulars of canon law on these subjects, but for a contemporary study on them in light of the Pio-Benedictine Code of 1917, cf. Francis J. Schenck, *The Matrimonial Impediments of Mixed Religion and Disparity of Cult*, Canon Law Studies 51 (Washington, D.C.: Catholic University of America Press, 1929).

35. Cf. Ready to L. J. Kelly, April 22, 1938, in Archives of Catholic University, NCWC/USCCB, Office of the General Secretary, Box 83:7 (hereafter ACUA, NCWC/USCCB, OGS). On Evian, cf. *Proceedings of the Intergovernmental Committee, Evian, July 6th to 15th, 1938, Verbatim Record of the Plenary Meetings of the Committee*, n.p., 1938. Cf., also, S. Adler-Rudel, "The Evian Conference on the Refugee Question," *Leo Baeck Institute Year Book* 13 (1968): 235–276; Saul S. Friedman, *No Haven for the Oppressed* (Detroit: Wayne State University Press, 1973); and the special issue devoted to Evian in the *Annals of the American Academy of Political and Social Science* 203 (May 1939).

36. Cf. Ready to Archbishop Joseph Rummel, April 2, 1938 in ACUA, NCWC/USCCB, OGS, Box 83:7. Ready met with Undersecretary of State Sumner Welles, who informed him that "the effort as far as this country was concerned would be limited to already existing immigration quotas" and that there would be "no thought of asking Congress to extend the quotas."

37. Cf. Ready to Rummel, May 18, 1938, in ACUA, NCWC/USCCB, OGS, Box 83:7.

38. Cf. Rummel to Cardinal Samuel Stritch, October 7, 1938, recounting events of the summer of 1938, in ACUA, NCWC/USCCB, OGS, Box 83:8. Already in 1937, Berning wrote to NCWC Administrative Board Chairman Archbishop Edward Mooney of Detroit that the German bishops were grateful for the assistance lent to their people and that he had informed Cardinal Pacelli at the Secretariat of State of the American bishops' cooperation through its CCRG. Cf. "German Bishop Thanks U.S. Hierarchy for Aid to Catholic Emigrants," NCWC news release, August 7, 1937, in CMS, NCWC, BIA, Box 83.

39. Report submitted to the NCWC Administrative Board, October 10, 1938, in ACUA, NCWC/USCCB, OGS, Box 83:8. The report indicated that Ready had an audience with Pope Pius XI, who expressed "deep sorrow" over the plight of the refugees.

40. Cf. Telegram to Phillips, consul at the American Embassy in Rome, undated, and McDonald to Lord Cecil (of Chelwood), July 14, 1938, in Columbia University Rare Books and Manuscripts Library, James G. McDonald Papers, Box 1, Folder: P. 15: "Evian."

41. Cf. McDonald to Galeazzi, June 14, 1938, in Columbia University Rare Books and Manuscripts Library, James G. McDonald Papers, Box 1, Folder: P. 15: "Evian."

42. McDonald's legacy is only now becoming available to a wider public and his humanitarian work is given further contextualization through publication of the first volume of his diaries and papers. Cf. Richard Breitman, Barbara McDonald Stewart, and Severin Hochberg, eds. *Advocate for the Doomed: The Diaries and Papers of James McDonald, 1932–1935* (Bloomington: Indiana University Press, 2007).

43. Galeazzi's role at the papal court was probably as high as any ecclesiastic working in the Vatican and McDonald exploited this role to great effect. McDonald, in turn, gave Galeazzi—and through him the Secretariat of State—*entré* to important contacts in America, both in the Protestant press and at the Federal Council of Churches of Christ. Moreover, McDonald served as a conduit to significant Jewish leaders around the world. For instance, in a letter he wrote to Galeazzi from Paris, McDonald pointed to the mutual cause presented by the post-*Kristallnacht* crisis: "As I told you when I came to see you last Friday morning, it is a group of Jewish leaders in New York who can do the most to bring Catholics and Protestants together in a common front against statism which endangers all three of the great religious communities. What surprises me most is that among the leaders of the great religious groups there has seemed to be so little realization of the need for and possibility of common action in defense of freedom of religion, whether this be in Germany, Russia, or Mexico." Cf. McDonald to Galeazzi, January 28, 1939, in Columbia University Rare Books and Manuscripts Library, James G. McDonald Papers, Box 1, Folder: Catholic Church.

44. McDonald to Rummel, October 31, 1938, and September 27, 1938, in Columbia University Rare Books and Manuscripts Library, James G. McDonald Papers, Box 2, Folder: Rummel (1934–1959).

45. Report submitted to the NCWC Administrative Board, October 10, 1938, in ACUA, NCWC/USCCB, OGS, Box 83:8.

46. Cf. McDonald to Taylor, November 11, 1938, in Columbia University Rare Books and Manuscripts Library, James G. McDonald Papers, Box 2, Folder: Taylor, Myron C. (1941–1953).

47. McDonald to Rummel, November 11, 1938, in James G. McDonald Papers, Columbia University Rare Books and Manuscripts Library, James G. McDonald Papers, Box 2, Folder: Taylor, Myron (1941–1953).

48. Cf. Donald Warren, *Radio Priest: Charles Coughlin, the Father of Hate Radio* (New York: Free Press, 1996), 109–110. Among the most comprehensive and damning publications on Coughlin's communications was a pamphlet designed to give rebuttal. See, General Jewish Council, "Father Coughlin: His 'Facts' and Arguments," (New York, 1939). Mussolini published a decree forbidding marriage of "Italian Aryans" with persons of "another race" on November 10, 1938. This further fomented antipathy between Mussolini and Pope Pius XI, who would be felled by consecutive heart attacks two weeks later. See further Frank Coppa, "Pope Pius XI's 'Encyclical' Humani Generis Unitas Against Racism and Anti-Semitism

and the 'Silence' of Pope Pius XII," *Journal of Church and State* 40:4 (1998): 775–795.

49. In addition to his work for the AJC and the Jewish Joint, Strauss was the president of Temple Emanu-El in New York, the largest Jewish congregation in America at the time. At this time he was partner in the banking house Kuhn, Loeb, and later became the head of the Atomic Energy Commission.

50. Cf. Strauss Papers, (P-632): Box 31.

51. McDonald to Strauss, November 21, 1938, in Columbia University Rare Books and Manuscripts Library, James G. McDonald Papers, Box 1, Folder: Strauss, Lewis L (1934–1959).

52. Cf. the correspondence in January 1939 that McDonald carried on with Dr. Samuel McRae Cavert, director of the Federal Council of Churches of Christ. McDonald praised Cavert for being such a positive leader against what McDonald termed "extreme totalitarian statism" in both Mexico and Germany and encouraged him to stand with Catholics at this precarious time. Cf. McDonald to Cavert, January 28, 1939, in Columbia University Rare Books and Manuscripts Library, James G. McDonald Papers, Box 1, Folder: Catholic Church.

53. Cf. Columbia University Rare Books and Manuscripts Library, James G. McDonald Papers, Box 1, Folder: Baerwald, Paul (1934–1961): Lazaron to Baerwald, November 30, 1938: "My dear friend: I noticed in the paper this morning a dispatch from London in which the following statement occurred: 'With new life injected into the proceedings, the inter-governmental committee on refugees will resume work Friday on the problem of getting 600,000 Jews out of Germany.' May I suggest the advisability of asking James McDonald to contact authorities in the Associated Press, United Press and International News Service requesting that in any dispatches referring to the situation the phrasing should be 'Christian and Jewish refugees'? I am sure the advisability of taking this step is obvious to you. These agencies can use the phrase 'Christian and Jewish refugees' in all of their dispatches. This would do a number of things: it will reveal the truth of the situation; it will make proper impression by repetition upon the American conscience; it will serve to counteract any propaganda that the situation is purely a Jewish problem. I think it much better that Mr. McDonald's committee take this step rather than that the American Jewish Committee should do it." McDonald replied to Lazaron, December 7, 1938: "Dear Rabbi Lazaron: Mr. Baerwald has forwarded to me your letter to him of November 30, and I enclose a copy of my communication to the United Press, Associated Press, and International News Service to show that I have complied with your suggestion. Thanks for calling the matter to our attention."

54. Cf. statistical summary of activities in the first three fiscal years of the CCRG's existence in CMS, NCWC BIA, General Correspondence, Box 9.

55. Leo House continues to operate on West 23rd Street in Manhattan.

56. CMS, NCWC, BIA, General Correspondence, Box 13.

57. Letter of "SW" [?] to Mohler, November 5, 1938, in CMS, NCWC, BIA, Box 83.

58. CMS, NCWC, BIA, General Correspondence, Box 23.

59. "Mystical Body of Christ," CMS, NCWC, BIA, General Correspondence, Box 83.

60. Mohler to Ready, April 2, 1938, in ACUA, NCWC/USCCB, OGS, Box 83:7.

61. Strauss Papers (P-632), Box 5, file: Henry Ittleson-Rosenwald, Wm. 1938. The "JDC" refers to the Joint Distribution Committee; the "UP" is the "United Palestine Appeal"; "Co-ordinating" refers to the Coordinating Foundation. My thanks to Richard Libowitz of St. Joseph's University, Diane Spielmann of the Center for Jewish History, and Adina Anflick of the American Jewish Historical Society for clarification of these abbreviations.

62. James Rosenberg to Lewis L. Strauss, October 24, 1938, in Strauss Papers (P-632): Box 5, file: Henry Ittleson-Rosenwald, Wm. 1938. On the function of the "Survey Committee," cf. memorandum dated January 14, 1938, in Strauss Papers (P-632): Box 41, folder: 1938.

63. News clipping attached to the letter of James Rosenberg to Lewis L. Strauss, October 24, 1938, in Strauss Papers (P-632): Box 5, file: Henry Ittleson-Rosenwald, Wm. 1938. Rosenberg was a confidant of, among others, Sen. Robert Wagner and helped lobby for the Wagner-Rogers bill to allow German Jewish children entrance into the United States.

64. A characterization made by Robert A. Divine, *The Reluctant Belligerent: American Entry into World War II* (New York: John Wiley and Sons, 1965), 55, and cited in David M. Kennedy, *Freedom from Fear: The American People in Depression and War, 1929–1945* (New York: Oxford University Press, 1999), 419.

65. Kennedy, *Freedom from Fear*, 413. Much of the problem related to émigrés had to do with the amount of wealth one could take with them. The Nazi government had restricted the sum to a paltry amount, creating instantaneous destitution for most Jews desirous of leaving. Even in the days following Kristallnacht, when it was apparent to all that Jews were being targeted, President Roosevelt maintained that quotas would not be relaxed for this particular group of Germans.

66. Kennedy, *Freedom from Fear*, 417.

67. Samuel Untermyer, *"No Pasaran" (They Shall Not Pass): Religion Answers the Nazi Challenge: Address of Samuel Untermyer Before the Temple and Synagogue Brotherhoods at Baltimore, Md., December 19, 1937* (New York: 1938), 1–32. Untermyer was, until 1938, head of the "Non-Sectarian Anti-Nazi League to Champion Human Rights." Cf. Richard Hawkins, "'Hitler's Bittersweet Foe': Samuel Untermyer and the Boycott of Nazi Germany, 1933–1938," *American Jewish History* 93:1 (March 2007): 21–50.

68. Cf., Jim Forest, *Love is the Measure: A Biography of Dorothy Day* (rev. ed. Maryknoll: Orbis Press, 2002), 73–74.

69. These policies have been examined in considerable detail. See, for example, Robert L. Beir, *Roosevelt and the Holocaust: A Rooseveltian Examines the Policies and Remembers the Times* (Fort Lee, NJ: Barricade Books, 2006); Vicki Caron, *Uneasy Asylum: France and the Jewish Refugee Crisis, 1933–1942* (Stanford: Stanford University Press, 1999); Maurice Davie, *Refugees in America* (New York: Harper and Brothers, 1947); Henry L. Feingold, *The Politics of Rescue: The Roosevelt Administration and the Holocaust, 1938–1945* (New York: Holocaust Library, 1980); Walter Laquer, *Generation Exodus: The Fate of Young Jewish Refugees from Nazi Germany* (Hanover and London: Brandeis University Press, published by University Press of New England, 2001); Louise London, *Whitehall and the Jews, 1933–1948: British Immigration Policy, Jewish Refugees, and the Holocaust* (New York: Cambridge University Press, 2000); Michael Marrus, *The Unwanted: European Refugees in the Twentieth Century* (New York: Oxford University Press, 1985); *Rescue Attempts During the Holocaust: Proceedings of the Second Yad Vashem International Historical Conference, Jerusalem, April 8–11, 1984* (Jerusalem: Yad Vashem, 1977); Robert Rosen, *Saving the Jews: Franklin D. Roosevelt and the Holocaust* (New York: Thunder's Mouth Press, 2006); A. J. Sherman, *Island Refuge: Britain and Refugees from the Third Reich, 1933–1939* (Berkeley: University of California Press, 1973).

70. On Evian, one might first consult the official record: *Proceedings of the Intergovernmental Committee, Evian, July 6th to 15th, 1938, Verbatim Record of the Plenary Meetings of the Committee*, n.p., 1938. Cf., also, S. Adler-Rudel, "The Evian Conference on the Refugee Question," *Leo Baeck Institute Year Book* 13 (1968): 235–276; Saul S. Friedman, *No Haven for the Oppressed* (Detroit: Wayne State University Press, 1973); and the special issue devoted to Evian in the *Annals of the American Academy of Political and Social Science* 203 (May 1939).

71. Razovsky was born in St. Louis in 1891. From 1920 to 1932 she was secretary of the immigrant aid department of the National Council of Jewish Women. Razovsky was involved with the famed "St. Louis" incident in which a ship carrying hundreds of German Jews was turned away from Cuba and the United States. In the aftermath of the war, Razovsky was a resettlement supervisor for those in the displaced persons camps. She died in 1968.

72. Ostermann to Mohler, November 4, 1938, in CMS, NCWC, BIA, Box 13: Cuba.

73. Pierre Blet, *Pius XII and the Second World War According to the Archives of the Vatican*, trans. Lawrence J. Johnson (Mahwah: Paulist Press, 1999), 141.

74. Ibid. I pass over the question this comment immediately generates, namely, should the Jewish organizations have been aware of the plight of formerly religiously Jewish non-Aryan Catholics, and what was the obligation owed to them in any case? Blet indicates the following starting

point for the Holy See in response to the refugees: "A first step on their behalf was a circular letter dated 30 November 1938 and sent to the pope's representatives in North and South America, Africa, the Near East, and Ireland in order to obtain means of subsistence for Jews who were forced to leave their homelands. Then, early in January 1939, another circular letter was sent to the archbishops of free countries; it invited these prelates to create national relief committees whose purpose would be to assist non-Aryan Catholics." Ibid., 141–142. In fact, in the United States, the American bishops did not wait for permission from the Vatican to pursue its own relief agenda.

75. Cf. "German Bishop Thanks U.S. Hierarchy for Aid to Catholic Emigrants," NCWC news release, August 7, 1937, in CMS, NCWC, BIA, Box 83.

76. This was not the first time that Groesser made himself known to Mohler and the NCWC. Already, in November 1936, he was alerting Mohler by letter to the anticipated movement of large numbers of Catholics out of Germany. Groesser had drafted a memorandum, which Mohler then relayed to Monsignor Michael Ready, the NCWC General Secretary, who placed it before the bishops at their November meeting. The result was the bishops' agreement to form the CCRG. Cf. Mohler's "Memorandum for the Record," November 17, 1936, in CMS, NCWC, BIA, Box 24: Groesser.

77. Cf. George Timpe to Mohler, March 10, 1937, in CMS, NCWC, BIA, Box 24: Groesser.

78. Cf. Mulholland to Mohler, December 22, 1937, referring to a *New York Times* article of the same date, "Priest Jailed in Reich." In CMS, NCWC, BIA, Box 24: Groesser. Inquiries were immediately made with the German ambassador, who offered placating words. Mohler returned Mulholland's favor with the following testimony: "It certainly is interesting to note that Father Groesser now is criticized from both sides. In the United States they classed him as being pro-Nazi; in Germany they arrest him, apparently for anti-Nazi activities. Whenever a man is so definitely pigeonholed by both sides one might readily believe that his actions were pretty nearly correct." Cf. Mohler to Mulholland, December 24, 1937, in CMS, NCWC, BIA, Box 24: Groesser. Groesser would remain in jail for months, until he died in his cell in Berlin in March 1940 of "unknown causes."

79. Spicer, *Resisting the Third Reich*, 107.

80. According to Spicer, "the real heart of the *Hilfswerk* was Dr. Margarete Sommer, a devout Catholic laywoman who courageously risked her life to run the *Hilfswerk* throughout the Nazi years. She not only endeavored to make sure that the *Hilfswerk* met the material and spiritual needs of those it assisted, but also built up a variety of contacts through which she gained extensive knowledge about the persecution, ghettoization, and murder of European Jews. At great personal danger, Sommer dauntlessly passed this information on to Preysing and his fellow bishops." Cf. Spicer, *Resisting*

the Third Reich, 132. Spicer then notes that it is "significant" that von Preysing established the Hilfswerk prior to *Reichkristallnacht* (November 9–10, 1938), but he is vague about why. In my view, it is significant precisely because the situation was getting utterly desperate and it was hoped that such a move might prevent future problems. It anticipated making links to overseas aid agencies like the NCWC. On the Hilfswerk's efforts, Wolfgang Knauft, "Einsatz für verfolgte Juden, 1938–1945: Das Hilfswerk beim Bischöflichen Ordinariat Berlin," *Stimmen der Zeit* 206 (1988): 591—603, and Michael Phayer, *Protestant and Catholic Women in Nazi Germany* (Detroit: Wayne State University Press, 1990), 204; Lutz-Eugen Reutter, *Die Hilfstätigkeit katholischer Organisationen und kirchlicher Stellen für die im nationalsozialistischen Deutschland Verfolgten* (Hamburg: Universität Hamburg, 1969); Lutz-Eugen Reutter, *Katholische Kirche als Fluchthelfer im Dritten Reich: Die Betreuung von Auswanderern durch den St. Raphaels-Verein* (Recklinghausen-Hamburg: Paulus, 1971).

81. Mohler to Ostermann, January 3, 1939, with memorandum of Mohler to Ready, December 30, 1938, in CMS, NCWC, BIA, box 13: Cuba.

82. CMS, NCWC BIA, General Correspondence, Box 8. It may be noted that several cases of assistance were handled that included Jewish families or individuals, which were usually brought to the attention of the NCWC by the Apostolic Delegate, Archbishop (later Cardinal) Amleto Cicognani.

83. CMS, NCWC BIA, General Correspondence, Box 9.

84. Perhaps the best statistical breakdown on the destinies of the refugees of Europe are to be found in Noakes, cited supra n. 6 and n. 18, as well as Rubenstein, *The Myth of Rescue,* esp. chapter 2, "The Myth of Closed Doors, 1933–1939."

85. Cf. von Dirksen's comment in *Documents on German Foreign Policy* (Washington, D.C.: United States Government Printing Office, 1949), Series D, v. 5, 908.

86. I pass over an enormous literature on intercontinental antisemitism, though one may consult with profit Doris Bergen, "Catholics, Protestants, and Christian Antisemitism in Nazi Germany," *Central European History* 27:3 (September 1994): 329–348.

CHAPTER 6

KRISTALLNACHT: THE AMERICAN ULTRA-ORTHODOX JEWISH THEOLOGICAL RESPONSE*

GERSHON GREENBERG

The responses to Kristallnacht by American-Jewish ultra-Orthodox thinkers established the fact that the shocking event would be confronted theologically, and that attempts would be made to absorb it into the structures and themes of religious thought. Their responses set the stage for the Jewish religious thought that responded to the catastrophe over the course of the war. Ultra-Orthodox Jewish thought through the Holocaust moved away from rational attempts to understand the catastrophe or to align the catastrophe with history. Instead, it moved onto the plane of metahistory.[1] That perspective dealt with the higher reality of covenantal relationship between God and the people of Israel, which was reflected in time-space historical events. The ultra-Orthodox thinkers placed a ring of silence around rational and historical deliberations, and then looked to traditional literature, believed to be rooted in divine revelation, for explanations. Both a source for ideas and a source for vitality and life itself, this literature became the basis for a wide variety of deliberations in the ghettos and towns of Nazi-occupied Europe, in Palestine, in America, and in England. Often, the deliberation was the final testimony of the author before his community and before God, the articulation and epitome of his spiritual being. The texts that have been discovered, identified so far by the scholarship, include many of the themes that began to be articulated with Kristallnacht: The identification of Nazi persecution with the realm of profanity, personalized over the course of Israel's metahistory by the likes of Haman; the growing catastrophe as an ultimate confrontation between the sacred and the profane, which would culminate in redemption; the instrumentalizing of Hitler by God to force the people of Israel back to their Torah-true selves; the culpability of assimilationist and secularist Jews for breaching the line between the sacred and the profane, releasing a latent hatred for Israel, and turning a cold war into a hot war; the suffering of the pious as unavoidable collateral damage of the punishment of Israel's sinners by God through the Nazi persecutor; the idea that such a calamity, so unnatural, could not have been produced by human hands alone; the nature of Israel's metahistory as an ongoing cyclical dynamic of ascent-descent-ascent; Israel's ability to have the troubles recede through prayer, fasting, and good deeds, and by unifying the nation, renewing Torah, penitent return to God, and restoring the Land of Israel (While Israel suffered disasters before, the characteristics and depth of the current calamity was unprecedented); Finally, the conviction that Kabbalistic dramas of the apocalypse were now under way.[2]

1. EASTERN EUROPEAN RESPONSES

Ultra-Orthodox Jewish thinkers in America identified themselves religiously with their brethren-in-religion in Europe, in the Land of Israel, and in communities across the globe. While they certainly related to the American context, their religious grounding remained universal. There was also a personal factor to the identity. Many of the teachers, fellow students, and family members of American ultra-Orthodox thinkers were in Europe and the Land of Israel. Accordingly, it is appropriate to introduce American reactions with those in Europe and the Land of Israel.

Eliezer Gershon Fridenzon, who died in the Warsaw Ghetto in the spring of 1943, served as the editor of *Beit Ya'akov*, a journal addressed to the Beit Ya'akov schools and Benot Agudat Yisrael organizations in Poland. He responded to the disaster on apocalyptic and metahistorical levels. In his first reaction (November 24–December 22, 1938), he wrote that the events of Kristallnacht constituted a volcanic eruption of barbaric, primitive evil that swallowed up Germany's culture, scientific study, and art. It was evil's last convulsion as it faced total destruction. Like a death-head (*toytn kop*), it rose from its grave to see the light of the world one more time before disappearing forever, and performed a "good-bye" dance of dread, insanity, murder, robbery, and sadistic torture (*kedei nokh ayn mol 'oyf a gezegnung' optsutantsen ir heslikhn imhdikn meshuga'im-tants*). The death-head mocked and spit at the majestic image of God—as it faced its black end. This was the Amalek (Israel's paradigmatic enemy; see, e.g., Deuteronomy 25:17–19) of darkness, in his inevitably losing battle with the light of God. The apocalyptic struggle involved a response by the people of Israel. Just as once he destroyed the Temple in Jerusalem, so Amalek was now setting synagogues and *Batei midrash* aflame, and as the response then was to build the yeshiva in Yavneh, so it was now to cultivate Torah education.[3] In his second reaction (December 23, 1938–January 20, 1939), Fridenzon turned to the metahistorical framework of the covenant. Israel had mistakenly hearkened to other nations, and God responded justly. But there was also the promise of hope under divine providence. Fridenzon held Jewish assimilationists responsible:

> The reformers [i.e., proponents of Reform Judaism] as well as all sorts of assimilators have been immersing themselves into [the world of] Gentile Germans, with thoughts of remaining forever bonded with anything German, every possible way, and that their position would be as solidly secure as that of the Germans themselves. . . . Thousands have been torn from their Jewish roots, having served the German "Molokh" of culture, scientific study and art. . . . Blindly, they have continued to dance the wild devil's dance of Jewish self-denial. And the punishment has arrived . . . a punishment of providence.

At the same time, the very presence of God, evidenced by Kristallnacht as divine retribution, gave reason to hope—"our consolation and hope for a better tomorrow." The God who punished, for Fridenzon, was the God who redeemed.

The punishment extended to pious Jews. The Nazis, who meted out the divine punishment, made no distinction between one Jew and the other (see Rashi ad Exodus 12:22). Beyond this, as the punishment belonged to divine providence, collective Israel was responsible for the sins of any individual Jew—for "all Israel are a surety for each other" (NumR., Parashah 10, Siman 5). Fridenzon stressed that it broke his heart to speak these words, let alone before the blood even dried. But not to speak would be worse and held more danger than did the horrible events themselves. Jews had to be awakened to the consequences of the great sin of falling blindly into the arms of strangers. Fridenzon wondered whether the Jews in England and America were learning anything from the historical tragedy that had befallen German Jews.[4]

In a letter issued on January 3, 1939, the Admor of Bobov, Bentsiyon Halberstam (1873–1941), observed that the expulsion of Jews from their countries of residence in the wake of Kristallnacht left them with nothing and subjected them to torrents of fury—all this was taking place during the very same enlightened era when people believed in the natural compassion and uprightness of the human being. This could not be explained in natural terms, and had to be under God and authorized by God:

> We believe in full faith that the creator Himself, may His name be blessed, has made, does make, and will make all events. Further, anything which befalls a nation or an individual belongs to providence, as does the substance of any worldly occurrence. This present generation is proud and boastful of the enlightenment which has spread its wings in all lands. The [enlightenment] has refined human nature to be sympathetic and righteous, and even compassionate towards animals. Who would believe that could become so cruel, so suddenly? Like ostriches in the wilderness [Lamentations 4:3], slaughtering the righteous, father and son, innocent weanlings? Does this not make us realize that this is not a matter of natural law or judgment?

Given the fact that the tribulations were from God, Halberstam (like Fridenzon) had reason to hope:

> We may draw balm and healing for our pain from [the plight itself]. The saboteurs of the vineyard [see Song of Songs] are authorized [to act by God]. This implies (le'umat zeh) that sudden salvation will come suddenly from above: 'Hide thyself for a little moment, until the indignation be over past' [Isaiah 26:20] and the light of Israel will arise.

Halberstam grounded his dialectical thinking on the fact that Israel's history was by nature one of descent and ascent. The people of Israel have undergone terrible persecutions and attempts to annihilate them. There was the rabbinic sage Akiva (50–135 CE) and his colleagues, their skin flayed while they were still alive, the Chmielnitsky pogroms of 1648–1649, and the Vienna expulsion (presumably that of 1690). In *Midrash Talpiyot*, Halberstam continued, the author Elijah ben Solomon Abraham Hakohen of Smyrna (1650–1779) wrote of tens of thousands of infants being buried alive and of the earth throbbing for three days from their convulsions, and of torturers pushing their hands into the wombs of pregnant women, mocking an examination for propriety according to biblical prescription (*Kashrut*).[5] But the Zohar declared that whenever there was suffering it was followed by the good (Zohar, Helek 3, Ki Tissa 188[b]), and the midrash stated, "Israel will always ascend from the lowest degradation" (ExodR., Parashah 1, Siman 9). In the current era, Halberstam concluded, recovery assumed the apocalyptic dimension of passage from the "footsteps of the messiah" (*Ikveta dimeshiha*) to redemption. To the extent that Israel recognized this dialectical process and remained confident about it, the people could endure the agony. As Halberstam said, "For our soul is bowed down to the dust; our belly cleaveth unto the earth. Arise for our help, and redeem us for Thy mercy's sake" (Psalms 44:26–27).

What was Israel's role? Jews must be charitable:

> Take pity on the unfortunate, support them as much as possible, until the time comes for their release from prison. God will recompense well the generous of the nation, those who extend a hand to the unfortunate through the present time. May their reward be total. One should not tire of giving. Those who have not yet fulfilled their obligations should open their hand in a spirit of generosity. The rich should increase their giving. The poor should not lessen their acts of grace (*Hesed*), each according to ability. As this was the era of *Ikveta dimeshiha*, we need to make the greatest effort to increase philanthropy (*Gemilut hasadim*), the third of the three pillars upon which the world stands.

Further, there must be greater piety in terms of biblical commandments (*Mitsvot*) and the relationship to God: "Our entreaty to God cannot be merely sanctimonious. Let us search our ways to improve our hearts concerning Him, to walk in all His ways, and to observe His *Mitsvot* with entire heart and desiring soul."[6]

Ikveta dimeshiha was also invoked by "B-n" in the *Beit Ya'akov* journal of March 21–April 18, 1939. The sufferings of *Ikveta dimeshiha* were so terrible that the rabbinic sages of the Talmudic era said, "Let [the sufferings of the messiah] come; but let me not see him" (b. Sanhedrin 98[b]). But they would be followed by the *Tikkun* (mending). Israel's participation was required for understanding the process under way and of performing *Teshuvah* (penitent return to God). "B-n" viewed the dynamic of suffering and messianic relief in atemporal, metaphysical terms, as distinct from linear-historical or metahistorical (Fridenzon and Halberstam). The dynamic was a secret ingredient of God's creation, a single, transcending relationship that revealed itself in a variety of contexts—for example, persecution of the *Asarah harugei malkhut* (the ten martyrs during the reign of the Roman emperor Hadrian, 117–138 c.e.) and now, Kristallnacht. Apprehension of the secret dynamic enabled one to see that current events mirrored other such passages, and that now it belonged to an eschatological movement from troubles to *Tikkun*. Otherwise, recognizing the infinite depth of divine thought, and the humanly incomprehensible character of God's direction of the world, the proper response was silence.[7]

In Vilnius, Hayim Ozer Grodzensky shared the belief that the troubles belonged to a metahistorical transition, one which carried the eschatological, apocalyptic dimension of passing from exile (darkness) to redemption (light). He focused on assimilation, which was the catalyst for the persecution, and the necessity of *Teshuvah*. In the hours following Kristallnacht, on November 10, 1938, Grodzensky spoke of the desperate situation of Jews on the Polish border. Expelled from Germany, the doors of the world were also shut to them. The people of Israel could do nothing to dissipate the enemy's rage, but they did have the power to change themselves. They must turn to God, rely upon Him ("Upon whom is it for us to rely? Upon our father, who is in heaven", b. Sotah 49^b), and perform *Teshuvah*. The midrash asked: "Why are Israel likened to sheep [Jeremiah 50:17]? Just as with a lamb, whose limbs feel pain from anywhere in the body, so with Israel. If only one of the people sins, all the people feel it" (LevR., Parashah 4, Siman 6). Each Jew must feel the pain of the other, and help the other, and provide bread to the hungry (Isaiah 58:7). Jews also must pray, and Grodzensky pleaded to God to bring the light of salvation to those who remained hopeful (*Asurei tikvah*). Thus, while the people could not bring about change through empirical means (of time and space), they could bring change through the metahistorical relationship with God, in terms of *Teshuvah*, charity, and prayer.[8]

In his May 31, 1939, statement, Grodzensky responded to the inflagration of houses of learning, and Torah scrolls, to relentless decrees, and to the plight of thousands of Jews who remained on the German-Polish border and were threatened with death. The current crisis was worse than Israel's medieval tribulations or the Chmielnitski pogroms. For the faith of those Jews that God would not abandon his people, which assured divine presence (the *Shekhinah*), was now absent. The assimilation and reform in Western Europe generated (*umisham yatsah*) persecution and expulsion, and the poisonous hatred (assimilation and persecution combined) was spreading eastward. Faith, expressed in terms of Torah and *Mitsvot* (Sabbath, *Kashrut*, family sanctity), was missing—precluding the understanding that the persecution, under God, resulted from assimilation. Nor did the people have the spiritual strength to endure. As in his November 10 statement, Grodzensky declared that the response to the distress had to be reliance on God and *Teshuvah* (Deut 4:29–30). *Teshuvah* was to take the form of strengthened Torah and *Mitsvot*, and of instilling the faith needed to endure. Then, not only would the tribulation be contained. Redemption itself would be evoked.[9]

These Eastern European reactions to Kristallnacht unfolded on the plane of metahistory. Fridenzon attributed the disaster of Kristallnacht to assimilation and the divine response to it, through the Nazi persecution. He paired this metahistorical interpretation with an apocalyptic, dualist battle between darkness (Amalek) and light, which terminated with the demise of evil; two processes, side by side, with metahistory enveloped by the apocalyptic drama. Halberstam could find no natural explanation and turned to God. Insofar as it was all under God, one could hope for relief. He articulated a metahistorical dialectic, in which the people of Israel's decline implied ascent, which culminated in the eschatological as well as apocalyptic transition from *Ikvetah dimeshihah* to redemption. Israel must endure as it always had, and concentrate on intensifying its relationship with God and performing *Mitsvot* and charitable acts. "B-n" identified the descent-ascent dynamic as a secret of creation. It was a metaphysical, rather than metahistorical matter, revealing itself in different contexts; an ongoing transtemporal passage from suffering to eschatological *Tikkun*. Grodzensky turned to metahistory, to the covenantal relationship with God. Pleading to God for help, and performing *Teshuvah* and charity, he was convinced, would affect historical events. Like Fridenzon, he tied the disaster to assimilation, and attributed the correlation to divine providence. Grodzensky despaired over the breakdown in Israel's faith, which blocked both comprehension of what was happening (in metahistorical terms) and the belief in the presence of God, which in turn assured God's presence. As for Fridenzon, Halberstam, and "B-n," the metahistorical process would become sublimated into the *Ikveta dimeshiha*.

2. PALESTINE

The Chief Rabbi of Tel Aviv, Mosheh Avigdor Amiel (1882–1946), echoed themes articulated in Eastern Europe: The troubles were not natural (Halberstam), they resulted from assimilation (Fridenzon, Grodzensky), and Israel did not have the Torah-faith resources to respond (Grodzensky).[10] Amiel wrote that the nations' hatred toward Israel and their intent to obliterate the Jews, coupled with the tacit approval or praise of other nations, had no natural or human explanation. The reason was to be found within the metahistorical arena of Israel's covenantal relationship with God. He said, "If a man sees that powerful sufferings visit him, let him examine his conduct" (b. Berakhot 5ª). Upon examination, the cause was obvious: assimilation. Judaism in Germany gave birth to the Reform movement; Reform led to assimilation, and assimilation to conversion to Christianity. The grandchildren and great-grandchildren of the reformers of 150 years ago converted; and the decline of Judaism over the 25 years since First World War was precipitous. The history of assimilation correlated with persecution from outside—for which Amiel found a precedent in the Jewish experience in Spain. Instead of the much-sought-after equal rights, the Jews got Hitler's doctrine of race (*Torat hageza*) and the intent to destroy, murder, and eliminate them (Esther 3:13).

Amiel cited Meir Simhah of Dvinsk (1845–1926), who identified a pattern where Jews entered a strange land, Torah became abandoned, and persecution followed. There were those who now thought of Berlin as Jerusalem, and Meir Simhah predicted that a whirlwind would come and uproot them into distant lands. While Meir Simhah believed that as in the past the people of Israel returned to Torah following their troubles, they would now return to their sacred values, Amiel remained pessimistic. In the past, suffering evoked the strengthening of Torah. The Mishnah, for example, was composed by Rab in the face of Israel's increasing troubles, and Rabina and Rav Ashi edited the Talmud in response to the nation's distress. Rashi (Rabbi Shelomoh Yitshaki, 1040–1105), the *Ba'alei hatosafot* (the Tosafists, medieval Talmud commentators), and Yehudah Halevi (1075–1141) all produced their great work in dangerous times, and the Zohar itself appeared in a troubled era. In this sense, the sufferings fell under the rubric of "sufferings of love" (b. Berakhot 5[a]). In the present time Jews and their Torah were under attack, but the Jews were not returning to Torah. In the past, when Torah was attacked ("What is the reason that you go forth to be stoned? Because I circumcised my son. What is the reason that you go forth to be burned? Because I have kept the Sabbath"; LevR., Parashah 32, Siman 1), the Jew had the ability to look down upon the oppression from the spiritual heights. He could annul the reality (*Bitul ha'yesh*) that negated Torah—for example, Hannah and her seven sons (see II Maccabees, ch. 7). Consciously or subconsciously, the persecutor would sense it. Not so now. Sufferings continued, with no Torah-spiritual response. The question, "How doth the city sit solitary?" (Lamentations 1:1) was not being asked; no one cried out to heaven asking "Why?" And without the questions being asked, Jews did not feel the need for *Teshuvah* ("Turn Thou us unto Thee, O Lord, and we shall be turned; renew our days as of old. Thou canst not have utterly rejected us, and be exceeding wroth against us"; Lamentations 5:21–22). The ability to endure and even turn back the suffering, drawn from Torah-faith, was missing.[11]

Amiel's response was mirrored by Y. A. Dvorkes in the journal *Diglenu: Bita'on Tenuat Hanoar Ha'agudati Be'erets Yisrael* in April 1939. The inhumanity, barbarism, and immorality of Germany, precisely in an era of cultural advance, was a coincidence between assimilation with quest for civil rights and the troubles. All this pointed to metahistorical explanations. Citing "Punishment comes into the world only on Israel's account" (b. Yebamot 63ᵃ), Dvorkes looked to Israel to set right its relationship to God. Israel had to perform *Teshuvah*, turning to God for God to turn to Israel: "My sons, present to me an opening of repentance no bigger than the eye of a needle, and I will widen it into openings through which wagons and carriages can pass" (Song of SongsR., Parashah 5, Siman 3).[12]

The dialectical relationship between ascent and descent, a metaphysical-level secret for "B-n," and the underlying dynamic of Israel's metahistory and eschatology for Halberstam, was also articulated in March 1939 by Bentsiyon Meir Hai Uziel (1880–1953), the Sephardi Chief Rabbi of British Mandate Palestine. Israel was the lone sheep, among 70 wolves (EstherR., Parashah 10, Siman 1), persecuted ever since the days of Pharaoh ("Omdim alenu lekhaloteinu," Haggadah Shel Pessah). But the people of Israel always survived and became revived, enduring the passage by its faith—that God was "true and faithful" ("Emet Ve'emunah," Tefillat Ma'ariv Lekhol), that there was power greater than worldly power (Psalms 33:16), and that God was "true and certain" ("Emet Ve'yatsiv," Tefillat Shaharit).[13]

Reuven Katz (1880–1963), the Chief Rabbi of Petah Tikvah, distinguished medieval and modern persecution. While in Spain and Portugal the intention was conversion to Christianity, the "contemporary Haman" blended religion into race, and conversion was not an option. Like Halberstam and Amiel, Katz pointed out that no natural explanation was possible specifically in a world where races were mixed, a racial attack on Israel made no sense. In the era of progress, of socialist and democratic government, the decree was issued to obliterate Judaism. In an era of great culture, the greatest tyrant in all of Israel's history arose against the nation. "Is all this meaningless? Do not such hard facts make us think? Is the higher hand not hidden in all this?" Without citing assimilation or any other sin, Katz identified the sufferings with God's love and intended to bring *Teshuvah*. In turn, the suffering and *Teshuvah* belonged to messianic redemption (Halberstam, "B-n," Grodzensky). The rabbinic sages asserted, Katz observed, that if the time came for redemption and Israel had not done *Teshuvah*, "God will set up a king over them, whose decrees shall be as cruel as Haman's, whereby Israel shall engage in *Teshuvah*" (b. Sanhedrin 97ᵇ), the sufferings serving as birth pangs of the messiah (*Hevlei mashiah*). The beast-man was out of control and the world was descending into a flood of fire, destruction, and obliteration. But the darkness implied light—just as the worst slavery in Egypt heralded redemption.[14]

3. AMERICA

Information about Kristallnacht reached the masses of ultra-Orthodox Jews in America, beginning November 11, 1938, through *Der Tog* and *Morgen Zshurnal-Togblat* dailies. [15] The editor of the monthly, *Hapardes Kovets rabani hodshi*, signaled that the tragedy would be absorbed on both levels, historical and metahistorical. He wrote in the November 24–December 22, 1938, issue that the disaster (*Shoah*) that Hitler and his murderers were inflicting upon German and Austrian Jews broke all limits of human behavior. Many of the 12,000 Jewish subjects of Poland, expelled from Germany and stranded on the German-Polish border, were being starved, tortured to death, and driven to insanity and suicide. Israel's sanctity was being shattered. Synagogues were being destroyed and Torah scrolls burned: "The evil Hitler vilifies and blasphemes the name of God and Israel, and decrees that the name of God be erased from the Tenakh. [Still,] we believe that Hitler's war against God will hasten his downfall." [16]

A. MORDEKHAI TSEVI SCHWARTZ

Several of the Eastern European and Palestinian motifs were mirrored in America. The perception that there was no natural explanation for the events (Halberstam, Amiel, Katz), the targeting of assimilation as the immediate cause of the disaster (Fridenzon, Grodzensky, Amiel), the conviction that Hitler was an instrument of the divine (Fridenzon, Katz), and the belief that *Teshuvah* could contain and alleviate the troubles ("B-n," Grodzensky, Dvorkes, Katz) were all present in the writings of Mordekhai Tsevi Schwartz. Schwartz served as *Av Beit Din* (head of religious court) in Tsh.[?] Cered (Transylvania), and then in London and in Hull. *Doresh Tov Le'amo*, which he published in London in 1917–1919, included approbations (*Haskamot*) from British rabbinical colleagues Avraham Yitshak Kook (then rabbi of Jaffa, Kook was stranded in Europe in First World War and officiated temporarily at Mahzikei Hadat synagogue), Shemaryahu Yitshak Blokh, Meir Tsevi Yung (1858–1921), Shmuel Yitshak Hilman (author of *Or Ha'yashar*, d. 1953) in London, and Yisrael Hayim Daykhes (1850–1937) in Leeds. Schwartz came to America that year, to serve as rabbi in Youngstown and Cleveland, Ohio. In *Derushei Hokhmah Veda'at*, responding to Kristallnacht and the May 1939 British *White Paper* addressed to British government policy on Palestine, he spoke of the unprecedented troubles, the tragic consequences of assimilation and reform, God's use of Hitler as instrument, *Teshuvah* and Torah as responses to catastrophe, and the imminence of redemption.

With tens of thousands of Jews homeless, synagogues being destroyed, Torah scrolls and rabbinic texts being burned, Jews imprisoned in concentration camps, and mothers being torn away from their children, Schwartz wrote, the tragedy was worse than anything since the middle ages. The abusive Nazis (*hanatsim hamenatsim*), devoid of human feeling and inherently hateful of Jews, have been assisted by the otherwise just and righteous nation of England—as if oblivious to its love for Tenakh. England shut its doors to Jews being expelled from Germany and Austria, leaving them to die from hunger and cold in no man's land. There was no natural explanation. How could some Austrian painter and low-ranked soldier, jailed in Germany for perverse activities, achieve such power in the enlightened German nation? How could he dissolve the *Reichstag*, annul state laws, dismiss judges and ministers at will, kill hundreds of army officers in a single night, and take over the treasury? The only explanation was that all this came from Heaven, from God. Schwartz cited: "Knowest thou not, that it is Heaven that has ordained this [Roman] nation to reign?" (b. Avodah Zarah 18[a]). The heavenly action was to be seen in terms of sin, punishment, and *Teshuvah*.

The people of Israel had sinned against Torah and violated *Mitsvot*. The crimes were compounded by obliviousness and somehow associated with past generations—in the spirit of transmigrating souls that kabbalists described (*gilgulim harishonim, kiferush hamekubalim*).[17] The Reform movement and other heretical behavior of Jews in Western Europe spread eastward (Grodzensky's point). There was assimilation, generated by Jewish attempts to ingratiate themselves to the Gentiles. Schwartz added a psychosocial dimension to the assimilation-persecution correlation. Violations of *Shabbat, Kashrut*, and family purity, the neglect of Torah study, and the rush into professions, seeking doctorates, all backfired, and Jewish property was stolen, Jews were beaten and placed into concentration camps. The neglect of Torah, the attempt to co-opt hatred through intimacy, generated only deeper enmity.[18] It was true, Schwartz conceded, that Jews would be hated whether or not they adhered to Torah. But assimilation served as a catalyst, without which the troubles might have been avoided. Once the assimilation took place, God entered into history with punishment to stop and reverse it. As a judgment from above, it was made on the basis of majority behavior and affected all Jews. Once God allowed the destroyer to injure Israel, no differentiation was left between the righteous and the wicked (Rashi ad Exodus 12:22). While the enemy served as His instrument, God hid His face (Deut 31:16–18). Schwartz identified contemporary perpetrators with Israel's archetypal enemies: Esau, Amalek, Haman. These enemies, rooted in the tree of the Garden of Eden, the source of evil (EstherR.,

Parashah 9, Siman 2), rose up against Israel over the generations ("Bekhol dor vedor," Haggadah shel Pesah) (as with Bentsiyon Meir Hai Uziel). They did so as divine instruments, to evoke *Teshuvah*—and have Israel cry out to God and return to Torah. The alternative to the life of Torah was suffering:

> The Holy One, blessed be He, overturned the mountain upon them like an inverted cask, and said to them, 'If you accept the Torah, 'tis well. If not, there shall be your burial.' Said Raba, 'Yet even so they reaccepted it in the days of Ahasuerus, for it is written that the Jews confirmed and took upon them' (Esther 9:27). That is, they confirmed that they had accepted long before (b. Shabbat 88ᵃ)

The intent of the suffering was to bring *Teshuvah*: "And when Pharaoh drew nigh. . . . He brought Israel nigh to the repentance which they showed" (ExodR., Parashah 21, Siman 5).

God would help. Once a Jew returned to God (Lamentations 3:40), God "dug an opening for his prayer from under the throne of glory" (EstherR. Parashah 9, Siman 7). Even more, Jews could then expect redemption (Midrash Shoher Tov: Tehillim. Perek 106, Siman 6) and that the nations would fall into catastrophe—the rabbinic sages observed that any catastrophe that came to the world was tied to Israel (b. Yebamot 63ᵃ). Without repentance Israel would never be redeemed:

> R. Eliezer said, If Israel repent they will be redeemed. If not, they will not be redeemed. R. Joshua said to him, If they do not repent they will not be redeemed. But the Holy One, blessed be He, will set up a king over them, whose decrees shall be cruel as Haman's. Whereby Israel shall engage in repentance, and he will thus bring them back to the right path (b. Sanhedrin 97ᵃ).[19]

The fact that Schwarz's motifs mirrored those abroad may be explained by the universal religious grounding of ultra-Orthodox Judaism. In addition, it is likely that he read *Ma'amar Ikveta Dimeshiha* (*Treatise on the Onset of the Messiah*), which Elhanan Wasserman of Baranowitch wrote and published during his 1938 sojourn in America. The body of the *Ma'amar* was completed before Kristallnacht—but when his son Simhah questioned the despairing conclusion, after Kristallnacht Wasserman added a few pages of a more optimistic nature. The *Ma'amar* was being studied in Baltimore synagogues. That it was well known was indicated by the fact that Wasserman asked Shimon Schwab (Baltimore) to publish a companion volume of sources (1941), and in the 1950s it was cited as proof of the connection between Zionism and Holocaust in New York yeshivas headed by Yitshak Hutner and by Mosheh Feinstein. Wasserman held that the disastrous events, the persecutions of Jews in Europe, constituted the darkness and evil that was to be purged for redemption to take place. The evil was internal (nationalism, religious, and secular; assimilation and *Haskalah* [Jewish enlightenment]; and the degradation of Torah and scholarship) and external (graduated persecution, measure-for-measure). The deeper the internal "Amalek," the deeper the external—the more Jews insinuated themselves into alien cultures, the harsher the repulsion. The persecution was the manifestation of divine wrath (Isaiah 10:5), in response to Israel's emulation of foreign cultures (Ezekiel 20:39). It would, Wasserman predicted, reach the point where Jews would become homeless, economically desperate, and dispersed to the point where not a single "kernel of corn" would remain in place after passing through the "sieve" (Amos 9:9). Israel could not stop the attacks from outside, as they came from God. All that was possible was to wait them out until Israel passed into the range of the absolutely persecuted—whereupon God would rescue His people (Deut 32:36).[20]

B. TOBIAS GEFEN

Tobias Gefen (1874–1970) framed Kristallnacht in empirically historical terms, and Hitler in political ones. The response he called for was to bring the different branches of Judaism together for united actions. He remained hopeful that the persecution would pass. Gefen studied at the Kovno and Slobodka yeshivas, and received rabbinical ordination in 1903 from Tsevi Hirsh Rabinovitch, Mosheh Doveshevski, and Ya'akov David Wilovsky (1845–1913, author of *Migdal David: Hidushim bekhamah inyanim bashas*). When pogroms broke out that year, he left for the United States. He served as rabbi in New York and Canton, Ohio, and then, beginning in 1910, in Atlanta—where he remained until his death.[21]

Gefen's religious thought absorbed the shock of Kristallnacht by drawing hope from rabbinic sources. In his November 19 sermon for the Torah portion Hayei Sarah, he recalled how Rabbi Akiva, lecturing to an audience despaired and weakened by the persecution of the Roman emperor Hadrian, instilled hope by recalling Esther's success in rescuing her people from Haman. Esther then reigned over 127 provinces—the number of years her archetype Sarah lived (GenR., Parashah 58, Siman 3). The week's Torah portion related that after Ephron reneged on his promise to Abraham of land as a gift, and he demanded 400 *Shekelim* for Sarah's burial plot, he became isolated as a leper (GenR., Parashah 58, Siman 7; Genesis 23:14-15). Gefen predicted that Hitler, who fined the victims $400 million for the Kristallnacht destruction, would also be driven into isolation: "He that hath an evil eye hasteneth after riches, and knoweth not that want shall come upon him" (Proverbs 28:22). FDR, Gefen added, already started the process. Gefen coupled his message of hope with a call for Jewish unity. To Hitler, all Jews were one; he did not distinguish one from the other. He identified Henryk Grynspan, who alone killed the minister von Rath, with all Jews—whom he then fined and murdered. For their part, Jews had to transcend the differences between Orthodox, Reform, and Conservative alignments and unify. As one, they must offer consolation, give charity, and prevail upon democratic countries to provide refuge. Then, God would end the captivity of His people. Gefen apparently remained hopeful through the war. When it ended in 1945, he wrote that the evil realm (*Sitra ahra*) had now fallen, and the world would not allow the blood of six million to be covered up (citing Psalms 79:10). With this he said, he could look forward to redemption (citing Ovadiah 1:21).[22]

C. MENAHEM RISIKOFF: THE ROLE OF THE PRIESTS

Menahem Risikoff (1868–1960) studied at the Slonim and Volozhin yeshivas and received rabbinical ordination from Shlomoh Kohen (Vilnius), Yosef Shlupfer (Slonim), Katriel Nathan (*Av Beit Din*, Augustov), and Eliyahu Adran (Grajewo). He published *Tiferet Menahem* on issues of ritual and ethics in 1894 in Vilna and, beginning in 1896, served as rabbi in Kazan (capital of the Tatarstan autonomous republic in Russia). He left for America when riots broke out in 1905 and served as rabbi in Ohev Shalom in Brooklyn until his death. Risikoff's works of responsa, Halakhic novellae, and biblical exposition (Derush) included *Divrei Menahem* (Grajewo 1910/11), *Sha'arei Zevah* (Jerusalem 1912/13), *Mitorat Tsevi Yosef* (New York 1926), *Sha'arei Ratson* (New York 1931), *Sha'arei Shamayim* (New York 1936/37), and *Sha'arei Mizrah* (place and date uncertain). There were numerous approbations, including ones by Avraham Yitshak Kook and Avraham Duber Kahana Shapira (Kovno).[23]

Precedents

Risikoff had a presentiment of the catastrophe. In his eulogy for Rav Kook, who was appointed Chief Ashkenazi Rabbi of Palestine in 1921 and died September 1, 1935, he explained that Kook's death could not be understood as a *Korban olah* (a Temple sacrifice where only ashes were left) that atoned for the generation's sins. For Rav Kook's greatness far exceeded the importance of the entire generation. The death rather fell under the category of "the righteous is taken away from the evil to come" (Isaiah 57:1). God let Abraham die, lest he live to see Esau's evil deeds. Now, knowing that Rav Kook's heart was too good and too tender to withstand the sorrow over the evils of anti-Semitism to come, God in His compassion (Habakkuk 3:2) took him to paradise immediately to enjoy the brilliance of His presence (the *Shekhinah*). Rav Kook died when he did, because God wished to spare him the suffering and punishment to come. As the rabbinic sages of the Talmudic era phrased it, "Let him [the sufferings of the messiah; see b. Sotah 49[b]] come, but let me not see him" (b. Sanhedrin 98[b]). Nor would God annul the pains of the messiah's birth, for they were indispensable to redemption, and redemption was not to be delayed.[24]

In his response to Kristallnacht, Risikoff spoke of the position of the priestly class, between history (below) and redemption (above). A decade earlier, he also spoke of such a position—although in a different sort of context. In his response to the 1929 pogroms in Hevron, Jerusalem, and Safed, when, he said, the souls of Torah students instilled with a spirit of holiness (*Ruah ha'kodesh*) were attacked by the profane ones (*Temeim*) and ascended to heaven like the soul of Isaac at the *Akedah*, there was, tragically, no mediator between Israel and God. In ancient days, when the Roman tyrant, quoting, "And he that stealeth a man and selleth him, or if he be found in his hand, he shall surely be put to death" (Exodus 21:6), declared that in the absence of those who sold their brother Joseph to an Ishmaelite caravan (Genesis 37:25), ten rabbis would atone for the sin, the ten martyrs during the reign of Hadrian asked for three days to ascertain if such atonement was decreed from heaven. If it was, they would submit to the decree—as it would be coming ultimately from the Merciful One. Then:

Trembling and shuddering, they directed their attention to Rabbi Ishmael, the High Priest, and asked him to pronounce God's name and ascend to learn whether the punishment was by divine decree. Rabbi Ishmael purified himself and reverently pronounced the name; he rose and inquired of one robed in linen, who said, 'Submit, beloved saints, for I have heard from behind the curtain that this would be your fate.' Rabbi Ishmael descended and told his colleagues the word of God. Thereupon the evil man commanded to slay [the ten] with force ("Eleh Ezkerah," Musaf Le'yom Kippur).

There were no such *Tsadikim* (pious ones) among the people of Israel now (1929) to mediate between heaven and earth, any *Tannaim* (teachers of the Talmudic era) who could, by the spirit of their mouths and lips, put the oppressors and scoundrels to death. Risikoff himself pleaded to God to accept the victims as sacrifices, as prayers of supplication for God to pour out His wrath upon the Gentiles ("Shefokh hamatekhah," Haggadah shel Pesah).[25]

Be'ita, Ahishena, Geulah

In *Palgei Shemen*, published after January 1939—although portions were completed already in 1912[26]—Risikoff expressed opposition to identifying the time of redemption. He cited Yitshak Ayzik Wildman (Haver) and *Av Beit Din* of *Shavel* (1789–1853), who reported that certain Jews expected redemption in 1839/40 but were ready to avoid despair should it not take place. For they knew that the messiah would surely come—whether according to human timing (*Be'ita*) or in a divine moment, an accelerated time that reaches timelessness (*Ahishena*) (b. Sanhedrin 98[a]). They would continue to wait for him daily. In fact, Wildman wrote, the moment of the end was to remain a secret until redemption was actual. It was a matter for God, and talking about it was useless (*dibur betelah habehirah*). As the rabbinic sages of the Talmudic era put it, "If the heart does not disclose its secrets to the mouth, how can the mouth disclose anything?" (Midrash Shoher Tov Tehillim, Parashah 9, Siman 2). R. Zera, for example, opposed those who talked publicly about the timing, and warned, "I beseech you, do not inherit a double *Gehinnom* [hell]" (b. Yoma 72[b]).[27]

But Risikoff did address the framework. The rabbinic sages distinguished *Be'ita* from *Ahishena*:

> R. Johanan also said, the son of David will come only in a generation that is either altogether righteous or altogether wicked. . . . R. Joshua b. Levi pointed out a contradiction: "It is written, the messiah will come in its time (*Be'ita*), while it is also written, I the Lord will hasten it (*Ahishena*). If they are worthy, I will hasten it (*Ahishena*). If not, the messiah will come at the end time (Be'ita)" (b. Sanhedrin 98[a]).

Risikoff brought the two together: The *Be'ita* would begin 300 years before the close of the sixth millennium and initiate a period for *Teshuvah* and purification through suffering. It would culminate with a nine-month period of intensified troubles and *Teshuvah*, followed by the *Ahishena* (in the month of *Av*), when the process would be accelerated to the extreme. Then, with the beginning of the seventh millennium, the Sabbath of the universe, ruled by God, would begin.[28] According to *Nahalat Ya'akov* by Ya'akov Avraham (d. 1699), the "*Perutah*" (a coin) and the "purse" ("Until the last *Perutah* has gone from the purse"; b. Sanhedrin 97[a]) referred respectively to holy sparks (*Nitsotsot*) and shards of vessels (*Kelippot*). *Perutah* was equivalent to 300 (*Pay*: 80 + *Resh*: 200 + *Vav*: 6 + *Tet*: 9 + *Hay*: 5), to 289 *Nitsotsot* plus two letters of God's name (*Yod* + *Hay* + *Vav* + *Hay*) amounting to 11 (*Hay*: 5 + *Vav*: 6). At a certain point the *Nitsotsot* would be liberated and purified of the *Kelippot*, leaving the now unnourished *Kelippot* to descend into oblivion, and the *Hay* and *Vav* to return to complete God's name ("God and His name would be one." Aleinu prayer). The process of purification resembled birth pains, lasting nine months. Those months would total 276 days, as indicated by "*Re'u*" (*Resh*: 200 + *Ayin*: 70 + *Vav*: 6) ("Lo it is yet high day, neither is it time that the cattle should be gathered together; water ye the sheep and feed them (*Re'u*)." Genesis 29:7). Calculating the 29-day and 30-day months of the annual calendar, the 276 total had to apply to the months *Kislev* through *Tammuz* (counting *Adar Alef* and *Adar Bet* as one month). During those nine months, the troubles would become so severe that with the coming of *Av*, lest Israel disappear completely, *Be'ita* would be transformed into *Ahishena*. Risikoff cited the situation in Egypt as an example: In an apparent reference to Isaiah Horowitz, *Shenei Luhot Haberit*, he observed that the children of Israel were rushed out (*Behipazon*) because they had already entered the forty-ninth gate of *Tumah* (profaneness, pollution) and were about to enter the fiftieth, where they would be lost hopelessly in *Tumah*. Risikoff attributed the concept of *Be'ita* to *Ahishena* transformation to the Besht (Ba'al Shem Tov Yisrael ben Eliezer, 1698–1760):

> There are [88] days in the [three] months leading up to *Kislev* [*Ellul*: 29, *Tishrei*: 30 and *Heshvan*: 29]. Then come the nine months [*Kislev* through *Tammuz*] cited in the *Gemara* (b. Sanhedrin 98[b]), ending with the [onset of the] month of *Av*. The Besht wrote, that the redemption would come speedily in our days, [at the onset of] the month of *Av*. . . . According to the Besht, what happens with *Be'ita* and *Ahishena* is this: The troubles [which accompany *Teshuvah*] during the 276 days become so difficult that it becomes impossible to endure them any longer. This impossibility is reflected by the fact that the *Be'ita* ends and *Ahishena* sets in [with the onset of] the month of *Menahem Av*. In Egypt the children of Israel were redeemed in a rush (*Behipazon*). Had they not been redeemed at that point, they would never be. It is a case of precluding any extension. Redemption will take place [at the onset of] the month of <u>Av</u> [starting when] *Be'ita* is transformed into *Ahishena*.[29]

The *Av* of *Ahishena*, the point of transition into the seventh millennium, would come, Risikoff believed, in 1939 (July 17–August 15, 1939). He cited a report in the daily *Morgen Zshurnal* of February 23, 1939, that the Besht himself cited *Av* 5699 as the moment for the fall of Nazism:

> *Mapuleh fun natsizm vet geshehn kumenden av layt ba'al shem's ketav yad. Spetsiele kaybel tsum morgen zshurnal. Varsha, dinstag-di idishe prese meldet, az men hot entdekt a nayes ketav-yad fun Ba'al Shem Tov, in velkhen es vert faroysgezagt dem oyfshtayg fun natsizm in oykh zayn mapuleh. Di mapule fun natsizm vet, layt dem ktav-yad, geshehn in hodesh av, 5699, das hayst dem kumenden yohr.*

The fall of Nazism will take place during the coming *Av* according to the Baal Shem's manuscript. Special cable to the *Morgen Zshurnal*, Warsaw, Tuesday. The Jewish press announces that a new manuscript of the Ba'al Shem Tov has been discovered, in which the rise and fall of Nazism is predicted. According to the manuscript, the fall of Nazism will occur in the month of *Av* 5699, which means the coming [i.e. in the coming months of this] year.[30]

Risikoff added that 1937/1938, equivalent to 5698 on the Hebrew calendar, was *Tartsah* (*Tav*: 400 + *Resh*: 200 + *Tsadi*: 90 + *Het*: 8). *Tartsah* included letters for murder (*Retsah*: *Resh* + *Tsadi* + *Het*) and for cleansing (*Titrahets*: *Tav* + *Resh* + *Het* + *Tsadi*)—indicating being cleansed by the troubles (*titrahets mitsarotekha*). The letters for the year 1938/39, 5699 on the Hebrew calendar were *Tav*: 400 + *Resh*: 200 + *Tsadi*: 90 + *Tet*: 9 (*Tartsat*), indicating *Tirahem rahameha tsidkatekha tuvekha*: May Your mercy unfold, Your righteousness and goodness. Further, the *Tet* indicated the completion of the nine months of suffering (citing, "The son of David will not come until the Roman power enfolds Israel for nine months"; b. *Sanhedrin* 98[b]). The letters *Resh* + *Tsadi* + *Tet* in *Tartsat* indicated the Sovereign of the World's establishing righteousness, through troubles and *Teshuvah* over the nine months (*Re'eh ribono shel olam tekayem tsidkat ha-tet hodashim*).[31] Risikoff also cited a report in a local (New York) daily that a certain famous kabbalist in Sarajevo predicted January 26, 1939, as the date of the messiah's arrival—when "the Gentiles would eat filth" (*un di goyim velen kayen di blate*). The absence of anticipation or regret, when that day came and went, was a sign, he said, of the weakening of messianic faith in Israel.[32]

Part of the trouble of *Be'ita*, according to Risikoff, was dishonesty, and this was evident in current events. Various governments had assured Austria and Czechoslovakia that they would defend them if needed. But when the time came, they did not. Had the two countries, with millions of people and heroic character, acted independently to defend themselves, they might have succeeded. Likewise, England promised to help Jews in the Land of Israel when needed, but when the time came, England turned to the Arabs—while the world remained oblivious to Israel's plight.[33]

The larger picture of *Be'ita* involved domination by Amalek-Haman, now in the form of Hitler. Risikoff referred to Nazis, swastikas, and Mussolini with their names spelled backwards—"Sitzan" (Nazis), "Akitsavs" (swastikas) and "Anilasum" (Mussolini)—as a way to obliterate them. He aligned Hitler ("H") with Amalek and Haman. Like Amalek, Hitler was evil for the sake of being evil. Amalek was jealous of Israel and sought to injure the people, even if it meant injuring himself.

Like a bee that stung and then died, Amalek-Hitler was ready to take out Israel's eye, even if it meant losing both of his own. There was no empirical reason for Hitler to chase Jews from Germany, leaving them naked, hungry, and driven to suicide—a *Hurban* of 600,000 people. He did so, simply because he was *Tumah*, compelled to destroy purity even if it meant his own death. Haman was out to conquer the world, especially Israel, and signed a treaty with Edom-Rome to do so, and Hitler was out to destroy Israel and rule the world. While Ahasuerus hated the Jewish religion but would have accepted conversion, Haman hated the Jewish race (*Geza*), and conversion was irrelevant. Hitler persecuted even those Jews with ancestors who had converted. Both Haman and Hitler made themselves into idols. According to Yitshak Alfasi (1013–1103), Haman made himself into an idol by engraving an image on his clothing and all but Mordekhai bowed down to him. Hitler wore a swastika on his coat, so that he and his racism would be made into idols. Haman wanted the world to believe in crime and murder, and Hitler wanted the world to accept the faith of the swastika, with all its crime, murder, and hatred for Israel. The intent of Hitler (Amalek-Haman) was foreseen by the rabbinic sages: "Grant not to Esau the wicked desire of his heart. This refers to Germanya (or Germumyah) as Edom. For should they but go forth they would destroy the whole world" (b. Megillah 6[a/b]).[34]

Risikoff left the matter of Hitler's instrumentality ambiguous. In *Palgei Shemen* he wrote that as Haman was sent by God to punish Israel and induce *Teshuvah* (b. Sanhedrin 97[b]), Hitler was sent by God to turn Israel back to its authentic, Torah-true self (*verasha zeh shenishlah min hashamayim*).[35] But a few months later, in *Hakohanim Vehalevi'im*, he declared that it was impossible to accept the idea that the contemporary Haman was sent to punish Israel for its sin. Such extreme suffering could never come from God—for God acted according to Torah (b. Avodah Zarah 4[b]). Hitler, Risikoff concluded, murdered on his own.[36]

Israel's Role: Prayer

As redemption came from God, and God did not change (Malachi 3:6, 24), redemption was certain. But Israel also had to act. To move from *Be'ita* to *Ahishena* to *Geulah* (redemption), charity (*Tsedakah*) was required. Risikoff anticipated an outburst of righteousness during the month of *Av*—when the good nations would act to redeem Jews and non-Jews from Hitler. As to the Jews themselves, Risikoff cited an instance where Nazis kidnapped Jews at night, took them by boat to some distant place, and demanded a ransom. The Jews paid. Indeed, were non-Jews to be in need, Jews would be the first to give.[37]

For the eschatological process to proceed, the people also had to pray. To begin with, Israel must pray to have the people return to their authentic selves: "And please, God, our Lord, make pleasant the words of Your Torah in our months and in the months of Your people" ("Veha'arev na hashem eloheinu et divrei toratekha befinu ubefi amekha," Birkat hatorah, Shaharit).[38] Risikoff cited a prayer from Tanna Debe Eliyahu (a midrash composed of Seder Eliyahu Rabbah and Seder Eliyahu Zuta, redacted in the tenth century), found in Mosheh ben Gershon (d. 1831), and *Mishpat Tsedek*, which articulated God's love for Israel, evidenced by His separating it from 70 other nations, and asked God to remember the patriarchal covenant. It then petitioned God to see how even Jews who were destitute continued Torah study and found money for instructing their children; to take into account how the elderly went daily to synagogues and houses of study, ever expecting salvation; and to keep in mind all the orphans and widows who performed *Mitsvot*. It implored God to strengthen the poor and the oppressed and to pity His people as once He pitied the lost of Nineveh (Jonah 4:11), and bring them from darkness, oppression, and slavery to redemption. All "For the sake of Your great Name."[39]

Risikoff composed a prayer, published in *Hakohanim Vehalevi'im*, expressing awareness of Israel's sin, which brought God to have them suffer. But as the people loved God throughout and now acknowledged their sin, and they were suffering so terribly, would God, who ever watched over them in secret, come forth from His hiddenness to bring redemption? The prayer articulated the affliction of the people, who were surrounded by death (Psalms 18:5), scorn, and derision (Psalms 44:14), abandoned and enslaved, removed from justice, their corpses ruled over by heretics. It pleaded to God not to hide His face in the day of distress (Psalms 102:3), but to respond speedily (Psalms 102:3) to the cries of Israel. It acknowledged that the people had sinned against Torah, and that the righteous God therefore handed them over to the persecutor ("Thou didst deliver them into the hand of their adversaries, who distressed them; and in the time of their trouble when they cried unto Thee, Thou heardest from heaven; and according to Thy manifold mercies Thou gavest them saviors who might save them out of the hand of their adversaries." Nehemiah 9:26–27). But while they sinned, they continued to love God—who never stopped watching over them, even if secretly:

> We know You watch over us and will save us. But only in secret, for we sinned before You. . . . In truth, even at the time that we sinned before You, deep love for You remained hidden in our hearts. . . . We always embraced and adhered to You, even when we sinned. For the image of

God is within us. We always knew, inside, that we were Jews, the seed of Abraham, Isaac and Jacob, the children of Your compassion. Gentiles and the evil Hitler know this. They watch our terrible sufferings, aware that we are the seed blessed by God, and that we will never, God forbid, betray our covenant. We remain righteous, unlike those evil ones who trespassed even the seven Noahide laws [Genesis 9:1–7] which You commanded.

Would God judge the people of Israel accordingly, as he judged forced converts (*Anusim*), in light of their exilic condition? "It is known full well to Thee, that our will is to perform Thy will and what prevents us? The yeast in the dough, and the subjection to foreign powers" (b. Berakhot 17ᵃ). Would the God of mercy, seeing how His people were being slaughtered, suffering at the hands of the evil nations, and now acknowledged their sin and revealed their hidden love for God, break forth from His hiddenness? The prayer concluded with thoughts of redemption:

Show us the revealed light of Your countenance. For in the light of Your countenance we shall see the eternal salvation which You promised us through Your Torah and prophets. In compassion, turn our eyes to Zion, with its messiah, righteous ones and high priests. Build our Temple, to worship You in awe.[40]

Israel's Role: The Priests
Risikoff identified himself with the priestly class: "I am the youth of the house of Aaron" ("*Anohi hatsa'ir leveit Aharon*"): "We Your servants, the sons of Aharon Your holy priest, come before You, in shame, impoverished and wretched."[41] As described in *Yalkut Reuveni* (a Kabbalistic midrash by Reuven ben Hoeshke Katz, d. 1673), the Levites had a special, emerald-like brilliance. The robe of the High Priest in the Temple had 12 jewels, each inscribed with a tribal name, and that of the Levites was on the emerald:

The emerald (*bareket*) sparkled [*barak* = to glitter] and shed light as a candle. It was the stone which Noah suspended in the ark: 'A light shall thou make to the ark' [Genesis 6:16]. The emerald was given to Levi . . . as the tribe of Levi shed light on Torah. Thus, when Moses [who received the Torah] was born, light filled the entire house [ExodR, Parashah 1, Siman 20]. The emerald had a special property, of making the fool wise and of lighting up the eye (Reuven ben Hoeshke Katz, "Tetsaveh," para. 44, in Yalkut Reuveni).

In order to move from *Be'ita* to *Ahishena* and *Geulah*, Risikoff believed, the priests (*Kohanim* and *Levi'im*) had to assume a position between the below (history) and the above (redemption). When the Temple was aflame, the rabbinic sages reported, a band of young priests ascended to the roof. Declaring that "Sovereign of the universe, as we were not worthy of the Temple, these keys are handed into Thy keeping," they cast the keys upwards toward heaven. The figure of a hand appeared from above to receive them, and they jumped down into the flames (b. Ta'anit 49ᵃ). Upon redemption, Risikoff continued, the keys would be returned to the priestly descendants of those martyrs (*Martirer*), to enact the passage of history (and metahistory) into the messianic realm. For a synagogue to be built, there had to be a *Shamash* (beadle), and for the Temple to be built, there had to be a *Shamashim*, envoys of the Merciful One (*Shiluhei de'rahmana*, b. Yoma 19ᵃ), and these were the priests (*Kohanim* and *Levi'im*).[42] According to the Kabbalists (*Mekubbalim*), they would be the first to meet the messiah.

Risikoff brought the drama into the present:

> Today, we also are living through a time of flood. Not of water, but of a bright fire, which burns and turns Jewish life into ruin. We are now drowning in a flood of blood. But, just as Noah's ark was rescued from the flood by merit of the tribe of Levi, so it will be with the flood of blood today. The tribe of Levi, and it alone, can rescue the Jewish people. Only it can bring their eternal salvation from today's flood of blood. Through the *Kohanim* and *Levi'im* help will come to all Israel. The Holy One of Israel, Thy savior [Isaiah 43:3].

Specifically, the Levites must transmit the prayers of Israel that were needed to evoke redemption.

> The tribe of Levi is the sanctified and elected tribe. It is incumbent upon it to stand between the Holy One blessed be He and Israel in order to bestow the abundance of blessing and holiness upon Israel. And also to mediate between Israel and the Holy One blessed be He, to introduce Israel's prayers and to recommend good things for Israel, before the Holy One blessed be He.

Risikoff had a practical plan: Elder *Kohanim* and *Levi'im* must issue a call through newspapers for all priests to gather on a weekday for a day of fast resembling Yom Kippur. They should don the *Kittel* (white linen robe), *Tallit* (prayer shawl), and *Tefillin* (phylacteries). The priestly blessing should be recited, as well as selected Selihot. These included the prefatory "Lekhah Hashem hatsedakah" (To Thee, O Lord, belongs righteousness); "Aykh niftah lefanekhah" ("Now shall we open our mouth before Thee," anonymous, Selihah, nr. 1); "Yashmi'enu salahti" ("O announce to us, I have forgiven" by Shelomoh bar Shmuel Berabi

Yoel Hazak, nr. 16), to "Hashem Elohei Tseva'ot" ("O Lord, God of hosts," by Rashi, nr. 23); "Elohim yireh lo" ("God will show him," by Yoel ben Yitshak Halevi, nr. 30); "Ezak el elohim koli" ("My voice cries to God" by Shelomoh Nahman Hakatan, nr. 36); "Avlah nafshi vehashakh ta'ari" ("My soul has been wicked, and my face is clouded with grief," anonymous, nr. 40); and "Ya'azov rasha netivo" ("The evil one should leave his path," author unknown, nr. 57). Also "Torah hakedoshah hithaneni bevakashah" ("O holy law, pray urgently," by Shimon bar Yitshak, nr. 58); "Amnam anahnu hatanu vehe'evinu" ("Surely we have sinned and trespassed," by Gershon ben Yehudah, nr. 79); "Atah helki vetsur levavi" ("You are my portion, and the creator of my heart," by Eliyah bar Shemayah, nr. 81); "Hashem elohei yisrael atah tsadik elohah selihot" ("O Lord God of Israel, thou art righteous, O God of forgiveness," by Eliyah bar Shemayah, nr. 88); and "Ezon tahan vehasket atirah" ("Give ear, O Lord, to our supplication, and heed our entreaty," anonymous, nr. 89). Finally "Hashem, Hashem, El Rahum Vehanun" ("The Lord, the Lord, is merciful and gracious," found throughout the Selihot); "Eykh ne'enhah bemashber" ("How Israel sighs from disaster," anonymous, nr. 94); "Amon pithei teshuvah" ("Wide are the doors of penitent return," anonymous, nr. 96); "Mikveh yisrael moshi'u be'et tsarah" ("Hope of Israel, who rescues the people in the time of trouble," by Mosheh bar Shmuel bar Avshalom, nr. 97); "Adon din im yedukdak" ("Lord, may our judgment be careful" by Zevadiyah, nr. 98); and "Yeratseh tsom amkha" ("May the fasting of your people be acceptable," by Yitshak bar Avigdor, nr. 99).[43] The *Shofar* was then to be sounded, and the priests were to study *Musar* (morality) and do *Teshuvah*. Every priest aged 13 and above should inscribe his name and that of his wife and children in a book to cite proof of priestly descent back to three generations based on *Verein* and *Shtetl* records.[44] In a work published later, in 1948, Risikoff detailed the worship and sacrifices to be performed by the priests in the rebuilt Temple of redemption, along with the laws pertaining to *Pidyon ha'ben* (redemption of the first born), *Tumah* (impurity), *Even shetiyah* (the stone from which God drew out the world), and the *Olah* sacrifice. Although applicable only with actual redemption, study of these laws served as substitute for the actual implementation as long as Israel remained in exile. The study also brought the messiah closer.[45]

D. COMMUNAL PRAYER

The motifs articulated by Schwartz, Gefen, and Risikoff also surfaced in the context of the prayer and fast days called by the Union of Orthodox Rabbis of the United States and Canada. Kristallnacht was seen as an attack upon

Israel's covenantal holiness. While unprecedented in its magnitude and character, it nevertheless belonged to the metahistory of Israel's sin-suffering relationship, which could be reversed by *Teshuvah*. God's presence and His mercy, though hidden, remained throughout the troubles.

On Sunday, November 20, 1932, the members of the Union met in New York to respond.[46] Their meeting coincided with the national day of worship called by FDR—for which David de Sola Pool (She'erit Yisrael Sephardic synagogue, New York) and Richard Sizoo (Collegiate Reformed Church) composed a prayer that begged God to have mercy on the victims, expressed hope that the suffering would be so nobly born that the oppressors themselves would learn about the dignity of the soul and forgiving love, and wished that all humankind would recognize its oneness, internally and with God, and thereby bring justice to the earth.[47] After resolving that Bernard Dov Revel (President of Yeshiva University) would send a letter to FDR expressing gratitude to him for his efforts "on behalf of persecuted German Jewry and other oppressed groups," and imploring him "to intercede with His majesty's government that the doors of Palestine be opened to Jewish victims of recurring medieval darkness, thus assuring new hope, sanctuary and faith to the Jewish martyrs of inhumanity,"[48] the members called for a day of fasting, repentance, prayer, and charity to reverse the evil decree ("Letsom, liteshuvah, utefillah utsedakah ma'avirin et roa hagezerah," Hazarat Hashats Le'musaf Yom Beit De'rosh Hashanah. See GenR., Parashat 44, Siman 13) on Monday, November 28. Their call followed a similar one by Hayim Ozer Grodzensky for September 18, 1938, responding to the destruction of Jewish life and property in Austria on a scale unknown since medieval times, where Shaharit was to include recitation of Selihot, Avinu Malkeinu, Anenu (fast day supplication), Psalms 130:7, unspecified words of rebuke (*Divrei kibushim*), and Minhah selected prophetic texts.[49] The Union President Joseph Konvitz and the Secretary Yehudah Layb Seltser wrote in the journal *Hapardes* that Kristallnacht was an attack upon the sanctity of the people of the covenant. It was an assault upon the people, killing children and the elderly, leaving thousands to wander in hunger and cold, and upon the vessels of holiness, destroying synagogues, *Batei midrash* (houses of learning), and Torah scrolls, dragging rabbinic scholars and pious Jews through the streets. Konvitz and Seltser aligned the Torah burnings with persecutions under Hadrian, when Haninah ben Teradyon, wrapped in a Torah scroll, was set aflame and the letters ascended to heaven (see b. Pesahim 87[b] and b. Avodah Zarah 18[a]). They called for a response that spoke to the metahistorical dimension of the assault. As the Jews once responded to Haman's genocidal decrees with fasting, sobbing, and sackcloth (*Esther* 24:16; b. Ta'anit 15[a]), so Jews should respond today. American Jews had sinned, they violated the

Sabbath, desecrated the synagogue, mocked family purity, and married and divorced illegitimately. Now they had to do *Teshuvah*. Once they did, God would respond and the suffering would ebb (Jeremiah 3:7, Psalms 120:1). Throughout, however, God's presence remained, and His *Shekhinah* lamented over Israel's suffering (see b. *Berakhot* 3ª).[50]

At the main service, held at Yeshiva University's Rabbi Yitshak Elhanan Seminary (RIETS), the ark was draped in a white curtain (*Parohet*) as was customary for High Holidays, and had the tone, as one observer put it, of services on 17 *Tammuz* (commemorating the destruction of the Temple). The Selihot recited at Shaharit affirmed the just God, the tie between sin and calamity, and the effectiveness of confession and prayer in ending the troubles. Over the course of the day, recitations of Job 35:5 and Psalms 16:8 ("Shiviti"), 20:2, and 22:21 articulated God's real presence despite His apparent absence, and pleas for His response to the troubles. A *Hazkarah* (memorial prayer, presumably El Mole Rahamim) mourned the holy martyrs of Hitler's concentration camps (*kedoshim . . . martirer . . . al kiddush Hashem*). In his address, Konvitz identified the tragedy as a rebuke for Israel's sins ("*di tokhehah geht an mit ihr program*"). Revel observed that the tragedy was unprecedented, that the "human beasts" came from a cultured, not a backward nation, and he thanked God for not letting the Jews become as degraded as the persecutors.[51]

There were parallel events that same Monday in Boston. Adat Yeshurun synagogue in Roxbury, Massachusetts, where 3,000 gathered to fast and worship, lamentations from the Yom Kippur liturgy were recited, the *Shofar* sounded, and Joseph Dovber Soloveichik called for stricter adherence to traditional hours for family and spiritual life, and for dedicating the month of *Kislev* (November 24–December 22, 1938) to gathering funds for persecuted Jews.[52]

In Chicago, the decision to gather and the gatherings themselves took place rapidly, within a 24-hour period. The *Merkaz Harabanim* convened on November 21, led by Avraham Yitshak Kardon. The 45 members recited Psalms, and M. G. Goldtsvag recited a *Hazkarah*. A call was then issued by those present:

'Arise, cry out in the night. . . . Pour out thy heart like water' [Lamentations 14:1]. Broken, shattered and despaired, we stand before the unprecedented, horrible misfortune which has befallen our people. 'The hurt of the daughter of My people' [Jeremiah 8:11]. Come together this evening in the synagogues in every neighborhood of the city. Let our cries of pain be heard, let us open the gates of compassion with our tears. . . . Young and old, man and woman, come this evening into the synagogue, close the businesses, put your work aside, and let us pray to the Sovereign of the world for

compassion, and that He protects and rescues the dispersed of Israel. . . .
'Thy brother's blood crieth unto Me from the ground' [Genesis 4:10]. And
no one may remain at home tonight. May the father of mercy hear our
cry. May He see our tears and rescue us from all our troubles, and lead us
upright to our Land.

At 7:30 p.m. on Tuesday, November 22, six days before the ceremonies
in New York and Boston, services were held simultaneously at 14 sites.
After an opening address about the seriousness of the situation, Psalms
were read responsively (Psalms 13, 20, 22, 43, 44, 57, 69, 71, 74, 75,
79, 80, 83, 94, 118, 121, 123, 130, 142), and then Selihot. The Selihot
included (1) "Thou art a God slow to anger, and art called Lord of
mercy, and hast shown the way of *Teshuvah*" ("El erekh apayim ata uva'al
harahamim," anonymous, nr. 1); (2) "And the Lord passed before Moses
and proclaimed, the Lord is a merciful and gracious God; slow to anger
and abundant in kindness and truth; He keeps kindness for thousands of
generations, forgiving iniquities" ("Vaya'avor Hashem al panov vayikra,"
anonymous); (3) "Israel, thy people, offer supplication, for they are distressed and need help; their adversaries prolong their yoke on them, yet
with all that has befallen them, they still bless Thy name" (Yisrael amkha
tehinah orkhim, by Yitshak Hakohen ben Meir, a response to 1096 massacres, nr. 14); (4) "The waters compass us about even to the soul. We
have sunk into the depths of the floods. The waters of the sea pass over
us, the roaring waves of the deep cover us. Our splendor has turned into
deformity, and we retain no strength any more; we are trembling because
of our sins, we are deeply distressed because of the multitude of our
transgression" (Afafunu mayim ad nofesh, by Amittai b. Shefatyah, end
of ninth century); (5) "Give ear, O Lord, to our supplication, and heed
our entreaty; cause Thy anger to cease, and abate Thy wrath; let those
who come to implore Thee in the bitterness of their soul find help in Thy
great name (Ezon tahan vehasket atirah, anonymous, nr. 89)." The Torah
scrolls were then taken out, and the 13 attributes (Hashem, Hashem,
El rahum vehanun) (running throughout the Selihot) and the Shema
Kolenu ("Hear our voice, Hashem our God, pity and be compassionate
to us") recited. The services ended with the sounding of the Shofar, the
Hazkarah (presumably El Mole Rahamim) and Avinu Malkeinu.[53]

CONCLUSION

In Eastern Europe the *Beit Ya'akov* journal editor, Eliezer Gershon Fridenzon,
the Admor of Bobov, Bentsiyon Halberstam, and the world Orthodox
leader Hayim Ozer Grodzensky, channeled the tragedy of Kristallnacht into

the covenantal framework, as it displayed itself metahistorically. No natural explanation for the disaster was conceivable. Specifically, they articulated the themes of sin (assimilation) and divine punishment; Nazism's instrumental role where pious and nonpious Jews were not distinguished from one another; cyclical descent into suffering and ascent into redemption; and the apocalyptic struggle of Amalek-Hitler and Israel (*Ikveta dimeshiha*). How were Jews to respond? Through education, awareness of the consequences of sin, charitable deeds, *Mitsvot, Teshuvah*, and prayer. Several of these themes were echoed in the Land of Israel: the impossibility of any naturalistic explanation, cycles of descent and ascent, assimilation, the divine instrument of punishment, the absence of Torah strength to respond, and the need for *Teshuvah*, apocalyptic struggle, and redemption. Some motifs were added: the distinction between medieval and modern persecution, whereby race was now involved and conversion was not a way out, and the coincidence between the explosion of barbarism and modern cultural progress.

In America, drawing apparently from Wasserman's *Ma'amar*, Schwartz reiterated the theme of assimilation–divine punishment–*Teshuvah* and integrated the concept of Hitler's identity with Haman and the assertion that nations that stood by indifferently were complicit with it. Gefen moved from the metahistorical framework, to the extent that he spoke of Akiva and Hadrian, Henryk Grynspan, and Hitler's political isolation by the countries of the world, and focused on the need for the various branches of Judaism to unify so as to be able to act on behalf of the refugees—although he still referenced Sarah, Ephron, Esther, and Haman. Menahem Risikoff probed the eschatological process from *Be'ita* to *Ahishena* to *Geulah*, in terms of intensified suffering and *Teshuvah*, and drew from kabbalistic sources and the Ba'al Shem Tov (Besht) to predict the messiah's arrival in summer 1939. He called upon *Kohanim* and *Levi'im* to play a mediating role between history and redemption, praying together to accelerate *Geulah* and, in effect, recover the Temple keys that their ancient predecessors handed up to God before the Temple's destruction. The fast days held in New York, Boston, and Chicago articulated the dynamics of sin-*Teshuvah* and *Geulah*. Kristallnacht was interpreted by Union of Orthodox Rabbis (UOR) and *Merkaz Harabanim* spokesmen as an attack upon the Jews as human beings as well as upon the holiness of Israel. They addressed the crisis within the metahistorical framework, speaking of the attack in terms of Torah-martyrdom (Haninah ben Teradyon) and response in terms of *Teshuvah* for sin so as to evoke divine intervention. The prayers enacted the metahistory in ritual, articulating it and imploring God to respond. The core of reality remained the covenantal relationship to God, to whom the people were ultimately faithful, and who was ultimately merciful and compassionate.

The American ultra-Orthodox response to Kristallnacht evidenced rootedness in the theological premises of Eastern European Orthodoxy-centered thought. But there was also a degree of distinctiveness in the attention given to historical realities. Schwartz spoke of Hitler's background and the specifics of his takeover. Gefen spoke of his political isolation. Risikoff distilled metahistory into history with his program for priestly action to mediate redemption. The broad-based days of fasting, with their attention to charity, also reflected a distinctive attention to the concrete—subject to further research as to their existence in the Land of Israel.

The theological reactions in America, which to a substantial extent mirrored those in Eastern Europe and Palestine, left many areas of ambiguity. For example If Hitler was an instrument of God, how could he be evil for evil's sake? If Kristallnacht precipitated a metahistorical covenantal crisis, what relationship did it have to the apocalyptic drama involving Amalek? Given the view that the events required transnaturalistic explanation, why did the sufferings take the particular historical forms that they did? In the years to follow, these issues would be probed—and in the face of increasingly tragic conditions. They would be probed, in the tradition of the Kristallnacht thinkers, and within and around the framework delineated by them.

NOTES

* This study was completed at the Institute for Advanced Study, Hebrew University, in 2007/2008. I am indebted to the staff of the Hebraica Section of the Library of Congress and Jewish National University Library, Hebrew University, for exceptional assistance in gathering materials for this study.

1. On metahistorical responses to the Holocaust, see Gershon Greenberg, "Introduction," in *Wrestling with God: Jewish Theological Responses During and After the Holocaust* (Oxford, England, Oxford University Press, 2007), pp. 11–26. Judith Baumel and Jacob Schacter write:

> In their effort to maintain faith in God in the face of often incredible suffering, Jewish victims of tragedy in all centuries felt constrained to view their experiences as part of a continuum and not as something radically new and different. Although they may have objectively believed that the magnitude of their suffering was unprecedented, they never presented it as such, for fear that this might indicate that God was finally breaking His covenantal bond and severing His close relationship with His people, a thought they simply could not abide and one that their faith would not allow them to accept. Whatever cataclysmic event they experienced was

never seen in isolation, as sui generis, but, on the contrary, was portrayed as just the latest example of the age-old, consistently recurring phenomenon of God's punishment for Jewish sin. Indeed, the Jewish collective memory was so long and sharp that any time it confronted even a tragedy of major proportions, it was able to place it into paradigms of previously experienced tragedies and destructions. In fact, the greater the tragedy, the more potentially dangerous it was to Jewish faith and, hence, the greater the effort to absorb it and subsume it under already established patterns and archetypes. Such a conception, in which even the unprecedented was assigned a precedent, was a comforting and reassuring one, allowing for the classical covenantal construct to remain intact. This continuity with the past provided great hope for the future.

Judith Baumel and Jacob J. Schacter, "The Ninety Three Bais Ya'akov Girls of Cracow," in *Reverence, Righteousness and Rahamanut: Leo Jung*, ed. Jacob J. Schacter (Hoboken, NJ: Aronson, 1992): 109.

2. On the history of Orthodox Jewish religious thought through the Holocaust, see *Wrestling With God: Jewish Theological Responses During and After the Holocaust*, ed. Steven T. Katz, Shelomoh Biderman, and Gershon Greenberg (Oxford: Oxford University Press, 2007). Substantive theological responses to Kristallnacht on the part of Reform, Conservative, and Reconstructionist Judaism have yet to be identified.

3. The notion of an internal Amalek was unusual. But it can be found, for example, in Levi Yitshak of Berditschev, "Derush Lepurim," in *Kedushat Levi*, vol. 1 (Brooklyn: Me'irat Eynayim, 2002/3): 188. E. G. Fridenzon, "Far der antshaydung," *Beit Ya'akov* 16 nr. 152 (24 November–22 December 1938). Avi Patt directed me to this source.

4. The theme of evil's fright at the prospect of its demise upon the end of history, sending it into a rampage, may be found in Zadok Rabinowitz (Zadok Hakohen of Lublin), *Sefer Yisrael Kedoshim* (Benei Berak, Israel: Yahadut 1966/67): 48$^{a/b}$. E. G. Fridenzon, "Nokh alets farblendinishn," *Beit Ya'akov* 16 nr. 153 (22 December 1938–20 January 1939): 1.

5. Elijah ben Solomon Abraham Ha-kohen, of Smyrna (1650–1729), "Anaf Gerushim: Umelitsot Gadol al Yisrael," in *Midrash Talpiyot* (Lublin, Poland: N. Herszenhorn i. Sz. Sztrazberger Ptg., 1927): 104^a–104^b. Halberstam cited documents of decrees and expulsion from Vienna, which were added at the end of the Hazekuni text—presumably Hezekiah ben Manoah (Thirteenth century), *Hazekuni: Perush al hamishah humshei Torah* (Cremona: V. Konti, 1559). I have been unable to find this in any of the editions. See David Kaufmann, *Die letzte Vertreibung der Juden aus Wien und Niederösterreich, ihre Vorgeschichte (1625–1670) und ihre Öpfer* (Vienna: E. Konegan, 1889), and A. F. Pribram, ed., *Urkunden und Akten zur Geschichte der Juden in Wien*, 2 vols. (Vienna and Leipzig: Wilhelm Braumueller, 1948).

6. Bentsiyon Halberstam, "Igeret Hakodesh Me'et Kohen Kadosh Admor Hakadosh Maran Mibobov Shlita: Be'ezrat hashem 3 leseder lishuatekha

kiviti hashem 5699 bobov hashem tsuri vego'ali," in Hayim ben Shlomoh Czernowitz, *Sha'ar Hatefilah*, ed. Hillel Grinfeld (Tel Aviv: Tarbut Ptg., 1955): 157–159.

7. On Asarah Harugei Malkhut see Solomon Zeitlin, "Legend of the Ten Martyrs," *JQR* 36. nr. 1 (1947): 1–16; Harry A. Fischel, "Martyr and Prophet," *JQR* 37 nr. 3 (1947): 265–280 and 37 nr. 4 (1947): 363–386. R. Boustan, *From Martyr to Mystic: Rabbinic Martyrology and the Making of Merkavah Mysticism* (Tübingen 2005); Louis Finkelstein, "The Ten Martyrs," in *Essays and Studies in Memory of Linda R. Miller*, ed. Israel Davidson (New York, 1938): 29–55; and M. Herr, "Kiddush Hashem Veriko Ha'aktu'ali Bime'ah Hasheniyah Lisefirah," in *Milhemet Kodesh Umartirologyah Betoledot Yisrael Uvetoledot Ha'amim* (Jerusalem: n.p., 1967/68): 73–92. B-n (presumably Binyamin or Bentsiyon), "An aktuel vort," *Beit Ya'akov* 16 nr. 155 (21 March–18 April 1939): 1–2.

8. See also Y. Havas, "Al Haperek . . . Simanei Hageulah," *Hayesod* 8 nr. 1264 (5 May 1939): 1. Hayim Ozer Grodzensky, "Kol Kore Le'ezra Miharidefot Vehagerushim," *Dos Vort* nr. 731 (11 November 1938): 1, rpt. in *Ahiezer: Kovetz Igrot*, vol. 1, ed. Aharon Sorsky (Benei Berak: Netsah 1970): 276–277.

9. Grodzensky, "Be'ezrat and Hashem [31 May 1939]," in *Sefer Ahiezer: Kolel She'elot Uteshuvot*, vol. 3 (Vilna, Lithuania: Sh. F. Gorba Ptg., 1939): prefatory page.

10. On non-Orthodox responses in Palestine see Shulamit Volkov, "The Kristallnacht in Context: A View from Palestine," *Leo Baeck Institute Yearbook*, 35 (1990): 279–296. Also, Editor, "Pera'ot Ayumot Bi'yehudei Germanyah: yehudim mukim be'ahzariyut. Batei kenisiyot mutsatim veneherasim—5000 yehudim ne'asru bevina-Goebbels 'margia' umavtiah 'tehukat nakam'," *Hatsofeh* 2 nr. 264 (11 November 1938): 1, and Editor, "Gezerot Hashemad Al Yehudei Germanyah: 'Kenas shel milyard mark— nishul muhlat mikal anfei haparnasah. Segirat kal ha'itonim hayehudim. Alfei yehudim ne'asrim umeunim. Kal yehudei frankfort bakele. Shemuot al gezerat 'geto.' Sa'arat hitmarmarut be'eropa ube'amerika," *Hatsofeh* 2 nr. 265 (13 November 1938): 1.

11. Meir Simhah Ha'kohen of Dvinsk, "Behukotai," in *Meshekh Hokhmah*, vol. 3 (Jerusalem: Hotsa'at Haskel, 1977): 771–773. Mosheh Avigdor Amiel, "Nehapesah Darkenu: Hirhurei teshuvah," *Hatsofeh* 2 nr. 288 (9 December 1938): 7; 2 nr. 300 (23 December 1938): 6; 2 nr. 318 (13 January 1939): 6. On Amiel and Katz see Gershon Greenberg, "Ontic Division and Religious Survival in Wartime Palestinian Orthodoxy and the Holocaust (Hurban)," *Modern Judaism* 14 (1994): 21–61. On the literature of suffering and love, see Mosheh ben Gershon, *Mishpat Tsedek: Leva'er inyan kabalot yisurim be'ahavah* (Benei Berak: Mishor 1986/87). Dvorets drew a comparison with Spain from a different perspective. In the expulsion from Spain, boats were filled with Jews and set to sea. Now Jews were able to escape and seek refuge—only to be returned to the inferno or into the depths of the ocean. This was one month before the voyage of

the St. Louis. Dvorets, "Al haperek . . . Akhzariyut Aymim," *Hayesod* 8 nr. 263 (20 April 1939): 1.

12. Y. A. Dvorkes, "Tekufateinu: Hirhurim la'matsav," *Diglenu* (3 April 1939): 15.

13. Bentsiyon Hai Uziel, "Mo'ed Hadash Aviv," *Ha'yesod* 8 nr. 261 (March 1939): 2.

14. Reuven Katz, "Hevlei Geulah," *Ha'yesod* 8 nr. 259 (3 March 1939): 2. On messianic expectations see also Y. Havas, "Al Haperek . . . Simanei Hageulah," *Ha'yesod* 8 nr. 1264 (5 May 1939): 1.

15. On the overall American Jewish response, beyond the theological, see Sander A. Diamond, "The Kristallnacht and the Reaction in America," in *YIVO Annual* 14 (1969): 196–208; and Alfred Gottschalk, *The German Pogrom of November 1938 and the Reaction of American Jewry* (New York: Leo Baeck Institute, 1989). On pre-Kristallnacht responses to growing dangers see Avraham Margoliyot, "The Problem of the Rescue of German Jewry during the Years 1933–1939 and Reasons for the Delay in Their Emigration from the Third Reich," in *Rescue Attempts During the Holocaust*, ed. Yisrael Gutman and Efrayim Zuroff (New York: KTAV, 1978): 247–266. Also Hayim Liberman, *In tol fun toyt* (New York: H. Liberman, 26 September – 25 October 1938) and Shmuel Menahem Halevi Fayn, "Di asarah harugei malkhut," in *Di sikhere veg: Beobakhtungen un erklehrungen oyf di problemen im judentum* (St. Louis: Quality Ptg., 1938): 38–42.

16. E.g., Editor, "Natsi pogrom brayngt toyt un hurban," *Der Tog* 24 nr. 8697 (11 November 1938): 1–2. Editor, "Moradige pogrom kvalie in daytshland brayngt toyt un farvistung oyf di iden," *Morgen Zshurnal-Togblat* (*MZ-T*) 38 nr. 11,267 (11 November 1938): 1–2. Editor, "Natsis tsvingen rosh hakahal untertsutsinden a shuhl," *MZ-T* 38 nr. 11,270 (16 November 1938): 1, 3. Editor, "Al hurban hamikdash" *Hapardes* 12 nr. 9 (24 November–22 December 1938): 2–3.

17. On transmigration of souls see e.g., Hayim Vital, "Sha'ar Shishi," in *Sha'ar Hakavanot*, vol. 1 (Jerusalem: Mekhon Da'at Yosef): 1.

18. Schwarz said he would have preferred to advocate for Israel before God, as in his "Kunteras Melits Yosher: Al yisrael lifnei avihem shebeshamayim," in *Doresh Tov Le'amo: Helek Rishon* (London: Y. Groditsky Ptg., 1917): 131–132. But it was also a *Mitsvah* to admonish Israel when necessary, and thereby awaken *Teshuvah*.

19. Martin Herman (Mordekhai Tsevi) Schwartz, "Yafe li'yemei hateshuvah ulekhal et," *Derushei Hokhmah Veda'at* (St. Louis: Quality, 1939/40). Schwartz, however, did not share the categorical dualism of Wasserman between Torah and outside knowledge. See "Leparashat Shemot . . . Hokhmat Hafilosofiyah Veshitot Hahakhamim: 'Hume' Ve'Kant," in *Doresh Tov Le'amo. Helek Sheni* (London: Y. Groditsky, 1919): 37–55. Schwartz also wrote *Kunteras Lehavdil Bein Hatame U'ven Hatahor: Neged hakunteras taharat hakodesh shel hagaon harav yisrael hayim daykhes* (Seini: n.p., 1927); *Foundations of Jewish Belief: Designed to Elevate and Strengthen*

Belief in God and the Divine Origin of the Torah (New York: Spero Fdtn., 1947); *Shirah Hadashah* (Brooklyn: Balshon Ptg., 1966); and *Avodat Tamid: Shirei kodesh le'hol* (New York: n.p., 1953).

20. Elhanan Wasserman, *Ma'amar Ikvetah Dimeshiha: A belaykhtung fun der yetstiker tekufah* (New York: n.p., 1938). Simon Schwab, *Beit Hasho'eva: Vehu kovets ma'amarim al ikveta dimeshiha* (New York: Ha'ahim Shulzinger, 1941). Schwab related to me that the *Ma'amar* was studied in Baltimore synagogues (interview, Washington Heights, December 1989). Hayim Wasserman of the Council of Young Israel Rabbis in Jerusalem related that the Holocaust was tied to the Zionists during his yeshiva days at Mesivta Tiferet Yerushalayim (headed by Mosheh Feinstein) and Yeshivat Hayim Berlin (headed by Yitshak Hutner), both in New York, in the mid-1950's (Interview, Jerusalem November 2007). On Eliezer Simhah Wasserman's role see Gershon Greenberg, "Elhanan Wasserman's Response to the Growing Catastrophe in Europe: The Role of Ha'gra and Hofets Hayim upon His Thought," *Jewish Thought and Philosophy* 10 nr. 1 (2000): 171–204.

21. See Louis Gefen, "Biography of Tobias Gefen," in *Lev Tuviah* (Newton, MA: Rabbi Tobias Gefen Memorial Fund, 1988): 19–40, and Dov Levin, "Dimuto Shel Harav Tuviah Gefen: Mirahok umikarov," idem, pp. 9–16.

22. The first Sabbath after Kristallnacht was that of Parashat Vayera (12 November). Tobias Gefen, "Derush le'parashat hayei sarah 5,699," in *Nahalat Yosef* (New York: Moinester, 1945–1946): 60–64.

23. Other *Haskamot* were by Meir Dan Plotski (Krasnosielc), Mosheh Betsalel Luria, Eli Aharon Milaykovsky, Aharon Ya'akov Perlman, Yosef Slonima, Yisrael Hayim Daykhes, Eliyahu Mosheh (Zheludok), Aryeh Layb (Snipuskes), Menahem Mendel (Shchuchyn), Tsevi Hirsh Mah Yafit (Vilkoviski), Mosheh Mordekhai Epstein (Jerusalem), Meir Shapiro (Piotrkov), Meir Dan Rafael (Ostrov), Hayim Yehudah Layb Oyerbakh, Shlomoh Hakohen (Vilna), Lipman David ben Moreinu Harav *Resh Yod* [?] of Kollelot Hasidim (Jerusalem), Mosheh ben Moreinu Harav *Yod Alef* [?] (Riga), Mosheh Franko Haham Bashi (Jerusalem), Eliyahu M. Panizal, Shmuel Nissim, Hayim Eliyahu Halevi, Shalom Hadayah, Hayim David Surnago, Hayim Ya'akov Burlah, Shimon Ashriku, all of the Sefardi community (Jerusalem), Hayim Yosef Sonenfeld, and Shaul Hayim Halevi Hurvits (Jerusalem), Mosheh Betsalel Luria, and Yitshak Yosef Silberberg (Krasnosielc). Risikoff said he was known by the name *Yod-Alef-Mem-Hay-Dalet-Nun-Vav-Nun-Het-Hay-Yod-Mem*—which I could not decipher. See Mosheh Betsalel Luria, "Haskamot Hageonim," in Risikoff, *Divrei Menahem* (Grajewo: Avraham Mordekhai Fyorka Ptg., 1910/11). Shmuel Noah Gottlieb, *Ohalei-Shem* (Pinsk: M. M. Glauberman, 1912): 297–298.

24. Rizikoff, "Lezekher olam yehiyeh tsadik," in *Sha'arei Shamayim*, vol. 1 (New York: Ha'ahim Shulsinger, 1936/37): iv–v.

25. Risikoff, "Hesped al hapera'ot shehayu bi'yerushalayim ubehevron ubetsefat behodesh av, bishenat 5689," in *Sha'arei Ratson* (New York: n.p., 1931): 310–318. Risikoff referred to the "El Mole Rahamim," which was recited for murders and destruction of synagogues, *Batei midrash* and *Sifrei Torah* in Morocco. Risikoff, "Vezeh nusah 'El Mole Rahamim' she'amru az," in *Divrei Menahem* (Grajewo: Avraham Mordekhai Fyorka Ptg., 1910/11): 59ᵃ–59ᵇ.

26. Gottlieb, *Ohalei Shem*, pp. 297–298. Rizikoff, *Palgei Shemen* [Job 28:6] (New York: n.p., 1939): 8. *Palgei Shemen* includes FDR's 28 May 1938 greetings for Rizikoff's fiftieth wedding anniversary (31 May) and Rizikoff's letter of praise for FDR. *Palgei Shemen*, pp. i–iv.

27. Yitshak Ayzik of Shavel, *Divrei Yitshak* (Piotrkov: n.p., 1909): *Derush* 8; and p. 97. I could not verify the source. Risikoff, *Palgei Shemen, Siman* 136, pp. 147ᵇ–150ᵇ.

28. Risikoff, *Palgei Shemen, Siman* 109, pp. 103ᵇ–105ᵇ.

29. Ya'akov Avraham, "Parashat Vayigash," in *Nahalat Ya'akov* (Lemberg: n.p., 1724): 23ᵇ col. 2–24ᵃ col. 1. See Hayim Vital, "Sha'ar 39: Derush alef," in *Ets Hayim* (Jerusalem: Yeshivat Hamekubbalim, 1995): 65ᵃ. Horowitz wrote:

> All the things related to freedom on this [Passover] night have to do with the freedom of the soul, with our being redeemed from the *Kelippot*. We were sunken into 49 aspects of *Tumah*, and we were brought out to freedom [*Massekhet Pesahim: Matsah Shemurah* 1, p. 183ᵃ]. . . . The matter of *Hipazon* [in a rush] was that of a great rescue for Israel. For Israel was sunken into *Kelippot* with 49 aspects of *Tumah*. Had the Holy One blessed be He not brought out Israel just at this moment, the people would have sunken and descended completely, and would not have ascended God forbid, and we and our children would have been enslaved. [Massekhet Pesahim: Matsah Shemurah 14," p. 266ᵃ].

> Isaiah Horowitz, "Matsah Shemurah," in *Shenei Luhot Haberit Hashalem: Massekhet Hulin, Shabbat, Pesahim*, vol. 2 (Jerusalem 1993): 183ᵃ, 266ᵃ. Risikoff, *Palgei Shemen, Siman* 147, pp. 171ᵃ–173ᵇ.

30. Risikoff, *Palgei Shemen, Siman* 147, 170ᵇ–173ᵇ.

31. Risikoff, *Palgei Shemen, Siman* 110, p. 108ᵇ.

32. The "Daily local paper" presumably referred to *MZ-T* or *Der Tog*. I was unable to find the source. Risikoff, *Palgei Shemen, Siman* 136, p. 150ᵃ.

33. Risikoff, *Palgei Shemen, Siman* 110, pp. 107ᵇ–108ᵇ.

34. Risikoff cited *Tanna Derabi Eliyahu Rabbah* for his description of Amalek's self-destructive jealousy, but I was unable to verify. Nor could I find the source for the treaty between Haman and Edom-Rome. Risikoff cited Alfasi, *ad Megillah* 10, *Ein Ya'akov* for his statement about Haman's idolatrous garment. Risikoff, *Palgei Shemen, Siman* 25, pp. 35ᵃ–36ᵇ. I am grateful to Yohanan Shtern-Petrovsky at the Institute for Advanced Study for deciphering the reversed spelling of "Sitzan," etc. Risikoff, *Palgei Shemen, Siman* 110, pp. 106ᵃ–107ᵇ.

35. Risikoff, *Palgei Shemen, Siman* 110, pp. 106ª–107ᵇ.
36. Risikoff, *Hakohanim Vehalevi'im o Hitorerut Liteshuvah* (New York: Ha'ahim Shulsinger Ptg., 19 September 1939–2 September 1940): 12ª–12ᵇ.
37. I was unable to verify the incident of the kidnapped Jews. Risikoff, *Palgei Shemen, Siman* 147, pp. 171ª–173ᵇ.
38. Risikoff, *Palgei Shemen*, pp. 8ª–8ᵇ.
39. Mosheh ben Gershon in *Mishpat Tsedek: Leva'er inyan kabalat yisurin be'ahavah ve'inyan hateshuvah ve-khu* (Benei Berak: Mishor, 1986/87). The "Tefilah Nora'ah" is not included in this edition. Risikoff, "Tefilah Nora'ah," *Palgei Shemen*, p. 204ª.
40. Risikoff, "Tefillah," in *Hakohanim Vehalevi'im*, pp. 11ᵇ–12ª.
41. Risikoff, *Tiferet Menahem*, title page; and "Tefillah," in *Hakohanim Vehalevi'im*.
42. I have been unable to find the Kabbalistic source for the idea that the Levites would be the first to meet the messiah. Risikoff, *Hakohanim Vehalevi'im*, pp. 4ª–4ᵇ.
43. Risikoff, *Hakohanim Vehalevi'im*, p. 11ª. *Seder Selihot: Keminhag lita raysin vezamut* (Vilna, Lithuanua: Ha'almanah Veha'ahim Rom Ptg., 1870/71). Composed between the eight and thirteenth centuries, some of the Selihot addressed specific crises, and focused on divine *Hesed* and rescue from oppression; others were transgenerational, and articulated the principles of divine forgiveness for trespass, and atonement for sin. Editor, "Basefer hazeh," in *Selihot: Keminhag lita, raysin vezamut* (Vilna, Lithuania: Ha'almanah Veha'ahim Rom Ptg., 1870/71): from the piece.
44. Risikoff, *Hakohanim Vehalevi'im*, p. 5ᵇ–6ª.
45. Risikoff, "Petah Sha'ar," in *Likutei Dinim: Torat Hakohanim Ve'avodat Beit Hamikdash Vehakorbanot* (New York: Moinester, 1948): 5–10. A comparison between Kristallnacht-related prayers across the globe is a subject for separate study. See for example "Tefillah Mi'yuhedet Mihaag Shene'emrah Bekhal Shabbat Veyom Tov Aharei Gezerat 5699: Leil habedolah 9–10.11.1938" ("Na November 1938 zegt men op Sjabbos en Joum Touf"); "Seder Tefillah Vetahanunim Lehitpalel Ulehithanen Lifnei Avinu Shebeshamayim Al Hasharurot Hanora'ot Be'artsot Germanyah: Or leyom 27 marheshvan 5699 (20.11.38)" in *'Kol Bekhiyot:' Hashoah Vehatefillah*, ed. Judith Tydor Baumel (Ramat Gan: Bar Ilan University, 1992): 125, 130–133.
46. The meeting was led by President Joseph Konvitz, Gedalyah Bublick, as well as by Ya'akov Levinson, Yehiel Mikhal Harlap, [?] Abin, [?] Kaplan, [?] Premsky, and [?] Gavrieli. A *Hazkarah* (memorial prayer was recited, presumably El Mole Rahamim), and a campaign to raise ransom money (*Kofer nefesh*) for German and Austrian refugees was launched. Editor, "Rabanim zaynen gozer ta'anis, foderen ofene tihren in erets yisroel: Biterer gevayn brekht oys oyf rabanim konferents ven men iz mazkir nesh-amos di idishe kedoshim fun daytshland," *Morgen Zshurnal* (23 November 1938): 3. In his own writings, Bublick divided Israel (biblical religion) off

from the rest of the world (barbarism). Bublick, "Tsvay gegnerishe veltn: Vegn dem bukh *Di velt naytikt zikh in religie,*" *Beit Ya'akov Literarishe Shrift far Shul un Haym* 16 nr. 152 (November and December 1938): 7–8; and "Der sona fun iden iz der sona fun di menshhayt," *Der Mizrahi Veg* 38 nr. 267 (13 November 1938).

47. David de Sola Pool and Richard Sizoo, "Ever-living, Ever-loving God," *New York Times* 86 nr. 29,518 (18 November 1938): 31. The Yiddish translation appeared as Editor, "A tefilah far di karbonos fun religieze un rasen-redifus," *Der Tog* 24 nr. 8706 (20 November 1938): 1. See also Editor, "Haynt a tog fun tefilos in shulen und kirkhen far karbanos fun natsi-redifus," *Der Tog* 24 nr. 8706 (20 November 1938): 1. Editor, "Natsis shekhten oys 14 iden in a moshav zekenim: Milionen in amerika zaynen mispalel for iden," MZ-T 38 nr. 11,274 (21 November 1938): 1. Ehad Harabanim, "Kharak-teristishe fragen un der entfer oyf zay," *Hamesilah* 3 nrs. 10–11 (October – November 1938): 18-21. Reportedly, 75 million Americans participated.

48. *The Commentator* 8 nr. 5 (30 November 1938): 1. See further Karen L. Riley, "Kristallnacht, Roosevelt and American Jewry: An Analysis of Selected White House Documents Following the 9 November Pogrom," in *The Netherlands and Nazi Genocide: Papers of the 21st Annual Scholars Conference* (eds.) G. Jan Colijn and Marcia S. Littell (Lewiston, NY,1992): 307–335. Roosevelt also asked Americans to use Thanksgiving Day (24 November 1938) for prayer, eliciting praise from the Orthodox Jewish Press. See Editor, "Prezident rozvelt ruft tsu tefilah far ale farfolgte," MZ-T 38 nr. 11,273 (20 November 1938): 1, 3. On the Orthodox response to the 1939 (MacDonald) White Paper see Yerahmiel Kumin, "Toledot: Di fayne goyim," in *Karnei Or* (New York: n.p., 1945): 179–181; and Hayim Liberman, *Oyb ikh vel es dir forgesn, England* (New York: n.p., 17 June 1939).

49. Elhanan Wasserman (Baranowitch) and Grodzensky were the dominant figures in the Ultra-Orthodox Jewish world. Grodzensky, "Kol kore leta'anit tsibur," in *Ahiezer: Kovets igerot,* ed. Aharon Sorski, vol. 1 (Benei Berak, Israel: Netsah, 1970): 274–275.

50. Yosef Konvitz and Yehudah Layb Seltser, "Letsom, liteshuvah, utefillah, utsedakah," *Hapardes* 12 nr. 9 (Kislev 5699/24 November–22 December 1938): 3. Yosef Konvitz and Yehudah Layb Zeltser, "Ruf fun agudas harabonim far dem ta'anis tsibur komenden montag," MZ-T 38 nr. 11, 278 (25 November 1938): 5. Sh. Erdberg, "In der ortodoksisher Velt," *Der Tog* 24 nr. 8704 (18 November 1938): 5. Editor, "Haynt a tog fun tefilot in shulen un kirkhen far karbanos fun natsi-redifus," *Der Tog* 24 nr. 8706 (20 November 1938): 1. Editor, "Rabanim hoyben on kofer nefesh kampayn," *Der Tog* 24, nr. 8718 (2 December 1938): 1. There were 30 cantors, including Yehoshua Vayzer, Pinhas Yosinovsky, Kapov-Kagan, David Mosheh Shtaynberg, Eliyahu Kretshmar, and David Roytman. On the Halakhic aspect of the fundraising efforts, see Jacob Levinson, "She'elah: Nishalti mitalmid hakham ehad besha'at hamilhamah, heyot shekal

perutah shenigbat be'ad negu'ay hamilhamah be'eropa. She'elah: nishalti halakhah lema'aseh al devar ha'relif," in: *Davar Be'ito: She'elot uteshuvot behalakhah* (New York: n.p., 1946/47): 50–56, 57–59. On Kristallnacht and assimilation, see further Aharon Petshenik, "Al hanisim veal hasevunot," *Der Mizrahi Veg* 3 nr. 2 (December 1938): 2; and David Graubart, "Mihuts tisakhel herev," *Hapardes* 12 nr. 9 (December 1938): 4–7.

51. My attempts to get the address from Yeshiva University, Agudat Yisrael and Agudat Harabanim in New York City were unsuccessful. Revel (1885–1940), born in Kovno, studied at the Telsiai yeshiva and came to America in 1906. See Michael Zylberman, "Concern from Afar: The Participation of 'Yeshivah' Students and Faculty in World War II Service and Holocaust Relief and Rescue Efforts," *Chronos* 1, nr. 1 (2000); see also B. A. Poupko (ed), *Edenu: Sefer Zikaron Lezekher Rabeinu Hagaon Dov Revel, Rosh Yeshivat Rabenu Yitshak Elhanan* (New York: n.p., 1952); and Aaron Rakefet-Rothkopf, "The Final Years," in *Bernard Revel: Builder of American Jewish Orthodoxy* (Philadelphia: JPS, 1972). Mirsky was a professor at Yeshivah University. See further "Orot Mi'ofel: Sihot umiderashot lehag ha'urim," *Hado'ar* 3 nr. 894 (16 December 1938): 6; Samuel K. Mirsky, "An Autobiography," in: *Samuel K. Mirsky Memorial Volume* (New York 1970): 279–296; and Tuviah Preschel, "Kitvei Prof. Shmuel Mirsky: Reshimat Bibliografit," in *Sefer Yovel*, ed. Simon G. Bernstein (New York: s.n., 1958): 539–558. The Yeshiva University's *Ha'nir* is unavailable. As the war progressed, Konvitz set the issue of Israel's sinning aside and spoke of the catastrophe as part of Israel's *Akedah* nature. Joseph Konvitz, "Vayikra malakh hashem [Parashat Vayera]," in *Divrei Yosef*, vol. 2 (New York: n.p., 1947/48): 24–25, ed. Hayim Karlinsky and "Hanerot halalu anu madlikin," in *Divrei Yosef: Derashot al hatorah*, ed. Hayim Karlinsky (Jerusalem: Mossad Harav Kook, 1998): 64–65.

There were similar services at the oldest Ashkenazi synagogue in New York, Beit Hamidrash Hagadol on Norfolk Street and Shomrei Emunah in Boro Park—where FDR was praised for his stance on behalf of Jews. Editor, "Ve'idot vekinusin," *Hado'ar* 5 nr. 892 (9 Kislev 5699–2 December 1938). Sh. Erdberg, "Shuler un shtiblekh gepakt nekhten inderfri un in ovent iber dem ta'anis-tsibur far di daytshe iden," *Der Tog* (29 November 1938): 1–2. Editor, "Ta'anis far daytshe iden gehalten mit tefilos in shulen un yeshivos," *MZ-T* (29 November 1938): 1–2. Editor, "Haynt ta'anis tsibur iber gants amerika far di daytshe iden," *MZ-T* (28 November 1938): 1. Other days of fasting and prayer were reported in the *JTA Daily News Bulletin* (15 November 1938): 4; (16 November 1938): 1; (17 November 1938): 6; (21 November 1938): 6, according to Haskel Lookstein, *Were We Our Brothers' Keepers?, The Public Response of American Jews to the Holocaust 1938–1944* (New York: Hartmore House, 1985): 230, note 94.

A notable response to the RIETS service came from the editor of the Yeshiva College undergraduate newspaper, *The Commentator*, protesting the absence of any call for action.

[To] have allowed such an assembly to pass without having advanced some concrete proposals to carry on an aggressive fight against the forces that would destroy us, is to have committed a sin of omission, particularly in view of the general support such proposals would have received. No mention of stringent enforcement and extension of the boycott on all Nazi goods was made; no drive for funds to rescue human souls from the inferno of Europe was undertaken or advocated, no committee to cooperate with other agencies endeavoring to alleviate these deplorable conditions were established. The opportune moment for having formulated these plans may have passed, but the opportunity of still realizing them has not.

52. Over 30 rabbis and cantors participated in the Adas Israel services. The gatherings were organized by the Boston Council of Orthodox Rabbis and the Jewish Orthodox Community Council. In addition to Soloveichik, the arrangements committee included D. M. Rabinowitz, J. Borwick, A. Gorovitz, R. V. Landau, T. Jacobson, and A. Rose. There were also services at West End Beit Hamidrash and Agudat Yisrael Synagogue. Editor, "Orthodoxy Here Fasts and Mourns: Many Attend Special Services at Roxbury Synagogue," *Jewish Advocate* (Boston) 82 nr. 20 (2 December 1938): 1.

53. I could not find Anonymous, *Vaya'avor Hashem*, or Ami Hai ben Shefatyah, *Afafunu*, in *Selihot Leyamim Hanora'im Kefi Minhag Pozna* (Krotoschin: B. L. Monasch and Sohn, 1845), *Selihot: Keminhag Lita* or in *Selihot Mikal Shanah Keminhag Elzas* (Roedelheim: J. Lehrberger and Co., 1850). See also *Selihot*, translated and annotated by Abraham Rosenfeld (New York: Judaica, 1978). Editor, "Letsom liteshuvah utefilah utsedakah," *Hapardes* 12 nr. 9 (November–December 1938): 3. Editor, "Toyzenter shikago'r iden velen haynt ovent in di shuhlen beten far di korbonos fun natsi terror," *Idisher Kuryer* (22 November 1938): 1, 3. Other services were held at Anshei Keneset Yisrael, Anshei Shalom, Sha'arei Tefillah Benei Reuven, Benei Mosheh, Estraykh-Galitsien Shul, Tiferet Tsiyon, Austin Community Center, Beit Midrash Hagadol Anshei Darom, Benei Yisrael, Bikur Holim, Anshei Mizrah, Keter Ma'arav, Beit Yitshak, and Loop Orthodox Synagogue.

CHAPTER 7

PERSECUTION, PROPHECY, AND THE FUNDAMENTALIST RECONSTRUCTION OF GERMANY, 1933–1940

MATTHEW BOWMAN

By the 1930s, the fundamentalists of America's Protestant churches had been driven to ground. In a series of titanic struggles throughout the 1920s—ranging from the cultural spectacle of the Scopes trial to procedural battles for control of denominational conventions—they had attempted to assert primacy in American religion and culture. But they failed. However, failure suited them; the role of prophetic minority fit neatly with the apocalyptic pessimism of their worldview. They began to build a shadow culture, in the world but not of it, a network of Bible schools, radio stations, and journals. These institutions were particularly strong among Presbyterian and Baptist fundamentalists; the premiere journals affiliated with schools or organizations, such as the *Sunday School Times,* the *King's Business,* and the *Moody Bible Institute Monthly,* reached tens and even hundreds of thousands of readers. Smaller journals, such as Arno Gaebelein's *Our Hope* and H. C. Barnhouse's *Revelation,* were respected for the reputation of their editors. Through all these mediums, fundamentalists watched the crises of the Great Depression unfold, certain that their prophetic perspective, based on intricate interpretation of the biblical texts of Daniel, Ezekiel, and Revelation, explained the world better than the solutions and arguments offered by their secular counterparts. Particularly, they studied the crisis in Europe intently, certain that patterns revealed in the Bible and leading toward the Second Coming were unfolding in Rome, in Moscow, and in Berlin.[1]

Because of the rigorous literalism of the biblical model that the fundamentalists forced the world into, it is easy to accuse them of oversimplification, of lack of nuance, and of possession of only the loosest grip on reality. It is true that their biblical orientation lent the fundamentalists two patterns of thinking: first, they believed that international events were explained and predicted in some detail in the Bible, thus leading them to a certain variety of fatalism. Second, they interpreted the world in moral and religious terms—political or economic calculations were entirely secondary. Tragedies occurred because of rejection of God or Satanic persecution; triumphs were the fruits of true Christianity. Accusations that fundamentalists lived in a black-and-white world were thus somewhat justified.[2] However, this did not mean that their thought was simple, uninformed, or unsophisticated; it merely meant that the world in which they lived was governed by its own set of laws, laws that nonfundamentalists did not entirely understand. Far from the caricature of willful ignorance with which they were often labeled, the fundamentalists placed a great deal of emphasis on seeking knowledge about the world around them and staying informed on current events; the fulfillment of prophecy in history was of paramount importance to their worldview. As Charles Trumbull wrote: "Next to a saving knowledge of the Lord Jesus Christ as one's personal savior, a knowledge of God's prophetic program for the age in which we are living, and for the age to come, is of supreme importance."[3]

They had found this knowledge in the Bible. In its pages lay a framework for the history of the world—a constant redemptive struggle between God and Satan played out in human lives. It began with Genesis; with what James Gray called the "protoevangium," God's promises to Adam, Eve, and the serpent of Eden immediately after the Fall, wherein lay the essence of history. As Gaebelein described this scene: "Two things are prominently stated: there is to be a conflict from now on, a conflict which will go on through the ages, and in the second place the conflict will end in the bruising, or crushing, of the serpent's head. Here is the forecast of history and God's redemptive program." For the fundamentalists, then, history was to be played out in a supernatural struggle between good and evil; this endowed even the most banal or seemingly secular events with implicit cosmic significance. And, in the case of events so dramatic as Kristallnacht and the other persecutions of the Jews, the fundamentalists found nothing less than direct fulfillment of prophecy. The Jews were not merely another religious minority; they were the people of

God, ordained by the prophets Isaiah and Jeremiah to endure through suffering; the Germans not merely a nation, but a vivid example of the power of Satan predicted to be unleashed upon the world by Paul and John the Revelator. In short, in the events in Germany of the 1930s, the fundamentalists saw the cycling gyre of the end times. As Carpenter argues, "The most astonishing sign of the times for fundamentalists, and the one they were most ready to explain in prophetic terms, was the rise of anti-Semitism and the widespread persecution of the Jews."[4]

The German persecution of the Jews was then central to the course of sacred history, and the fundamentalists watched it with great interest. By the early 1930s, more than half a dozen national fundamentalist journals were reporting on events in Germany, and they made a great deal of effort to inform their readers of exactly what was going on. In early 1939, for example, the journal *Revelation* reported that German Jews were being shipped to and murdered in the Buchenwald concentration camp—something that the national consciousness would be only vaguely aware of for several more years. Several months earlier, *Revelation* and several other journals had accurately reported the number of German Jews arrested and the property damage sustained during Kristallnacht. More than one historian has concluded that readers of the fundamentalist journals were better informed of German persecution than readers of more mainline journals such as the *Christian Century*.[5]

Why were fundamentalists so concerned about these events? Many historians, such as Timothy Weber, Yaakov Ariel, and Carpenter, have explored the central importance of the place of Jews in fundamentalist theology, and that place was anything but simplistic. Unlike most Christians, American fundamentalists were not supersessionists; that is, they did not believe that Jesus Christ and the grace of his atonement voided God's covenant with Abraham. Thus, the Jews remained in a unique, and even special, relationship with deity; they might be persecuted, but never forgotten, and God would continue to favor them through the end of times. From their movement's beginnings, fundamentalists like Arno Gaebelein and William Blackstone were fascinated with Judaism, devoting great amounts of time and paper to a study of the faith and advocating for fundamentalist cooperation with (and sometimes evangelism of) the Jews. Some, like Blackstone, became ardent Zionists; others, like Gaebelein himself, became versed in the Talmud. The centrality of Judaism in fundamentalist cosmology had profound relevance for the way the fundamentalists apprehended what was going on in Germany; Hitler's persecution of the Jews meant that his government was ultimately doomed, for God still protected his chosen people. As Gaebelein wrote, Hitler "is a poor student of history if he believes he can succeed with his anti-Semitism. He should remember a great anti-Semite whose name also begins with an H. That man Haman almost reached his satanic object, but God acted."[6]

Soon after the Nazi government began passing laws restricting Jewish participation in the German economy in the months following Hitler's accession to power, *Revelation* noted that "[o]ur greatest interest in the German situation is from the point of view of the Bible student."[7] The fundamentalist reading of the chiliastic texts of the Bible allotted a central role to the Jews and the state of Israel in the events of the End Times. The *Moody Monthly* warned that "the spirit of anti-Semitism is the spirit of the Anti-Christ." intimating that, in light of the suffering of the Jews in Europe of the 1930s, the rise of that figure could not be far off. The fundamentalist writer and prophecy expert Louis Bauman argued explicitly that anti-Semitism would trigger the Last Judgment; Christ would return to save his people when the Jews of restored Israel defied the Anti-Christ, for, as Bauman reminded his audiences, God had promised the Jews his protection and favor—as Jeremiah wrote, "All they that devour thee shall be devoured." However, until then, history would descend into what Bauman described by quoting Jeremiah, "The Time of Jacob's Troubles." Anti-Semitism would flourish, and, as Gaebelein wrote, "Can political schemes stop Antisemitism? . . . [The] question would have to be answered with NO! There is but one answer to all these questions concerning the promised hope for Israel, for the nations of the earth and for all creation. That answer is: The Lord Jesus Christ." The persecution of the Jews was inevitable; it was to be mourned, but no fundamentalist believed that it could be reversed short of the Second Coming of Christ himself, because it was predicted in scripture and confirmed by man's rejection of God.[8]

Because of the latter, the fundamentalists—particularly Gaebelein and William Bell Riley, president of the World Christian Fundamentalist Union—were suspicious of secular, or as Riley termed them, "atheistic" Jews, on the principle that those most favored of God are the worst corrupted—and indeed, a minority of fundamentalists believed that the Anti-Christ himself would emerge from their ranks. Secular Jews, however, were impeding God's work in less monstrous ways as well. For example, to Gaebelein, the Zionist movement of Theodor Herzl was doomed to failure and only impeded the prophesied refounding of Israel, for Herzl had abandoned Orthodox Judaism and hope for the Messiah. The infamous forgery known as *The Protocols of the Elders of Zion* circulated widely among some fundamentalists in the early 1930s, particularly those shaken by the official atheism of the Soviet Union, and those eager to find apocalyptic conspiracy emerging, as did the *Protocols*, from Russia.

Though the *Protocols* was increasingly denounced by publications like the *Moody Monthly* and *Revelation* as the decade went on, it appealed greatly to the conspiratorial orientation of many fundamentalists—though they always qualified such theorizing with assurances that Jews as a "race" were still the chosen people. For some, therefore, Hitler's persecutions were justified because they were stamping out atheistic Jewish corruption, manifest in international communism. This was, of course, merely a subset of corrupt Jews—a telling categorization, revealing of the double-mindedness that fundamentalism's careful parsing of the world into black and white engendered.[9]

This was not to say, of course, that fundamentalists did not believe that the perversions running rampant in Germany were satanically inspired—for their black-and-white worldview led them to, in the end, collapse all types of evil into one, fostered at its root by Satan, and Hitler's Germany was certainly a hotbed of it. However, while Italy seemed personified in the simultaneously sinister and attractive personality of Mussolini himself, a devil in human form, Germany, for the fundamentalists, was more than just Hitler. It was an entire culture gone wrong, corrupted by the all-pervasive version of evil of the twentieth-century world the fundamentalists found themselves in—an evil they referred to by the shorthand of "modernism." The *Sunday School Times* defined modernism as "primarily, and in its worst form, the worship or deification of man"; it was a denial of God, and the fundamentalists located it in the arrogance of academic study of the Bible, in the ignorance of God's will for the Jews that led to anti-Semitism, and in attempts to impose top-down institutionalized religion. Indeed, the *Sunday School Times* went on to define it as "essentially, a denial of the Bible"—the shorthand for all these things.[10] Modernism was not the supernatural evil of demonology or the Anti-Christ; rather, it was the all too natural evil of human beings, forgetting God and succumbing to Satan.

George Marsden has argued that fundamentalism is best understood as evangelicalism mobilized against certain elements of nineteenth-and twentieth-century culture—the new science of theory and hypothesis that replaced the old Baconian methods of induction and fostered Darwinism; the newly professionalized academia who viewed scripture as just another historical document, a popular culture that emphasized leisure and permissiveness, new political movements that stressed collectivism and statism, a liberal Christianity that sought to adapt evangelical faith to the modern world.[11] All of these things were collapsed into "modernism," and all were rooted ultimately in a culture's failure to take God and the Bible seriously—errors that to the fundamentalists meant essentially the same thing. When they lambasted the "modernism" that lay at the heart of Germany's troubles, the fundamentalists meant all of these things—just as they did when they spoke of the "modernism" of the United States. Germany, for the fundamentalists, was not an absolute "other," a state entirely dominated by supernatural evil the way they expected the Anti-Christ's revived Roman empire to be. It was not even the utterly foreign, corrupted atheistic state—Magog—that they were convinced the Soviet Union had become. In a way, then, the lack of a great evil role for Germany in biblical prophecy made it easier for American fundamentalists to think in complicated ways about the German people and culture, and to see in it the sort of declension that they feared modernism was inflicting on the United States. This made the evils of Germany simultaneously less demonically imposing, but also more insidious, because in Germany, the fundamentalists saw what they feared was happening in the United States.

Most historians have been content to leave analyses of the ways the fundamentalists thought about the German persecutions in this ambivalent position, characterizing it as a mixture of pessimistic fatalism and concern for the chosen people. The persecutions themselves were horrid events, but Jewish suffering had been ordained by God and history; the Jews were favored of God, but also potentially corruptible and, like all humans, flawed and deserving of punishment. The fundamentalists therefore condemned (for the most part) Nazi actions, studied them intently for clues of God's hand—but believed ultimately that only God's will could stop the suffering, and he had not yet elected to raise his hand. This, however, was not the whole story. Because of the dominance of theological calculation in the fundamentalist worldview, as well as the colossal shadow the Holocaust has cast over the 1930s and 1940s, it is in many ways natural for historians to focus, as the fundamentalists themselves did, on the significance of the Jews, their suffering as well as their eschatological roles. However, the fundamentalists were, if nothing else, thorough. While they sought to find prophecy about the future of Israel in the events of the German persecutions, at the same time they were reading those events for what they said about Germany itself, as they struggled to place that nation into the story told in biblical revelation. This paper, then, will explore the ways the fundamentalists used Nazi actions against the Jews to construct Hitler's Germany, the roles and interpretations that their prophetic and moral understanding of history assigned to it, its people, past, and present.

A casual reader of 1930s fundamentalist literature might be struck by what seems in retrospect to be a single colossal mistake: The fundamentalists, in the early years of Hitler's regime, did not seem to believe that he was a very important figure on the world stage. They were much more interested in his two great despotic rivals, Mussolini and Stalin; for those men, the fundamentalists could find significant analogues in the Bible. Germany, however, seemed to have no prophetic counterpart. The closest that fundamentalist interpreters of the Bible could come was "Gomer," depicted in Ezekiel 38 as a smaller nation that would follow Magog, the Prince of the North, in the tyrannical "Great Northern Confederacy" that would oppose the Anti-Christ in the battle of Armageddon. Magog, of course, was Russia, and the Soviet Union was easily pictured as the tyrannical state of Ezekiel. Germany, then, was expected to be subjugated to that nation at the end of times. This led the fundamentalists to some surprising insights as well as some massive blunders; on the one hand, for example, they predicted that Hitler would join an alliance with Stalin's Soviet Union when no one else thought this possible.[12]

On the other hand, however, they consistently underestimated both the strength of Hitler's Germany and the power the dictator himself held in that nation. As early as 1935, for example, *Revelation* wondered, "Is Hitler's Fall Near?" in a headline, arguing that the dictator had become merely a "bridge" over which opposing, and more powerful, forces in his government fought, and pointing out that a figure as virulently anti-communist as Hitler seemed to make the Great Northern Confederacy difficult to imagine. Following this view, fundamentalists frequently accused Hitler's associates and subordinates, rather than the dictator himself, of implementing the most objectionable policies of the Nazi state. Alfred Rosenberg, a prominent Nazi racial theorist and influential diplomat, and Julius Streicher, party Gauleiter and editor of the Nazi organ *Der Sturmer*, were particularly castigated; the fundamentalists became increasingly convinced that these two men were behind what Gaebelein called the attempt to "substitute the pagan gods of the heathen Teutons" for Jesus Christ. Gaebelein named them, not Hitler, as the culprits behind the campaign to nationalize Germany's churches, and referred to the Nazi government as the "Hitler-Rosenberg regime"; similarly, *Revelation* noted that "Rosenberg announced that Christianity must disappear from Germany"; Hitler's opinion not being mentioned. In a vicious bit of satire in the same issue, *Revelation* called Streicher "the leading anti-Semite in Germany." Streicher had pled innocence of Kristallnacht, claiming that he was so softhearted that he did not turn on the lights when he returned home late at night for fear of waking his pet bird. *Revelation* dryly commented, "And then we suppose that he goes to his desk and writes a paragraph about killing Jews." For the fundamentalists, then, the corruption of Germany was a communal affair, like the plague of communism in the Soviet Union. It did not stem entirely from the overpowering presence of Hitler—indeed, he personally was only one of a gang of criminals, and gained his power only because of persistence of the larger cultural rot he represented.[13]

In conformity to this point, despite much postwar identification of Hitler as the Anti-Christ, during the 1930s Mussolini loomed as a much more likely candidate for the role. The Anti-Christ was supposed to preside over a revived Roman empire, and Mussolini most obviously fit the bill. Consequently, Mussolini seemed to be the dictator who mattered in Central Europe, and Italy the more powerful state. Hitler was deemed more a curiosity than a serious champion of Satan; his Reich always portrayed as teetering on the brink of collapse. In November 1938, the *King's Business* made the contrast specific, announcing that "we do not believe, and therefore do not say, that Adolf Hitler will ever prove to be the man energized by Satan to perform the work of the Antichrist in the time of the end . . . should the church be taken out of the world today in accordance with 1 Thessalonians, Mussolini would stand before the world as the most likely candidate for that position." Accordingly, Louis Bauman in the *Sunday School Times* declared that "the master-mind of Europe is in Rome," and claimed that Mussolini was "too astute" to be drawn too deeply into Hitler's doomed war. The Italian would pick over the corpse of Hitler's failed empire, and rise from its ashes to create the revived Roman Empire—and possibly become the Anti-Christ. As late as 1940, it would not have surprised the fundamentalists for Hitler to collapse at any moment. Indeed, they even suspected it.[14]

On the other hand, fundamentalists offered frequent praises for American religious liberty and civil freedoms; they saw them rooted in the words of the Bible. As the *Moody Monthly* claimed, "The Jew made the United States of America possible. The early settlers came to study and obey the Hebrew Scriptures. Its original laws were taken from the laws of Moses. The inscription on the Liberty Bell is from Leviticus." However, their natural pessimism left them unconvinced that the United States was immune to declension, and the example of Germany made it even more plausible. For Germany itself was not supposed to turn out as it did. Like the United States, it had a uniquely blessed heritage. The fundamentalists referred to the German nation as the "land of Luther" almost as frequently as by its proper name. The German reformer was a particular hero of the fundamentalists, who lauded him for transcending the cultural particularities that they believed obscured the true gospel in his age as well as their own. The *Sunday School Times*, for example, published a commemorative article titled "The Voice of Wittenburg" on the anniversary of Luther's 95 Theses, exclaiming, "Unlike the other great men in Luther's day, Luther is a present figure . . . there is no better compass than the old faith, taught by Paul, restored by Luther.

We need it in the present eclipse [of] Modernism." The Germans, for the fundamentalists, were the inheritors of Luther's virtues, which they defined in terms familiar to themselves—Luther spoke truth to the powers of his day; he denounced corrupt religious culture, and he taught and valued the Bible. Further, the fundamentalists read him as an evangelical, a proponent of "heart" rather than "ritualistic" religion. But first and foremost for the fundamentalists, Luther was a man of the Book, a proponent and propagator of the Bible. *The King's Business* named Luther's translation of the Bible into German his most notable accomplishment, and the noted Presbyterian Walter Erdman argued in the *Moody Monthly* in late 1939 that the Germans were a "people who owe their common language, their unity, and their past progress to the circulation of the German Bible translated by Martin Luther." *The King's Business* in 1941 compared what Hitler's nation had become unfavorably with "Martin Luther's Germany," noting that "Martin Luther did not once claim self-sufficiency . . . but [was] the humble servant of Christ. Luther's translation of the Bible into the German vernacular in 1534 tremendously influenced the unification of the Germanic peoples." For the fundamentalists, it was paramount that a nation be built on a biblical foundation of humility and obedience; Germany, even more than the United States, was gifted with such potential, and Luther was the idealization of that nation's potential. In recreating him in their own image, most of these writers glossed over Luther's own anti-Semitism (Gaebelein alone acknowledged it, and concluded, "We are sure he did it out of ignorance"), because in the worldview they were constructing, anti-Semitism was tightly knit to a host of other evils of modernism that the shade of Luther was summoned to dispel from his homeland.[15]

Indeed, by the late 1930s, fundamentalists like Erdman were declaring soberly of the Germans, they "have forgotten their debt to the Book." As the 1930s crept onward, and it became increasingly clear that Hitler's programs—to assert state supremacy over religion, to strongly root nationalism in the center of German culture, and, most of all, to persecute the Jews—were only picking up speed, the fundamentalists reverted to the form that many had taken during the First World War: Germany was not merely governed by evil men, but their success was predicated on the rot that had penetrated to the very center of German culture, a rot that had brought the nation to its knees before the evils of modernism. Chief among these evils was a rejection of the nation's most fundamental heritage—the words of Luther's Bible.[16] How could this happen in Germany? By February 1941, the *King's Business* believed it knew. The journal ran an article asking, "Will America, Like Germany, Suffer Defeat?" The article tracked trends—the increased presence of modernism in the universities, a growing devaluation of the Bible and reliance on "rationalism"—that had, it claimed, emerged in Germany in the years before the First World War; although Germany's defeat "has not yet been consummated," the nation was gradually succumbing to "unbelief" and, correspondingly, had exchanged bad governments for worse, descended into a mania of anti-Semitism, and provoked a war it was doomed to lose. All this because Germany had rejected scripture: it had adopted "The Nazi New Testament," an edited version prepared by Hitler's pet academics that made Christ "Aryan" and sought to "delete every reference to the Jews." To understand the fundamentalist world-view, the key is to note the ways all of these evils collapsed in on each other: anti-Semitism was intricately related to the rejection of the pure New Testament at the hands of dissolute German scholars; an unbelieving nation succumbed to Hitler's tyranny; a cruel regime at home led to warmongering abroad. The danger here revealed, claimed the article, was that similar trends were apparent in the United States. The American seminaries were succumbing to liberalism; their nation had begun to forswear the Bible in favor of rationalistic science. The article even spoke darkly of Franklin Roosevelt's political intentions. What had happened to Germany could indeed as well "happen here."[17]

This mature opinion of Hitler's Germany as a state corrupted by modernism, however, did not emerge as a consistent opinion from the first days of Hitler's administration. This is in some ways surprising, because the fundamentalists had developed a powerful discourse of this type to describe imperial Germany during the First World War. It was a state debauched by the twin evils of modernism and natural selection, its faith destroyed by higher criticism and population subdued by militarism. In 1917, the fundamentalist William Bell Riley, echoing the opinion of many of his fellows, wrote, "The time used to be when Germany was the land of faith. For the last fifty years Germany has been equally famed as a land of infidelity under its new guise of 'Advanced Thought'—'Higher Criticism' now named 'Modernism!'" This was, however, not the rhetoric aimed at Hitler in his first years. Though the First World War had convinced the fundamentalists of Germany's corruption at the hands of modernism, the state of the world 15 years later made them reluctant to immediately give up hope on Hitler's Germany. The Russian Revolution had supplanted the German Empire as the focus of international modernism; its official atheism horrified the fundamentalists, and Hitler's scapegoating and repression of the German communists elicited some sympathy. The *Moody Monthly*, for example, urged moderation in early judgments on Hitler; its editor, James Grey, wrote, "[T]here are Jews and Jews just as there are Gentiles and Gentiles," and noted that several sources claimed that "Jews in Germany are not being punished as a race, but that Communism organized by Russian Jews is being punished by Hitler." Even Arno Gaebelein, who called Hitler "a regular Haman, a Jew hater," in March 1933 conceded that "Germany has awakened to find that as much money has been spent within her borders in building up communism . . . the Hitler victory in the recent election has resulted in the suppression of the Communist Party." As long as they believed Hitler was forcing communism back, the fundamentalists were willing to give him the benefit of the doubt. Indeed, their fatalism gave them a ready excuse; in early 1934, the *Moody Monthly*, at the same time it denounced Hitler's anti-Semitism as "a crime against humanity," acknowledged that "we believe God is using Germany today."[18]

This sort of self-conscious justification did not, for most fundamentalists, last long. Hitler's attempts to assert state control of the German churches in 1934 gave many of them increased pause, and his successes here convinced them that perhaps Germany was suffering from a problem more basic than an anti-Semitic ruler. The editors of *Revelation* described the "Hitler Church" in terms reminiscent of fundamentalist descriptions of Catholicism: it was an "organization shell, under Hitler, [that] does not represent the church of Jesus Christ. . . . There may be some saved but ignorant believers in it." The rise of the "Hitler Church" seemed baffling to fundamentalists sure that the spirit of Luther sustained Germany; it was the Reformation in reverse. However, they still held out hope. As Gaebelein wrote, "Thousands of the German youth. . . are loyal and staunch believers. In them it seems the courageous spirit of Martin Luther is remanifested. Not Hitler, but this strong evangelical movement, is the hope of Germany." For several years after Hitler took power, not only Gaebelein, but other fundamentalists as well, believed that the heirs to Luther would keep Germany in righteousness and resist what the *Sunday School Times* called the "paradox and nonsense" of the Nazi "Teutonic megalomaniacs who in their anti-Jewish fervor would cast the Old Testament out of the Church and repudiate the central doctrine of Christianity, atonement by the blood of Christ, as 'Pauline rabbinism.'" Here the *Sunday School Times* followed a common style of fundamentalist thought; the Nazis' anti-Semitism, amateur paganism, and lust for power were collapsed into a single type of evil—the Anti-Christianity of forgetting scripture. Later on, the journal equated its own Christianity with resistance to Nazi militarism, when it assured its readers that "[t]here are plenty of Christ's peace-men between the Vistula and the Rhine." The *Moody Monthly* noted the powerful anti-Nazi voice of Karl Barth in what it called "the battle of the Christian conscience against the state in Germany," and compared Barth's battle with the Nazi state with

Luther's struggle with Catholicism: "If Karl Barth might only become another Martin Luther what paens of rejoicing would go up to God!" However, this did not happen; instead, as Ernest Gordon reported with disapproval, "some responsible Germans even compare Hitler to Luther." That the grip of the Nazis only tightened thus as the 1930s continued, that anti-Semitism continued to rise and evangelicalism failed to wrest control of German culture back, made the fundamentalists sure that another, more basic, problem pervaded the nation. So they turned back to the old, reliable analysis of the First World War—and, increasingly, those accusations of a culture sick with modernism seemed on target.[19]

The emergence of modernism, the child of higher criticism of the Bible, was troubling enough to the fundamentalists; that it sprung from Germany, the land of Luther, was particularly disturbing. However, fundamentalists were sure that they had divined its roots. According to Gaebelein, Germans had made a fundamental mistake; as he stated, "The expression 'Christian civilization' is widely used in all Christendom. Did our Lord ever use the term? Did He tell His disciples ere He left them to go into all the world and to civilize all nations? He did not." Germany was "the heart of Europe . . . the land of Luther, of Schiller, of Goethe"; it had a great cultural heritage—but had become enamored of it. "Germany, sad to say," Gaebelein wrote, "has imbibed such a national pride which has developed into Aryan insanity, the delusion that to her belongs the place in the sun."[20] Hitler's Germany was committing the sin of idolatry; it had arrogantly replaced the fundamental authority of the Bible with a fascination with its own culture. In April 1939 the fundamentalists reeled with distress when the Nazis followed the economic and political devastation of Kristallnacht with cultural repression; as Leonard Sale Harrison wrote, the Nazis were "attempting, using their own words, 'to purge the Bible from all Jewish taint.'" The *Moody Monthly* reported that "the government through its ecclesiastical ministry has ordered the elimination of the name 'Jehovah' from all German churches, together with those of the Jewish prophets. . . . No longer may the churches use the Psalms . . . the Protestants have been warned that they must not use any Jewish names in any way or their church edifices will meet the fate of the Jewish synagogues—be burned to the ground."[21]

These offenses emerged from Hitler's ongoing struggle to control the Christian churches of Germany; that the fundamentalists so readily equated the plight of the Confessing Church there to that of the Jews is striking, and perhaps seems to smack of some degree of ignorance. However, the constant and consistent reports on the Jewish persecutions reveal that the fundamentalists were quite aware of Nazi anti-Semitism. Rather, the *Moody Monthly's* equivocation tells us something about the fundamentalist worldview; for them, Germany's anti-Semitism was intricately bound into larger forms of anti-Christian heresy. German theories of race doctrine, disrespect for the Old Testament, and ideas of cultural supremacy were representative of a larger sort of religio-cultural arrogance that despised the humility taught of true Christianity. The Germans had forgotten that true civilization was defined in terms of its loyalty to God—a measure that placed the orthodox Jews the fundamentalists deeply respected in great favor. As Harrison wrote, "To attack German Jews, Hitler continually uses the expression 'Aryan blood.' What does he mean by that expression? Is that superior to any other blood? Does he not know that when his ancestors were pagan idolaters, Jewish ancestors were enjoying the highest civilization?"[22]

That sort of godly civilization developed, the fundamentalists believed, from confidence in and obedience to the commandments of God, and the sort of perversions that afflicted German society developed from the absence of the Word. Higher criticism of the Bible, of course, was foundational to the developing culture of modernism the fundamentalists castigated; as Riley and Reuben Torrey, the successors to the great evangelist Dwight Moody, argued, it was the seed from which greater evils of all kinds emerged—cultural relativism, immorality, tyranny. As Torrey wrote, the "dethronement of the Bible leads practically to the dethronement of God; and in Germany and America, and now in England, the effects of this are declaring themselves." The relationship between the Bible and national morality in all sorts of fields was quite clear to the fundamentalists; Louis Bauman stated matter-of-factly that all Christians should oppose German persecution of the Jews because "love for the Jews came from a constant companionship of the Book." On the other hand, as the *Moody Monthly* pointed out, "Jew haters never learn anything from history. Jeremiah, like all the Old Testament prophets, was supernaturally exact when he said, 'All they that devour thee shall be devoured, and all that prey upon thee will I give for a prey.' (30:15)." The *Sunday School Times* noted grimly that "[w]ere it not for Adolf Hitler's consuming hatred for everything Jewish, he might halt long enough in his mad career to gain wisdom from a Jew whose great wisdom placed him at the head of two world empires. . . . Daniel might enlighten the German leader." Consciousness of the words of the Bible enlightened both Luther and the Reformed Puritans the fundamentalists placed at the founding of the United States; forgetting them led Hitler into the flawed policies that would doom his nation.[23]

Indeed, though the fundamentalists hardly needed overwhelming evidence, the struggle over the German churches increasingly convinced them that Germany was not merely reforming its Christianity through removing its Jewish elements, but rather rejecting that faith entirely. By the middle 1930s, the fundamentalists began to develop an unholy fascination with the crude outlines of the pagan Aryanism that Nazi thinkers like Rosenberg had begun to toy with. The *Moody Monthly* compared Hitler to Julian the Apostate, the Roman emperor who attempted to stem the spread of Christianity, and described the dictator as "a medium who frequently goes into a trance and paces his room most of the night in intercourse with the unseen, receiving directions." Gaebelein, coining the term "Aryanomaniac" to describe what he believed was Nazi religious fanaticism, observed darkly that Hitler "is either demon-led, Satan-inspired, or a maniac . . . it is said he constantly consults astrologers, spiritualistic mediums, and soothsayers." Harrison echoed this theory, accusing the Nazis of desiring "their mythical god Wodin to be put on a pedestal." In the fundamentalist mind, these efforts were more than a sort of top-down cultural engineering or theoretical exercise; rather, they were representative of the true state of the German soul, revealing of a poison that had seeped in long before the Nazis had seized power. As Walter Erdman wrote in the *Moody Monthly*, "The German state . . . will only tolerate a Christianity that is completely subservient to the government program, that is willing to suppress Christian emphasis on love and liberty and truth. . . . A Christianity in which Christ must be forced into a Nordic mold and His teachings altered to suit the character of the national policy." He noted that "[o]ver the portals of Heidelberg University the inscription 'To the Living Spirit' has been erased and replaced with the words 'To the German Spirit.'"[24]

What had led the Germans to this sort of heretical pride? Erdman asked a significant question: "Is it only a coincidence that it was in Germany that the application of the evolutionary theory to biblical criticism prepared the way for present conditions by producing a rationalistic theology and a discredited Bible?" For the fundamentalists, of course, nothing was a coincidence. The higher criticism had emerged first in German schools in the early nineteenth century; the Germans had failed to repudiate its dangers, and instead were seduced by them. Erdman's reference to evolution was important; the chaos that had overtaken Germany might have begun with what James Gray called "the destructive criticism of the Bible," but it did not end with it. Higher criticism alone did not produce the acids of modernity. As I have noted, the fundamentalists collapsed their evils together—what Torrey labeled the "fallacies of German rationalists" that led them to accept the higher criticism prepared the way for evolution, an even more destructive philosophy. Here were the stirrings of modernism, and the *Moody Monthly* laid out its genealogy: "Before Hitler, was Nietzsche, before Nietzsche, were the new German theologians. The tree of which neo-paganism is the awful fruit, was planted by those German professors of the last century, who, however, excellent their personal qualities, became the intellectual instruments of the powers of darkness." The fundamentalists found no significant difference between the biblical scholarship of the early nineteenth century, the gloomy philosophy of the late, and the fascist ideologies of the 1930s. In the most important ways—which, for the fundamentalists, had to do with their views of the Bible, and hence their susceptibility to evil—they were the same. There was no real difference in kind between the biblical scholars of the Tubingen school and the racial theorists of Nazi Germany, only a difference of degree. The latter were the natural fruit of the former; an evil that the fundamentalists found in its most undiluted form in the philosopher Friedrich Nietszche, whom the *Moody Monthly* described as "a clever philosopher and a genuine false prophet [who] maintains that by means of what we call evil, the elixir of supermanhood can be attained." This was the essence of modernism, a lack of humility before God; it is why Nietzsche was the man fundamentalists blamed most for the First World War, and why fundamentalists like Erdman found his ghost in the origins of the Second. He argued that "today, Goebbels, arch-propagandist and controller of national thought, echoes Nietzsche's words."[25]

The emergence of the Soviet Union had convinced the fundamentalists that the Russian nation would soon take on the role of the Ezekiel's Magog, and they had been sure that the Germans would eventually become the Soviets' subordinates for at least that long. Their growing disaffection with Hitler eased the cognitive dissonance of predicting an alliance between the communists and the man they praised for persecuting them. Indeed, following the train of fundamentalist thought through the 1930s reveals increasing confidence on the fundamentalists' part; the campaign to demonize Hitler allowed them to place the German dictator into the clear categories of evil already present in their worldview—categories dominated to that point by the communists. As the sins of Hitler's regime were increasingly spoken of in terms of "modernism," the fundamentalists managed to revision the world of the 1930s in ways they understood, as a struggle between unitary goods and unitary evils—fusing Nietzsche, higher criticism, Darwinism, German paganism, and Russian atheism in one grand anti-God ideology. The Nazi-Soviet pact of summer 1939 only confirmed their suspicions—but by that point, something curious had happened. The fundamentalists held firm to their convictions that in the end, Russia and the Anti-Christ would be the dominant forces of Europe; Germany would be the weak "Gomer" forced into alliance. Thus, not much, eschatologically speaking,

was expected of Hitler. He initially served as a staunch on the communism Russia was bleeding over the European continent, but eventually
Russia was expected to dominate his nation. He had visions of conquest,
but Mussolini, the much more likely Anti-Christ, was expected to fulfill
them. He was an anti-Semite and a heretic, but so was Stalin; he was a
cruel dictator, but so was Mussolini. But gradually, Hitler made himself
the center of eschatological speculation in Europe. He actually conquered
where Mussolini did not; he proved his ability to endure and extend his
power when many fundamentalists were predicting his decline. But most
of all, he built a regime that embodied the worst of the modernism that
fundamentalists feared; its anti-Semitism and anti-Christianity (which
the fundamentalists perceived as essentially the same thing) came to
define its terms. Communism was a great evil—but Hitler's fascism was
increasingly, in practice, becoming its equal, and spoken of in the same
breath. Hitler had defied prophecy, had seized for his state and ideology
a place beyond what the Bible had allotted him. Indeed, in February
1939, several leading fundamentalist leaders felt it necessary to remind
their readers that "the center of anti-Semitism today is Germany, but
from Germany persecution of the Jew has spread to nearly all portions
of the globe."[26]

As the *Sunday School Times* proclaimed, "All the isms—Nazism,
Fascism, Communism, Socialism, et al, may be listed under one general
caption, Confusionism. Satan is the supreme counterfeiter." The *Moody
Monthly* declared, "Communism is but international fascism and fascism
is but national communism. . . . They both hold in common the principle of the near-deification of the leader, of the superman, which must
needs mean man against God. . . . Darwinism uber alles." Certainly, the
political similarities between Hitler's Germany and Stalin's Russia did not
escape the fundamentalists' notice, but they saw more important similarities: James McComb wrote in *The King's Business* that "I do not believe
Hitlerism or Stalinism could have gained any headway in their respective lands if the majority of those who professed to believe the Bible had
actually believed it." As Riley complained, "That's what is the matter in
Russia: infamous atheism will not tolerate Christian speech! That is what
ails Germany—Men must not tell what God has done for them, nor
proclaim his saving truth!" If these two versions of modernism were the
same in their roots and in their natures, so were they the same in their
fruits: as the *Sunday School Times* proclaimed of Hitler and Stalin, Hitler
and Stalin are "bitter anti-Semites, haters of the Bible, mockers of Christ,
despisers of God, whose chief glory is their capacity to hate and to kill."
Anti-Semitism was not merely incidental here; it had, because of Hitler,
become representative—a telltale sign of modernism and hatred of

God, part and parcel of the diseases that afflicted the modernist state—violence, open blasphemy, and tyranny. The fundamentalists had ceased complaining of Soviet collectivism; instead, as the *Times* said, "Anti-Semitism . . . will prove utterly fatal to the Northern Colossus"; it was the disease which would lead to Armageddon, as the utterly corrupt human states, ignorant of Bible prophecy, inaugurated in the last days the final great war in futile attempts to destroy the Jews. And, in the years since Hitler's rise to power, it is perhaps not too much to say that Germany had replaced the Soviet Union as the center of prophetic fears.[27]

What had happened in six years to elevate Hitler's variety of modernism so? The church struggle had made the fundamentalists suspicious, certainly, but they were expressing hope about the potential of Luther's evangelical inheritance through the end of the 1930s. More striking was Hitler's anti-Semitism—and, by their own word, the drama of the Kristallnacht persecutions tipped the balance for many fundamentalists. In November 1938, they gave up hope on Germany. As Arno Gaebelein wrote, "An indescribable tragedy [has] passed into history, which reminds us of the cruelty committed against the Jewish people during the middle ages. . . . The mask is off. The good which was done in material things is now all undone, and poor Germany stands before an abyss." Gaebelein's use of words is intriguing; he speaks of good being undone, and compares Kristallnacht to the persecutions of the Middle Ages. That is, through its modernism, Hitler's Germany was actually regressing, undoing the Reformation and returning to a culture of superstition and primitive despotism. Indeed, he left little doubt that the demonic lay behind Kristallnacht, writing, "Yes, the mask is off behind which hid the face of another, the liar and murderer from the beginning." Further, Gaebelein demonstrated the peculiar reductionism of fundamentalism in other ways: "It is now definitely proved that these men try to destroy true Christianity in the land of Luther. . . . Because a Polish Jewish youth had killed a German who belonged to the German Embassy in Paris, vicious mobs of unbalanced, demon-inspired Nazis destroyed in one day properties belonging to the Jews." Here Gaebelein identifies the Nazi retribution against Jews as "definite proof" that they sought to destroy Christianity—indeed, proof of a degree they had never seen before—illustrating the deep, almost organic, connections the fundamentalists found among the elements of good and evil. For them, the Jews and Christians alike were chosen of God; their scriptures and faith were intertwined, and an attack on the faith of one was an attack on the other.[28]

This sort of deep identification of the Jewish plight with the cause of Christianity was not limited to Gaebelein. Louis Bauman, horrified at the events of Kristallnacht, dashed off a long pamphlet only a month after the riots, sounding the familiar alarms and laments at the degradation of German culture, while simultaneously exhibiting the close attention the fundamentalists paid to the events of Germany: "The present horror," Bauman wrote, "is only a part of a program of pogroms that has been in process of execution, ever since Hitler came into power [and] Agony upon Agony: Just six miles from Weimer, home of Goethe and the Republican German Constitution, is the new Buchenwald Concentration Camp." In "The Time of Jacob's Trouble," Bauman denounced the "hell-born despots of Berlin" and followed Gaebelein's inclination toward a sort of religious solidarity with the persecuted Jews, announcing that "[t]o utterly destroy freedom you must destroy Christianity. To destroy Christianity, you must first destroy its foundation—even the Jew. Thank God, the Hitlers are temporary! The Jew is eternal! . . . The foes of the Jew are inevitably the foes of the Christian."[29] This was a task easy for the fundamentalists at this point; their increasing tendency to conflate Nazism with communism had effectively dispelled the associations with the latter that had provoked the greatest fundamentalist suspicions of Jews. Further, fundamentalists had persistently identified Hitler's campaign against the German churches with the persecution of the Jews; they were, to men like Bauman, two branches of the same tree, one that had grown from the apparently fertile earth of Nazi loathing of God and the Bible. Hitler's campaigns had attained the sort of cosmic importance that the fundamentalists allotted to the representatives of good and evil on earth:

> The thing that is disturbing the world is not so much a battle between Aryan and non-Aryan, as it is a titanic struggle between conflicting philosophies . . . between totalitarianism and freedom, between regimentation and self-determination, between arbitrariness and arbitration, between demagoguery and democracy, between mobocracy and constitutionalism, between brute force and humanitarianism, between Bumbledom and political sanity, between pantheism and monotheism, between neopaganism and Christianity, between a god on earth and a God in heavens![30]

For Gaebelein, Bauman, and the rest, then, Kristallnacht was the capstone on a developing network of ideas and ideologies surrounding the Nazis; it brought the true picture and place of Germany, which had been hazy and confused, torn between the heritage of the First World War and the potential of Hitler's armies and German evangelicals to strangle communism, sharply into focus. With the Kristallnacht campaign, Hitler revealed that he was neither an ally in the war on godless communism nor a friend of Christianity; rather, his regime was merely another, though slightly more subtle, manifestation of the degraded culture of modernism. His war on the churches made fundamentalists suspect his intentions; his war on the Jews confirmed their fears, despite their early attempts to rationalize them. But Kristallnacht was too large a horror to ignore.

During the Battle of Britain in August 1941, the *Sunday School Times* mused that "even among Christians few people think of World War II as a religious war." But it was; "Europe's greatest since the Franks beat back the Saracens at Tours."[31] It had attained such stature because of the quality of the enemy; in the eight years since he had seized power, Hitler revealed himself to be the very personification of modernism, his state perhaps the single greatest enemy of God on earth, and for no greater reason than anti-Semitism. If Nazi paganism seemed the very stuff of fundamentalist nightmares, the persecution of the Jews was the worst of the Book of Revelation. This way of locating it—in the Bible—was the key to the fundamentalist construction of Germany, for to them, anti-Semitism was not merely prejudice against Jews. As Bauman's response to Kristallnacht demonstrated, anti-Semitism was embedded in a dense network of religious meaning; like a spiderweb, a tug on one thread bent other strands and demanded pressures of other kinds, and the entire construction was the stuff of Armageddon. Anti-Semitism was not important because it was a crime; it was important because it was a sign of the end times; it was evidence of ignorance of the Bible, and all that entailed; further, it shook the very foundations of Christianity itself. If this seemed to make the Jews themselves merely the pawns of history, the fundamentalists did the same to nations, seeking to subdue the actions of humanity to the patterns of meaning they found in God's Word.

NOTES

1. The best exploration of the events of this paragraph is Joel Carpenter, *Revive Us Again: The Reawakening of American Fundamentalism* (New York: Oxford, 2002), especially 97–105. Carpenter discusses journal circulation in 25–28.

2. For an example of such an accusation, see Harry Emerson Fosdick, "Shall the Fundamentalists Win?" *Christian Work* 102 (June 10, 1922): 716–722.

3. Charles Trumbull, "Introduction," to Louis Bauman, *Light from Bible Prophecy* (New York: Revell, 1940), 3.

4. On redemptive history, see Arno Gaebelein, *The Conflict of the Ages* (New York: Gaebelein, 1939), 31; James Gray, *A Text Book on Prophecy* (New York: Revell, 1918), 11–12; Carpenter, *Revive Us Again,* 97.

5. *Revelation* (February 1939), 55; on Kristallnacht, see *Revelation* (February 1939), 54–55, "Germany Brutally Fulfills Prophecy," *Sunday School Times* (November 26, 1938), 857. As early as May 1933, *Revelation* published an article containing some detailed research into Nazi attitudes toward Jews; the journal reprinted Hitler's declaration that "not a single Jewish hair is to be harmed" and openly scoffed at it, declaring its research indicated that Hitler intended quite the opposite. "The Jewish Travail," *Revelation* (May 1933), 170; Carpenter, *Revive Us Again,* 97, 99; Robert Ross, *So It Was True: The American Protestant Press and the Nazi Persecution of the Jews* (Minneapolis: University of Minnesota Press, 1980).

6. Timothy Weber, *On the Road to Armageddon: how evangelicals became Israel's best friend* (New York: Baker Academic, 2004) 133–48 passim; on Gaebelein's encounter with Judaism, see Michael Stallard, *The Early Twentieth Century Dispensationalism of Arno C Gaebelein* (Lewiston, NY: Edwin Mellen, 2002), 13–32; *Our Hope*, 39:11 (May 1933), 686.

7. "The Jewish Travail," *Revelation* (May 1933), 170.

8. *Moody Monthly*, 39:6 (February 1939), 316; Louis Bauman, *The Time of Jacob's Troubles* (Long Beach, CA: Bauman, 1938), 13; Arno Gaebelein, *The Hope of the Ages* (New York: Gaebelein, 1938), 71.

9. On the *Protocols*, Weber, *Road to Armageddon,* 132–42; Yaakov Ariel, *On Behalf of Israel* (Brooklyn, NY: Carlton, 1991); Gaebelein's theorizing from the *Protocols* can be found in his *The Conflict of the Ages* (New York: Gaebelein, 1933); he laments that "God is left out" of Hertzl's Zionism in *Hope of the Ages,* 172. Riley, exhibiting the curious double-mindedness characteristic of many fundamentalists, declares, "There is no race prejudice involved! None whatsoever!" in the midst of a ten-page discussion of the conspiracy of "atheistic Jews" in his *Wanted—A World Leader* (Minneapolis: Riley, 1939), 45, 41–51 passim; Carpenter, *Revive us Again*, 99, 97–105; *Revelation* denounced the *Protocols* in its February 1939 issue, the same that reported on Kristallnacht; in that issue, the editor, H. C. Barnhouse, declared that "hatred for the Jews is satanic," and stated flatly that "the charge of disloyalty" in the *Protocols* "is not true," 59. The *Moody Monthly* declared that "[n]o matter who its [the Protocols] human author or authors were, back of them was one author, and his name is 'that old serpent, called the Devil.'" *Moody Monthly*, 35:5 (January 1935), 230. The Texas fundamentalist J. Frank Norris never accepted the *Protocols*, and accused Riley of anti-Semitism for embracing them. See Weber, *Road to Armageddon,* 142. On the conspiracy of the *Protocols* as particularly appealing to fundamentalists, see Leo Ribuffo, *The Old Christian Right* (Philadelphia: Temple, 1984). An example of fundamentalists defending Hitler for persecuting "Communism organized by Russian Jews" rather than "Jews as a race" can be found in the *Moody Monthly,* 33:10 (May 1933), 392.

10. *Sunday School Times* (December 12, 1939), 914.

11. George Marsden, *Fundamentalism and American Culture,* 2nd ed. (New York: Oxford, 2005).

12. For Germany as Gomer, see *Our Hope*, 66:3 (September 1939), 234, where Gaebelein states bluntly, "Gomer is Germany." Also, Leonard Sale Harrison, *The Coming Great Northern Confederacy*, 2nd ed (London: Pickering, 1940), 21; Sale Harrison predicted the Soviet-Nazi alliance in the first edition, published in March 1939, several months before the treaty occurred. The "Questions" feature of the *Moody Monthly* 40:3 (November 1939), 148, addressed the inquiry "What authority have we for saying that Gomer is the progenitor of the Germans?" that the editors answered with reference to the Talmud. Louis Bauman declared in the *Sunday School Times* (December 23, 1939), 934 that "Germany will march as an ally of the northern colossus, probably because she will find herself in a position where she is unable to do anything else."

13. *Revelation* (December, 1935), 517; *Our Hope*, 65:7 (January 1939), 444–45; Arno Gaebelein, *The Hope of the Ages* (New York: Gaebelein, 1938), 66; Revelation (February 1939), 55, 54.

14. "The European Imbroglio," *The King's Business* (November 1938), 369; Louis Bauman, "Light from Bible Prophecy on the European War and Its Results," *Sunday School Times*, (December 2, 1939), 868.

15. *Moody Monthly*, 34: 6 (February 1934), 263; "A Voice from Wittenburg," *Sunday School Times* (November 4, 1933), 683; "Martin Luther's Germany," *King's Business* (February 1941), 47; *Moody Monthly*, 40:4 (December 1939), 183; *Our Hope*, 66:6 (Jan 1940), 479.

16. *Moody Monthly*, 40:4 (December 1939), 183.

17. "Will America, Like Germany, Suffer Defeat?" *King's Business* (February 1941), 46–48.

18. William Bell Riley, *The Menace of Modernism* (New York: Christian Alliance, 1917), 90; on fundamentalist response to the Russian Revolution and its treatment of Germany during the First World War, see Marsden, *Fundamentalism*. As Ribuffo, *Old Christian Right*, notes, fear of communism drove some fundamentalists in the 1930s—most notably, Gerald Winrod—to sympathy with fascism and anti-Semitism. For Grey, see *Moody Monthly*, 33:10 (May 1933), 392. *Our Hope*, 39:9 (March 1933), 551, 40:3 (July 1933), 40; "Anti-Semitism and the Protocols," *Moody Monthly*, 34:5 (January 1934), 209.

19. "The State and the Hitler Church," *Revelation* (October 1933), 394; *Our Hope*, 40:9 (March 1934), 549–50; Ernest Gordon, "The Church Crisis in Germany," *Sunday School Times* (January 13, 1934), 19; *Moody Monthly*, 34:4 (December 1933), 145–46.

20. Arno Gaebelein, *As it was—so shall it be* (New York: Gaebelein, 1937), 113, 119–20, 123.

21. Leonard Sale Harrison, *The Coming Great Northern Confederacy* (London: Pickering and Inglis, 1940), 42; *Moody Monthly*, 39:8 (April 1940), 441.

22. Harrison, *Confederacy*, 41.

23. Reuben Torrey, *The Higher Criticism and the New Theology* (New York: Gospel Publishing House, 1921), 111; Bauman, *Time of Jacob's Trouble*, 2;

Sunday School Times (June 29, 1940), 520; *Moody Monthly,* 34:6 (February 1934), 262.

24. "A Forerunner of Modern Apostates," *Moody Monthly,* 39:7 (March 1939), 373; *Our Hope,* 66:3 (September 1939), 222; Harrison, *Confederacy,* 36–37; Walter Erdman, "The Lie II," *Moody Monthly,* 40:4 (December 1939), 183.

25. Erdman, "Lie II," 183; Gray, *Text Book,* 69; Torrey, *Higher Criticism,* 39; *Moody Monthly,* 36:3 (November 1935), 121; *Moody Monthly,* 38:1 (September 1937), 4; *Moody Monthly,* 40:4 (December 1939), 183.

26. "An Appeal for Persecuted Israel," *Moody Monthly,* 39:6 (February 1939), 316. The article was signed by such leading fundamentalists as Mark Matthews, Clarence McCartney, Lewis Chafer, and Will Houghton. The first two were among the leading fundamentalist pastors in the nation; Chafer was probably the most important fundamentalist theologian of the 1930s, and Houghton had become the editor of the *Monthly* in 1935.

27. "Report on the International Prophetic Conference," *Sunday School Times,* (December 16, 1939), 909; "The Christian Answer to Communism and Fascism," *Moody Monthly,* 40:4 (December 1939), 181; James McComb, "Europe and the Bible," *King's Business* (May 1940), 167; William Bell Riley, *Re-Thinking the Church* (New York: Revell, 1940), 51; *Sunday School Times* (December 30, 1939), 953.

28. *Our Hope,* 65:7 (January 1939), 444, 463.

29. Louis Bauman, *The Time of Jacob's Troubles* (Long Beach, CA: Bauman, 1938), 15, 17, 7.

30. Bauman, *Time of Jacob's Troubles,* 27.

31. "Evolution and this War," *Sunday School Times* (August 2, 1941), 617.

NOTES ON CONTRIBUTORS

Victoria Barnett is Staff Director of Church Relations at the United States Holocaust Memorial Museum. She is the author of *For the Soul of the People: Protestant Protest against Hitler* (1992) and *Bystanders: Conscience and Complicity during the Holocaust* (1999), and editor/translator of Wolfgang Gerlach's *And the Witnesses were Silent: The Confessing Church and the Jews* (2000) and the new revised edition of Eberhard Bethge's *Dietrich Bonhoeffer: A Biography* (2000). She has written numerous articles and book chapters on the churches during the Holocaust, and is the author of an article on Dietrich Bonhoeffer published on United States Holocaust Memorial Museum's Web site (http://www.ushmm. org/bonhoeffer/).

Michael Berkowitz is Professor of Modern Jewish History in the Department of Hebrew and Jewish Studies at University College London. He is author of *The Crime of My Very Existence: Nazism and the Myth of Jewish Criminality* (2007), *The Jewish Self-Image* (2000), *Western Jewry and the Zionist Project, 1914–1933* (1997, 2000), and *Zionist Culture and West European Jewry before the First World War* (1993, 1996). He is editor or co-editor of four books, including *We Are Here: New Approaches to the History of Jewish Displaced Persons in Postwar Germany* (2009), edited with Avinoam Patt, and *Fighting Back? Jewish and Black Boxers in Britain* (2007), edited with Ruti Ungar. In 2007, he served as President of the British Association of Jewish Studies.

Matthew Bowman is a Ph.D. candidate in the history department at Georgetown University, writing a dissertation about lived religion during the fundamentalist crisis of the 1920s. He has published articles on the social gospel, antebellum evangelicalism, and Mormonism.

Gershon Greenberg has served as Visiting Professor of Jewish Thought at Hebrew, Tel Aviv, and Haifa universities, and as Professor of Philosophy and Religion at American University (Washington, D.C.). His research on the history of Jewish and Christian religious thought during the Holocaust has appeared in *Yad Vashem Studies, Holocaust and Genocide Studies*, as a three-volume Hebrew and Yiddish bibliograhy (Bar Ilan University), and in *Wrestling with God: Jewish Theological Responses during and after the Holocaust* (with Steven T., Katz).

Patrick J. Hayes received a doctorate in religious studies from the Catholic University of America in 2003 and has taught at Fordham University and St. John's

University. He is presently an Adjunct Professor at Fairfield University in Connecticut and an Archivist for the Baltimore Province of the Congregation of the Most Holy Redeemer (Redemptorists) in Brooklyn, New York. His research and writing focuses on the intersections of ecclesiology, church history, and social ethics.

Kyle Jantzen is Associate Professor of History at Ambrose University College in Calgary, AB, Canada. His first book, *Faith and Fatherland: Parish Politics in Hitler's Germany* (2008), examined clerical nationalism, church responses to National Socialist racial policy, and other issues in local church politics in the Third Reich. He is currently working on a survey of North American anti-Nazi radio broadcasts and a wider study of Canadian and American Protestant responses to the Nazi treatment of the Jews in 1938 and 1939.

Maria Mazzenga has served as Education Archivist at the American Catholic History Research Center and University Archives since 2005. After graduating with a Ph.D. in history from Catholic University in 2000, she taught U.S. history at Virginia Commonwealth University, George Mason University, and Catholic University, where she currently serves as adjunct instructor in history. She has written several articles on American Catholicism and on the U.S. home front during the Second World War and is currently working on a book on American Catholic responses to the Holocaust.

Index